The
Reference Shelf®

U.S. National Debate Topic 2012–2013
The Future of U.S. Economic Relations: Mexico, Cuba, and Venezuela

The Reference Shelf
Volume 85 • Number 3
H. W. Wilson
A Division of EBSCO Publishing, Inc.
Ipswich, Massachusetts
2013

GREY HOUSE PUBLISHING

The Reference Shelf

The books in this series contain reprints of articles, excerpts from books, addresses on current issues, and studies of social trends in the United States and other countries. There are six separately bound numbers in each volume, all of which are usually published in the same calendar year. Numbers one through five are each devoted to a single subject, providing background information and discussion from various points of view and concluding with an index and comprehensive bibliography that lists books, pamphlets, and articles on the subject. The final number of each volume is a collection of recent speeches. Books in the series may be purchased individually or on subscription.

Library of Congress Cataloging-in-Publication Data

The future of US economic relations : Mexico, Cuba, and Venezuela.
    pages cm. -- (The reference shelf ; volume 85, number 3)
  Includes index.
 ISBN 978-0-8242-1214-8 (issue 3, pbk.) -- ISBN 978-0-8242-1211-7 (volume 85) 1. United States--Foreign economic relations--Mexico. 2. Mexico--Foreign economic relations--United States. 3. United States--Relations--Mexico. 4. Mexico--Relations--United States. 5. United States--Foreign economic relations--Cuba. 6. Cuba--Foreign economic relations--United States. 7. United States--Relations--Cuba. 8. Cuba--Relations--United States. 9. United States--Foreign economic relations--Venezuela. 10. Venezuela--Foreign economic relations--United States. 11. United States--Relations--Venezuela. 12. Venezuela--Relations--United States. I. H.W. Wilson Company.
 HF1456.5.M6F88 2013
 337.7308--dc23

                                                                    2013010442

Cover: Mexican farmers take part in a march of hundreds of corn producers protesting against NAFTA (North American Free Trade Agreement). ©AFP/Getty Images

The Reference Shelf, 2013, published by Grey House Publishing, Inc., Amenia, NY, under exclusive license from EBSCO Publishing, Inc.

Printed in the United States of America

Contents

3

After Castro: Cuba's Revolution at Crossroads

4

Venezuela's Socialist Experiment

5

The Rise of Mexico

6

Poverty and Inequality in the Americas

Preface

The Future of U.S. Economic Relations: Mexico, Cuba, and Venezuela

Ever since the Monroe Doctrine was introduced in the early nineteenth century, the United States has consistently pursued a strong relationship with Latin America. This relationship has encompassed defense, security, trade, and economic development. In many cases, the United States has succeeded in building strong partnerships, but in other cases American efforts to create durable ties have experienced challenges. The United States and Mexico, for example, continue to grapple with issues related to immigration and the drug trade. Meanwhile, leaders such as Cuba's Fidel Castro and Venezuela's Hugo Chávez have worked to defy American influence and power in the region.

The historical tensions between the United States and Mexico, Venezuela, and Cuba have made building and maintaining deep economic ties between them a complex challenge. However, the death of Chávez in March 2013 and Castro's departure from an official role in the Cuban government have spurred conversations about how a new regional partnership might take shape. Meanwhile, the burgeoning trade relationship between the United States and Mexico continues to encourage efforts aimed at addressing issues such as security and immigration.

America's economic relations with Latin America remain a vital component of the world economy. In light of this fact, the National Forensic League included the question of whether the United States should launch a new effort at engagement with any or all of these nations in its 2013–14 program. The debate covers a range of issues: the capacity of regional political leadership; the economics of new trade initiatives and aid programs; and how to produce effective policy aimed at addressing poverty, security, and environmental sustainability.

The United States and Cuba

When revolutionaries led by Fidel Castro overthrew the regime of Cuban leader General Fulgencio Batista in 1953, the American government quickly recognized, the new government, although relations between Washington and Havana quickly soured when Castro called for the nationalization of hundreds of private businesses, many of them American, and imposed new taxes on American imports. President Dwight D. Eisenhower responded to Castro's policies by imposing a series of trade restrictions. The United States would go on to impose a full economic embargo on Cuba, allowing only food and medical supplies to be exported to the island. To offset Cuba's economic losses, Castro ingratiated himself with the Soviet Union, America's Cold War adversary.

In the early 1960s, the United States made repeated covert attempts to assassinate Castro and oust his regime. Under President John F. Kennedy, Eisenhower's economic embargo was made permanent. Castro remained defiant, speaking out against what he viewed as American imperialism. In 1962, Castro agreed to the establishment of Soviet missile bases in Cuba, triggering the twelve-day Cuban Missile Crisis and bringing the Cold War to the brink of a nuclear exchange. Although the standoff ended peacefully with the Soviets withdrawing their weapons, US officials would continue to hold Castro responsible for the crisis over the ensuing decades. In the 1980s and 1990s, US officials took steps to strengthen the American economic embargo, which included the adoption of the 1996 Helms-Burton Act, establishing penalties for countries that traded with Cuba.

Following the collapse of the Soviet Union in the early 1990s, Castro's Cuba has come to be viewed as a far less potent threat to American interests. While successive administrations have continued to criticize Castro for his alleged human rights abuses, many have criticized America's Cuba policy as being out of date. These criticisms have yielded some softening in US-Cuba relations. In 2001, for example, US officials approved the sale of food to Cuba after it was devastated by Hurricane Michelle. The policy has remained in place for more than a decade, providing Cubans with essential foodstuffs and generating hundreds of millions of dollars in profit for American companies.

Since the early 2000s, a number of the embargo's restrictions have been altered or lifted altogether. In 2011, the administration of President Barack Obama announced it would allow religious and academic groups to begin traveling to Cuba.

The aging Castro stepped down as Cuba's president in 2008. He left his official role in the Communist Party of Cuba in 2011. His brother, Raúl Castro, has since taken control of the reins of leadership, although Fidel's legacy continues to be strongly felt. The American economic embargo remains in place, and despite some opposition in the United States and Cuba, it is unlikely it will be dismantled in the near future. Nonetheless, many Cuban dissident groups argue that as the country enters its post–Fidel Castro period, opportunities for US officials to stimulate economic and political changes in Cuba will continue to present themselves.

The United States and Mexico

Whereas the US-Cuba relationship has been an adversarial one since the 1950s, the relationship between the United States and Mexico has been largely positive throughout the twentieth century. In 1994, the United States, Canada, and Mexico entered into the North American Free Trade Agreement (NAFTA), an accord that eliminated the majority of tariffs on the continent. NAFTA's provisions have been an economic boon for Mexico and the United States. Two-way agricultural trade between the two countries has increased by 150 percent since NAFTA's implementation. By 2005, total trade between the United States and Mexico was valued at approximately $16 billion, more than double what it totaled when NAFTA was first launched.

The economic benefits of free trade between the United States and Mexico have been all but overshadowed, however, by other cross-border issues. One of the most significant of these has been the drug trade. To be sure, the Mexican government has made great efforts to combat drug cartels operating in the cities and towns along the US-Mexican border. While these efforts have helped stem the country's once endemic violence and decreased the national murder rate, the challenges of drug-related political corruption and the influence of drug money on law enforcement remain.

Meanwhile, the United States government continues to invest resources to combat Mexican drug cartels from the American side of the border. Nevertheless, smuggling remains rampant, as cartels employ a wide array of tactics, including aerial delivery and subterranean tunnel systems. Violent crime continues as well, posing challenges to state and local police departments as well as federal agencies assigned to protect the border. While some in the United States criticize the Mexican government's antidrug initiatives, Mexican officials criticize American efforts to stem the demand for illegal drugs in the US population.

Another contentious issue in US-Mexico relations is immigration. Many US officials have decried the steady influx of Mexican migrants across the border, claiming they are illegal aliens that overburden public services and job markets. The presence of both legal and illegal Latin American immigrants in the United States has created a potent political constituency. In light of the influence wielded by Latin American voters in the 2012 president election, political leaders from both political parties have been speaking to the immigration issue in more muted terms. The issue of immigration has become less contentious as robust economic growth in Mexico has caused a decrease in the number of people opting to relocate to the United States.

US-Mexican relations have entered a new phase in recent years. Leaders on both sides of the border have at times in the past allowed heated, politicized rhetoric on challenging issues to create strains on the economic partnership between the two countries. However, US president Barack Obama and Mexican president Felipe Calderón avoided employing such tactics. Obama has been reluctant to embrace stronger anti-immigration laws until comprehensive reform to the country's overall immigration system is put into place. Before leaving office in December 2012, Calderón avoided criticizing US immigration laws directly, while making antidrug initiatives the focal point of his presidency. Experts believe that the promise of mutual economic growth through bilateral trade will result in continued efforts by the United States and Mexico to build on their existing relationship. Soon after taking office in December 2012, Mexico's newly elected president, Enrique Peña Nieto, met with President Obama to discuss increasing economic and security ties between the two countries.

The United States and Venezuela

The relationship between the United States and Venezuela throughout the late twentieth and early twenty-first century has been characterized by both antagonism and interdependence. In the late 1940s, for example, the United States is believed to have been involved in a military coup that removed from power the democratically elected government of President Rómulo Gallegos and replaced it with a junta that was thought to be more likely to ensure American access to Venezuela's oil resources.

Since the 1940s, oil resources have been at the center of US-Venezuela relations. Some Latin America experts describe the American opinion of Venezuela's government until the late 1990s as "open-minded"—neither warm nor hostile. However, the arrival of Venezuelan President Hugo Chávez in 1999 and his raucous criticism of American foreign policy resulted in a significant change in US-Venezuela relations. Chávez became known for his blunt and bombastic approach to foreign policy, and although the United States was Venezuela's biggest trading partner, he was unafraid to criticize the post–September 11, 2001, policies of President George W. Bush. In response, Bush recalled the American ambassador from Caracas, effectively halting diplomatic relations between the two countries. Meanwhile, Chávez ramped up his anti-American rhetoric in order to engender public support of his socialist ideals.

Despite the rhetorical barbs and diplomatic maneuvering between Caracas and Washington during Chávez's tenure as Venezuela's president, economic relations between the two countries continued apace. In fact, very few sanctions were levied on Venezuela even in the face of Chávez's heated speechifying. Throughout the late 2000s, Venezuela remained America's fourth-largest oil supplier. Although Chávez used oil revenues to increase public spending in the name of his unique brand of socialism, he also alleged that the CIA was behind a coup that briefly ousted him from office. He also made repeated allegations that US officials were seeking to assassinate him.

The end of the first decade of the twenty-first century saw changing dynamics in US-Venezuela relations. Bush finished his second and final term as president in 2008. His successor, President Barack Obama, was viewed throughout the world as a proponent of a more progressive American foreign policy. After taking office, Obama was not inclined to engage in his predecessor's war of words with Chávez, although he did not appoint an ambassador to Venezuela. In 2011, Chávez was diagnosed with cancer, and although he continued to lead, his deteriorating health presented opportunities for those seeking a warming of relations.

Chávez's death in 2013 has cast relations between the United States and Venezuela into flux. It is likely that full engagement between the two countries remains a distant prospect. Chávez's successor, Nicolás Maduro, has continued his legacy of anti-American rhetoric. Many experts believe that Venezuela is becoming increasingly undemocratic and that this trend will continue to complicate economic relations between Washington and Caracas. The United States remains Venezuela's largest economic contributor, while Venezuelan oil continues to play an important role in the American economy. While diplomatic relations between the two countries are likely to remain tumultuous, economic relations will likely remain unchanged.

1

Latin America in the Twenty-First Century

Presidents and Heads of State wave during the sixth Summit of the Americas in Cartagena, Colombia, Sunday, April 15, 2012. From left to right front row are: Colombia's President Juan Manuel Santos, Chile's President Sebastian Pinera, President Barack Obama and Guatemala's President Otto Perez. Second row from left, Honduras' President Porfirio Lobo, Mexico's President Felipe Calderon and Panama's President Ricardo Martinelli. Third row from left, St. Kitts and Nevis' Prime Minister Denzil Douglas, St. Lucia's Prime Minister Kenny Anthony, Trinidad and Tobago's Prime Minister Kamla Persad-Bissessar, Venezuela's Foreign Minister Nicolas Maduro. Fourth row from left, Argentina's President Cristina Fernandez, Barbados' Prime Minister Freundel Stuart, Bolivia's President Evo Morales and Canada's Prime Minister Stephen Harper.

The Future of US–Latin American Relations

Since the early 1820s, when the Monroe Doctrine established the first official policy of the United States regarding Latin America, the relationship between the United States and the countries of the Caribbean and Central and South America has evolved and become increasingly complicated. In terms of trade, the United States has enjoyed its status as one of Latin America's largest and most consistent partners. The United States entered into the North American Free Trade Agreement (NAFTA) with Mexico in 1994, for example, and into another free-trade agreement with Chile in 2004. In fact, of the twenty countries with which the United States shares free-trade agreements (as identified by the US trade representative), eleven are in Latin America.

In political terms, however, despite the strength of these economic ties, the United States has received less consistent positive feedback from a number of Latin American governments. The US government has long enforced a trade embargo on the communist regime in Cuba, for example. Meanwhile, the US and Venezuelan governments have been locked in a war of words for more than a decade. In recent years, many Latin American governments have accused the United States of imperialism, joining Cuba and Venezuela in their public criticism of US foreign policy in Latin America.

The recovery from the 2007–2009 global recession, coupled with leadership transitions in many Latin American governments (and in the United States as well), have led the US government to pursue a general policy of reengagement with Latin America. The aforementioned free-trade agreements and similar trade programs provide a vehicle for other types of bilateral and multinational cooperative programs that focus on social arenas, such as combating poverty and creating opportunities for economic development in rural areas. The US government and its Latin American partners may also find a renewed sense of cooperation in the war on drugs. Approaching these issues, however, is contingent on the notion that both the US and Latin American governments can change long-standing perceptions they have of one another. Such a shift in perception could strengthen relationships and enhance the effectiveness of US–Latin American cooperative programs.

Addressing Poverty and Economic Development

Latin American economic growth over the last several decades has been characterized by periods of expansion and contraction. For example, in the 1970s, most of the countries in this region experienced economic stability and widespread growth. In the 1980s, however, most countries in Latin America were gripped by recession. In the 1990s, growth began again at a moderate level. Concurrent with these economic growth fluctuations were changes in poverty rates and economic status.

According to a 2003 study published in the *Journal of Applied Economics* regarding poverty and economic growth in Latin America, poverty levels during the 1970s fell as the Latin American economies grew. During the 1980s, poverty rates increased again, with disparities widening between the socioeconomic classes. During the 1990s, poverty rates dipped slightly while class inequality remained static.

With regard to Latin America, its economic development, and the relationship it shares with the United States, poverty and class inequality are important factors to consider. The North American Free Trade Agreement, for example, immediately opened doors for economic development in Mexico. While the Mexican economy benefited enormously from the establishment of new factories and businesses in the northern states and in Mexico City, many of Mexico's poorest states in the south (such as Oaxaca, Chiapas, and Yucatan) remained beyond NAFTA's influence. Furthermore, the unskilled laborers working at the increasing number of factories along the US border, although finding employment, were consistently receiving meager wages for the hours they worked. Thus, although Mexico benefited greatly from NAFTA's introduction in 1994, a disproportionate percentage of the population was unable to share those benefits.

Free-trade agreements immediately relax economic policies for the participants. Tariffs, regulations, and restrictions are quickly eliminated in order to facilitate trade and commerce. One study by Anabel Gonzalez, chair of the World Economic Forum's Global Agenda Council on Trade, suggests that Latin American countries are frequently so incentivized by the prospect of free trade with the United States that they are willing to effect a wide range of changes. The result is increased trade, but the gap between upper- and lower-class citizens is perpetuated.

In this regard, Gonzalez and others argue, an opportunity exists. By including in free-trade agreements the establishment of programs that work to establish and bolster a middle class, improve vocational training in high-poverty areas, or otherwise lay the groundwork for bilateral antipoverty and development initiatives, the United States and its Latin American partners may see widespread economic growth in the latter. Such growth could even generate greater returns on the agreement for the United States.

The War on Drugs

The so-called war on drugs—an ongoing, US-led effort to halt the production, trafficking, sale, and use of illegal drugs—has raged since the mid-twentieth century. Latin America has long been a major source of such drugs, and drug cartels (criminal organizations dedicated to drug production, transportation, and distribution) are prevalent throughout the region, playing a major role in Latin America's violent crime rates.

The war on drugs has two main theaters. First, in the United States, federal, state, and local governments are, through law-enforcement efforts and social programs, attempting to lower demand for drugs by treating addiction and arresting drug dealers. The second theater is in areas, mainly in Latin America, that serve as the source of drugs. For decades, the US government has partnered with the governments of

Mexico, Venezuela, Columbia, and others to locate and prosecute members of drug cartels.

The war on drugs in the Latin American theater has produced some modest results; law enforcement has succeeded occasionally in breaking up smuggling operations. In 2012, for example, a suspected drug smuggling king, Daniel Barrera of Columbia, was captured in Venezuela (Barrera had allegedly built a major cocaine-trafficking network over the course of twenty years). However, because many cartels are involved in corruption at all levels of government, authorities have been unable to completely dismantle a drug cartel since the 1980s, when the US government successfully helped defeat Columbia's major cartels. The problem, as experts conclude, is that if an individual like Barrera is captured, another smuggler will likely move in to replace him. Even in the case of Columbia, the flow of drugs did not stop—new cartels arose in Mexico from preexisting trafficking organizations.

In recent years, Latin American leaders have shifted their focus with regard to combating drug cartels. Mexican authorities, for example, stepped up their efforts against the cartels during the administration of President Felipe Calderón. In 2006, Calderón arrived in office and quickly moved to send tens of thousands of Mexican troops into the country's streets to engage the cartels. Violence escalated as a direct result, with civilians frequently caught in the crossfire. Meanwhile, few major accomplishments were recorded—the cartels were simply too well connected, paying politicians and law-enforcement officers large sums of money to look the other way. Even the soldiers assigned to engage the cartels were susceptible to bribery, given their low wages. Calderón's efforts fell far short of his goals, as did his popularity as president.

In 2012, Calderón's successor, Enrique Peña Nieto, moved away from direct military engagement with the cartels. The violence was only worsening—if the military was successful in capturing or killing a prominent cartel leader, the resulting power vacuum would inevitably foster gruesome violence. Peña Nieto signaled his continued dedication to the war on drugs, but out of concern for public safety, he has focused on halting the flow of drugs through Mexico rather than on the production of these drugs.

The key to an effective and successful war on drugs in Latin America, experts believe, is cooperation. With the ratification of free-trade agreements, the United States and its Latin American partners can use this momentum to renew the antidrug effort. One recent study suggests that many Latin American governments, despite their partnerships with the United States, are too small and have too few resources to effectively fight the cartels. Calderón's failed combat strategy—undermined by his own military's lack of financial resources—provides evidence for this conclusion. On the other hand, the study argues, multinational agreements between Latin American nations can pool money, resources, and technologies.

An example of the benefits of this multinational (as opposed to bilateral) approach may be found in the 2008 Mérida Initiative. The United States, along with partners in Mexico, Central America, Haiti, and the Dominican Republic, shared about $1.4 billion to strengthen the border between the United States and Mexico and to empower the participating governments (particularly Mexico) to combat organized crime. In 2010, the Mérida Initiative had seen enough successes that the US government renewed and even expanded the program to focus on political and judicial corruption.

Perceptions

As stated earlier, the relationship between the United States and Latin America has become increasingly complicated over the last several years. One of the key factors contributing to this complicated relationship is the perception of Americans regarding Latin America, and vice versa. In Latin America, for example, the prevailing view among many countries is that the United States is asserting itself in Latin America in a spirit of imperialism rather than partnership. This attitude was arguably voiced loudest in recent years by President Hugo Chávez of Venezuela. Chávez directed his anti-American rhetoric at then–US president George W. Bush, however, and not necessarily the American people. Still, when Chávez died in early 2013, his vice president claimed that US operatives had poisoned Chávez.

While Chávez was one of the loudest leaders alleging US imperialism, he was by no means alone. To be sure, throughout the twentieth century, the US government intervened, sometimes through clandestine military operations, in Latin America to combat socialism as it spread in nations like Bolivia, El Salvador, and Nicaragua. With Fidel Castro mostly out of Cuban government and Chávez succumbing to cancer in 2013, it is possible that some of the anti-American rhetoric could be dialed down and political reconnection could occur. Then again, given that Chávez's successor, Nicolás Maduro, will likely continue to accuse the US government of interference, and that Bolivian president Evo Morales has made similar claims, the perception of the United States as an imperialist power could continue.

One of the misperceptions among Americans regarding Latin America is the idea that these countries are ineffective at addressing some of the key issues facing them (including poverty and drug-related crime). For example, when then–secretary of state Hillary Clinton visited Mexico in 2009, the *New York Times* posed the question of whether Mexico was a "failed state" due to its apparent inability to combat the drug trade or stem illegal immigration. This attitude does little to allay Latin American concerns about US imperialism and interference.

Additionally, a prevailing misperception among US leaders is that the establishment of socialist regimes in Cuba, Venezuela, and Bolivia (and these governments' ties to one another and other socialist regimes) is a matter for concern in and of itself, given other regimes' records on human rights. President Barack Obama expressed such concerns in 2011, alleging that the Venezuelan government was not protecting democracy, particularly the freedom of the press and the right to free speech. He also criticized the fact that Chávez's government had formed ties with Iran and Cuba, two longtime ideological rivals of the United States.

Recent pragmatic approaches to US–Latin American relations, which include free-trade agreements and multinational cooperative programs, may signal a change in both camps away from such rhetoric. Then again, there have been major changes in the governments of some of Latin America's key nations (most notably the death of Chávez, the departure of Castro, and the election of a new president in Mexico). The US political landscape is also undergoing some changes, such as recent legislation aimed at comprehensive immigration reform. Such shifts are indicative of the clear crossroads at which US–Latin American relations stand.

Gini Back in the Bottle: An Unequal Continent Is Becoming Less So

The Economist, October 12, 2013

Michael Jackson brought Santa Marta a moment of fame. In February 1996 the King of Pop landed by helicopter at the top of one of Rio de Janeiro's most notorious *favelas*. Politicians tried to stop him, but Mr. Jackson had permission from the drug barons who ruled the slum. He danced down the steep paths between shacks clinging precariously to the mountainside, surrounded by a cheering crowd of Rio's poorest citizens, and belted out his hit single "They don't care about us." The music video was played around the world. It trained a spotlight on Rio's poverty and inequality.

Sixteen years later Santa Marta is once again a showcase, but of a better sort. It was the first *favela* to be "pacified" under a government plan to wrest control of Rio's slums from the drug lords. The place was stormed by the army in 2008. It now has a police station, and is peaceful. It is a thriving example of the boom at the bottom of Brazilian society.

Meet Salete Martins, a bubbly 42-year-old, whose family moved to Santa Marta from Brazil's northeast when she was eight. By day she works as a trainee tour guide, showing visitors around her neighbourhood for a city-financed non-profit group called Rio Top Tours. At night she studies tourism at a local college. At weekends she sells Bahian food from a bustling stall near the *favela's* entrance. And in between she flogs a popular line of beauty products. Her monthly income is around 2,000 reais ($985), four times as much as she made selling sandwiches three years ago and more than three times the minimum wage. She plans to launch her own tour-guide company before the end of this year.

Ms. Martins's success is striking, even in Santa Marta. But it mirrors a trend that has swept the whole of Latin America. Poor people's incomes have surged over the past decade, leading to a big drop in inequality. In most Latin American countries the Gini coefficient in 2010 was lower than in 2000. The region's average, at 0.5, is down from almost 0.54 a decade ago, and lower than at any time in the past 30 years . . ., though still high relative to other regions. Judging by evidence from Argentina, the only country in Latin America to publish statistics on tax returns of top earners, the richest 1% are still pulling ahead of the rest. But that concentration is more than made up for by the narrowing of gaps further down the income scale.

Both shifts are reflected in popular culture. "Mulheres ricas" ("Rich women") is a new reality-TV show about Brazil's ultra-wealthy ("I bathe in mineral water every

day," said one woman in an early epi-
sode). But the country's most popular
prime-time soap is "Avenida Brasil,"
which documents life among the newly
minted middle classes. Although Latin
America saw only half the average GDP
growth of emerging Asia over the past
ten years, its poverty rate fell by 30%.
Around a third of the decline is due to
improvements in income distribution.

In education, the big challenge is to complement quantity with quality. Latin America has now reaped the benefits that come from simply getting more children into school for longer.

How did a continent that had been
egregiously unequal since the *conquis-
tadores'* land grab suddenly change course? Not because of radical nationalization
and redistribution. Latin America has a few asset-seizing hard-left governments,
notably Argentina and Venezuela, but inequality has also fallen in countries following a more orthodox economic course, such as Chile and Colombia. Nor is the
turnaround just a side-effect of the commodities boom. Inequality has fallen in
countries that rely heavily on exports of commodities, such as Peru, but also in those
where manufacturing plays a bigger role, such as Mexico. Nor can demography be
the main cause. Poorer Latin American families have become smaller, which reduces
inequality, but these changes were well under way in the 1980s and 1990s.

According to Nora Lustig, an economist at the University of Tulane and one of
the first to document the narrowing of the region's income gaps, two things have
made a big difference. First, the premium for skilled workers has been falling: a
surge in secondary education has increased the supply of literate, reasonably well-
schooled workers, and years of steady growth have raised relative demand for the
less skilled in the formal workforce, whether as construction workers or cleaners.
Second, governments around Latin America have reinforced the narrowing of wage
gaps with social spending targeted at people with the lowest incomes. These include more generous pensions and conditional cash transfers—schemes that offer
payment to the poorest families in return for meeting specific conditions, such as
making sure their children go to school.

The most striking change has been in education. In the past Latin American
governments lavished cash on universities. State primary and secondary schools
were underfunded and of appalling quality. That bias in favour of tertiary education, perversely, most benefited the children of the rich, who had attended private
primary and secondary schools. But since the early 1990s education spending has
become much more progressive, with a huge expansion in public secondary education among the poor. According to Karla Breceda, Jamele Rigolini and Jaime Saavedra, three economists at the World Bank, Latin American governments, on average,
now spend a larger share of GDP on education for the poorest 20% of children than
does the United States.

More progressive spending has produced results. Some countries have seen an
increase of 20 percentage points in the share of children finishing secondary school.

Another study for the World Institute for Development Economics Research in Helsinki by Guillermo Cruces, Carolina García Domench and Leonardo Gasparini showed that the gap between rich and poor in secondary-school enrollment has fallen in all countries except El Salvador, Honduras, Guatemala and Nicaragua.

Many Latin countries are also championing pre-school education. Rio's city government, for instance, has dramatically increased its network of nursery schools since 2009, building 74 new ones in the past three years. Any child from a family below the poverty line is guaranteed a free place in a nursery from the age of six months.

A nudge in the right direction

Conditional cash transfers (CCTs) reinforce this focus on schooling. These stipends cost relatively little (typically 0.2–0.8% of GDP) but influence the priorities of many. About a quarter of Brazil's population now gets some money from Bolsa Família, the country's CCT scheme. State and local governments piggyback on top. In Rio, for instance, the city supplements Bolsa Família payments for 700,000 of its poorer families. If children do exceptionally well in exams, a bonus is paid. If they miss school, the payment stops. Ms. Martins realized her 14-year-old was skipping school only when her monthly stipend was docked. Several academic studies in Mexico show that kids in CCT schemes stay at school longer.

Better education is boosting social mobility. Historically, the link between parents' and children's education has been closer in Latin America than anywhere else. In Peru, for instance, almost 70% of a child's educational achievement can be predicted from its father's schooling. But a forthcoming report from the World Bank suggests that the current generation of Latin American children are both better educated than their parents and moving relatively faster up the education ladder. And, like India's poorest castes, disadvantaged indigenous people have made big gains.

These newly educated workers enjoy far better prospects in the formal workforce than their parents did. State pensions have become more generous. Countries from Argentina to Bolivia have introduced non-contributory pension schemes—in effect, a promise of government support for the elderly. Minimum wages across the continent have soared. Brazil's has risen by more than 50% in real terms since 2003. And since pension benefits are linked to the minimum wage, the two trends reinforce each other.

The precise contribution of better education, better opportunities for less skilled workers and bigger social spending differs by country. An analysis by Ms. Lustig, Luis López-Calva of the World Bank and Eduardo Ortiz-Juarez of the United Nations Development Programme suggests that narrower wage gaps explain most of the reduction in inequality throughout the region. According to calculations by Marcelo Neri, of the Institute for Applied Economic Research, government transfers explain about one-third of the drop in inequality in Brazil.

So far, so good. But will these gains last? In education, the big challenge is to complement quantity with quality. Latin America has now reaped the benefits that come from simply getting more children into school for longer. But most of the state schools are still much less good than their private equivalents. Virtually all middle- and upper-class children still go to private primary and secondary schools. Until those gaps in quality have been eliminated, educational inequities will persist. They are behind the recent wave of protests over education in Chile.

The more immediate challenge is how to pay for all this. Latin American states have traditionally not been progressive in outlook. Put crudely, governments raised revenue from the more affluent, then spent it on generous public pensions for those same people. Even now, 60% of transfer spending in Bolivia, for example, goes to people who are not poor. Mr. Saavedra calls it a "fragmentary social contract." Governments fail to provide good public services, and middle-class people rely on private education and health care. But they do get generous pensions in return for their taxes.

The long boom of the 2000s allowed a painless change to this social contract. Sustained growth brought in enough tax revenue to boost both education spending and transfers at the bottom without pushing up tax rates. The boom also allowed huge increases in minimum wages without apparent damage to employment. But as growth slows and the real value of minimum wages rises, that combination is becoming unviable.

If the improvements in inequality are to be maintained, let alone continued, tough choices will have to be made. Middle-class entitlements will need to be squeezed. Much like the United States, many Latin countries will have to decide whether to invest in poorer kids or continue to pay generous pensions to richer old people. In both places the social contract needs to be remade. For evidence that this is possible, turn to Sweden.

Analysis: Obama Faces Latin America Revolt over Drugs, Trade

By Brian Winter
Reuters, November 9, 2012

President Barack Obama will face an unprecedented revolt by Latin American countries against the U.S.-led drug war during his second term and he also may struggle to pass new trade deals as the region once known as "America's backyard" flexes its muscles like never before.

Washington's ability to influence events in Latin America has arguably never been lower. The new reality is as much a product of the United States' economic struggles as a wave of democracy and greater prosperity that has swept much of the region of 580 million people in the past decade or so.

It's not that the United States is reviled now—far from it. Although a few vocally anti-U.S. leaders like Venezuela's Hugo Chavez tend to grab the media spotlight, Obama has warm or cordial relations with Brazil, Mexico, and other big countries in the region.

Most Latin American leaders were rooting, either privately or publicly, for his re-election on Tuesday.

That said, even close allies are increasingly emboldened to act without worrying about what "Tio Sam" will say or do. Nowhere is that more evident than on anti-narcotics policy.

In 2012 as never before, many governments challenged the four-decade-old policies under which Washington has encouraged, and often bankrolled, efforts to disrupt the cultivation and smuggling of cocaine, marijuana and other drugs in the region.

The reasons for the unrest: Frustration with what many perceive as the pointless bloodshed caused by the "war on drugs," plus a feeling the United States has not done enough to reduce its own demand for narcotics—if, that is, it's even possible to curb demand.

Those are hardly new complaints but they used to be aired in private. In April, several presidents voiced doubts about anti-drug policies at a regional summit that Obama attended. At the U.N. General Assembly in September, the leaders of Mexico, Colombia and Guatemala—historically three of the most reliable U.S. partners on drug interdiction—called on world governments to explore new alternatives to the problem.

New Assertiveness

Obama and other U.S. officials have energetically lobbied against legalization of drugs or letting up in the fight against powerful smuggling gangs. Yet some leaders and well-connected observers across Latin America expect substantial shifts in the next few years.

"The taboo is broken," said Moises Naim, a senior associate at the Carnegie Endowment for International Peace in Washington. "2012 will go down as the year when Latin American governments became assertive and began making changes of their own accord."

It remains unclear what exactly the changes will look like or how many countries will embrace them.

Some leaders, such as Guatemalan President Otto Perez, have openly proposed legalizing or "decriminalizing" certain drugs. Others have pushed for less dramatic changes such as legalizing only marijuana or, like Mexico's Felipe Calderon, have spoken in vague terms of a "less prohibitionist" approach.

Uruguay has gone furthest, proposing a bill this year that would legalize marijuana and have the state distribute it. That move was regarded as too extreme by many in the region, although this week's decision by voters in Washington and Colorado states to legalize marijuana for recreational use showed that, even in the United States, the status quo is changing fast.

"Nobody knows where this is going yet," said Fernando Henrique Cardoso, a former Brazilian president and part of an influential group of statesmen who have met behind the scenes with current leaders to advance the debate.

"I'd describe this as a phase of timid, controlled experimentation," Cardoso told Reuters. "It's going forward, and it seems there will be changes ... Nobody seems very concerned with how the United States will react."

Democracy Is Complicated

Cardoso, 81, remembers an era of powerful U.S. ambassadors and so-called "banana republics"—when Washington often played a hand in installing leaders across Latin America and deposing those who incurred its wrath.

That period basically ended with the conclusion of the Cold War. Still, as recently as a decade ago, the United States still enjoyed more leverage than it does now—thanks to trade, foreign aid, and loans from groups like the International Monetary Fund in which Washington plays a major role.

The United States' economic slump has contributed to the changing dynamic. But so has a wave of broad-based economic growth in Latin America that has lifted some 50 million people into the middle class since 2003, allowed countries such as Brazil to pay off debts to the IMF, and made the region broadly less subject to foreign pressure.

Although there are exceptions, Latin America as a whole has also become more democratic. That makes it more complicated for Washington to shape events than it was during the 20th century, when one U.S. secretary of state famously described a Caribbean dictator as "a son of a bitch, but he's our son of a bitch."

"Laugh if you want, but there's no one son of a bitch for us to go talk to anymore in these countries," said Shannon O'Neil, a Latin America expert at the Council on Foreign Relations in New York. "There are still some people in Washington who don't fully understand that these democracies are just as complicated as ours is ... and that ends up hurting us sometimes."

She said the more robust democracies help explain the recent pushback against drug policy. "What you're seeing is a popular outcry against the violence, and these governments are responding to it."

U.S. envoys are now respectful of countries' sovereignty but still circle the region and warn about the dangers a change may pose. Obama said just before the April summit that legalizing drugs would not do away with violent cartels and "could be just as corrupting, if not more corrupting than the status quo."

Some countries such as Peru have heeded such warnings and are intensifying their drug crackdown. Alvaro Uribe, who was a stalwart U.S. ally as president of Colombia from 2002 to 2010 and meets regularly with some of the leaders feeding the debate, said it may result in fewer changes than some think.

"A lot of it is lip service," Uribe told Reuters. "In private, few speak of substantial changes."

Uribe, Cardoso and others agree that Mexico's incoming President Enrique Pena Nieto will be a key piece to the puzzle because of his country's size and proximity to the United States, as well as Mexico's status as the prime battleground for drug violence. Some 60,000 people have died in Mexican drug violence in the past six years.

> *The United States' economic slump has contributed to the changing dynamic. But so has a wave of broad-based economic growth in Latin America that has lifted some 50 million people into the middle class since 2003, allowed countries such as Brazil to pay off debts to the IMF, and made the region broadly less subject to foreign pressure.*

Pena Nieto is likely to discuss drug policy when he meets Obama before taking office in December. Aides have said Pena Nieto opposes legalization, although Chihuahua state governor Cesar Duarte—an ally of the incoming leader—told Reuters that Mexico should legalize the export of marijuana and consider other changes following the votes by Washington and Colorado.

A Big Push on Trade

On the other big issue the United States cares most about in Latin America—trade—the road ahead also looks bumpy.

Naim said Obama administration officials have told him they want to make a major push for free trade throughout the hemisphere during a second term. "They'll try to start with the big countries," Naim said. "Whoever wants in can join."

The push may find receptive ears in countries such as Mexico and Peru on Latin America's Pacific coast, which tend to be more open to trade, in part because of their relative proximity to Asia. Several of those countries already enjoy trade deals with the United States, but stand to gain from a broader agreement.

However, new trade talks have faced huge barriers in recent years because of strains on the global economy and Latin American countries are likely to be even more insistent on negotiating thorny issues like U.S. agricultural subsidies than they were in the past.

That's in part because they have other options. China's trade with Latin America soared from near nothing in the past decade and now accounts for about 11 percent of trade in the region. The U.S. share has fallen from 53 percent to 39 percent.

O'Neil said the most likely outcome may be a "divide down the hemisphere" in which Brazil, Argentina, Venezuela and a few other countries stay out of any new trade deal. Together, they account for about 60 percent of Latin America's economic output.

The more fertile ground for cooperation may lie in less glamorous, but still important issues like energy policy, education and intellectual property rights. Even there, though, it's clear the relationship is ever more one of equals.

"Latin America, especially Brazil and Mexico, represent a huge opportunity for the United States—if they can take advantage of it," said Andres Rozental, a former Mexican deputy foreign minister. "But the era of unilateralism and the almost monolithic influence of the Americans in the world is just not what it was."

(Additional reporting by Pablo Garibian and Dave Graham in Mexico City; Editing by Kieran Murray and Bill Trott)

The Shameful Legacy of the Monroe Doctrine: Militarizing Latin America

By Conn Hallinan
Counterpunch.org, January 16, 2013

This past December marked the 190th anniversary of the Monroe Doctrine, the 1823 policy declaration by President James Monroe that essentially made Latin America the exclusive reserve of the United States. And if anyone has any doubts about what lay at the heart of that Doctrine, consider that since 1843 the US has intervened in Mexico, Argentina, Chile, Haiti, Nicaragua, Panama, Cuba, Puerto Rico, Honduras, the Dominican Republic, Guatemala, Costa Rica, El Salvador, Uruguay, Grenada, Bolivia, and Venezuela. In the case of Nicaragua, nine times, and Honduras, eight.

Sometimes the intrusion was unadorned with diplomatic niceties: the U.S. infantry assaulting Chapultepec Castle outside Mexico City in 1847, Marines hunting down insurgents in Central America, or Gen. "Black Jack" Pershing pursuing Pancho Villa through Chihuahua in 1916.

At other times the intervention was cloaked in shadow—a secret payoff, a nod and a wink to some generals, or strangling an economy because some government had the temerity to propose land reform or a re-distribution of wealth.

For 150 years, the history of this region, which stretches across two hemispheres and ranges from frozen tundra to blazing deserts and steaming rainforests, was in large part determined by what happened in Washington. As the wily old Mexican dictator Porfirio Diaz once put it, the great tragedy of Latin America is that it lay so far from God and so near to the United States.

But Latin America today is not the same as it was 20 years ago. Left and progressive governments dominate most of South America. China has replaced the U.S. as the region's largest trading partner, and Brazil, Argentina, Uruguay, Paraguay, and Venezuela have banded together in a common market, Mercosur, that is the third largest on the planet. Five other nations are associate members. The Union of South American Nations and the Community of Latin American and Caribbean State have sidelined that old Cold War relic, the Organization of American States. The former includes Cuba, but excludes the U.S. and Canada.

On the surface, Mr. Monroe's Doctrine would appear to be a dead letter.

Which is why the policies of the Obama administration vis-à-vis Latin America are so disturbing. After decades of peace and economic development, why is the

U.S. engaged in a major military buildup in the region? Why has Washington turned a blind eye to two successful, and one attempted, coups in the last three years? And why isn't Washington distancing itself from the predatory practices of so-called "vulture funds," whose greed is threatening to destabilize the Argentinean economy?

As it has in Africa and Asia, the Obama administration has militarized its foreign policy vis-à-vis Latin America. Washington has spread a network of bases from Central America to Argentina. Colombia now has seven major bases, and there are U.S. military installations in Honduras, Costa Rica, Ecuador, Guatemala, Panama, and Belize. The newly reactivated Fifth Fleet prowls the South Atlantic. Marines are in Guatemala chasing drug dealers. Special Forces are in Honduras and Colombia. What are their missions? How many are there? We don't know because much of this deployment is obscured by the cloak of "national security."

The military buildup is coupled with a disturbing tolerance for coups. When the Honduran military and elites overthrew President Manuel Zelaya in 2009, rather than condemning the ouster, the Obama administration lobbied—albeit largely unsuccessfully—for Latin American nations to recognize the illegally installed government. The White House was also silent about the attempted coup against leftist Rafael Correa in Ecuador the following year, and has refused to condemn the "parliamentary" coup against the progressive president of Paraguay, Fernando Lugo, the so-called "Red Bishop."

Dark memories of American engineered and supported coups against governments in Brazil, Argentina, Chile and Guatemala are hardly forgotten on the continent, as a recent comment by Argentine economics minister Hernan Lorenzino made clear. Calling a U.S. Appeals Court ruling that Buenos Aires should pay $1.3 billion in damages to two "vulture fund" creditors "legal colonialism," the minister said, "All we need now is for [Appeals Court Judge Thomas] Griesa to send us the Fifth Fleet."

Much of this military buildup takes place behind the rhetoric of the war on drugs, but a glance at the placement of bases in Colombia suggests that the protection of oil pipelines has more to do with the marching orders of U.S. Special Forces than drug-dealers. Plan Colombia, which has already cost close to $4 billion, was conceived and lobbied for by the Los Angeles–based oil and gas company, Occidental Petroleum.

Colombia currently has five million displaced people, the most in the world. It is also a very dangerous place if you happen to be a trade unionist, in spite of the fact that Bogota is supposed to have instituted a Labor Action Plan (LAP) as part of the Free Trade Agreement (FTA) with Washington. But since the Obama administration said the Colombian government was in compliance with LAP, the attacks have actually increased. "What happened since [the U.S. compliance statement] is a surge in reprisals against almost all trade unions and labor activists that really believed in the Labor Action Plan," says Gimena Sanchez-Garzoli of the Latin American watchdog organization, WOLA. Human Rights Watch reached a similar conclusion.

The drug war has been an unmitigated disaster, as an increasing number of Latin American leaders are concluding. At least 100,000 people have been killed or

The drug war has been an unmitigated disaster, as an increasing number of Latin American leaders are concluding. At least 100,000 people have been killed or disappeared in Mexico alone, and the drug trade is corrupting governments, militaries and police forces from Bolivia to the U.S. border.

disappeared in Mexico alone, and the drug trade is corrupting governments, militaries and police forces from Bolivia to the U.S. border. And lest we think this is a Latin American problem, several Texas law enforcement officers were recently indicted for aiding and abetting the movement of drugs from Mexico to the U.S.

The Obama administration should join the growing chorus of regional leaders who have decided to examine the issue of legalization and to de-militarize the war against drugs. Recent studies have demonstrated that there is a sharp rise in violence once militaries become part of the conflict and that, as Portugal and Australia have demonstrated, legalization does not lead to an increase in the number of addicts.

A major U.S. initiative in the region is the North American Free Trade Agreement (NAFTA), even though it has led to increases in poverty, social dislocation, and even an increase in the drug trade. In their book *Drug War Mexico* Peter Walt and Roberto Zapeda point out that deregulation has opened doors for traffickers, a danger that both the U.S. Customs Service and the Drug Enforcement Administration (DEA) warned about back in 1993.

By lowering or eliminating tariffs, NAFTA has flooded Latin America with cheap, U.S. government subsidized corn that has put millions of small farmers out of business, forcing them to either immigrate, flood their country's overstressed cities, or turn to growing more lucrative crops—marijuana and coca. From 1994, the year NAFTA went into effect, to 2000, some two million Mexican farmers left their land, and hundreds of thousands of undocumented people have emigrated to the U.S. each year.

According to the aid organization, Oxfam, the FTA with Colombia will result in a 16 percent drop in income for 1.8 million farmers and a loss of income between 48 percent and 70 percent for some 400,000 people working under that country's minimum monthly wage of $328.08.

"Free trade" prevents emerging countries from protecting their own industries and resources, and pits them against the industrial might of the U.S. That uneven playing field results in poverty for Latin Americans, but enormous profits for U.S. corporations and some of the region's elites.

The White house has continued the Bush administration's demonization of president Hugo Chavez of Venezuela, in spite of the fact that Chavez has been twice elected by large margins, and his government has overseen a major reduction in poverty. According to the United Nations, Venezuelan inequality is the lowest in Latin America, poverty has been cut by a half, and extreme poverty by 70 percent. These kinds of figures are something the Obama administration supposedly hails.

As for Chavez's attacks on the U.S., given that the U.S. supported the 2002 coup against him, has deployed Special Forces and the CIA in neighboring Colombia, and takes a blasé attitude toward coups, one can hardly blame the Chavistas for a certain level of paranoia.

Washington should recognize that Latin America is experimenting with new political and economic models in an attempt to reduce the region's traditional poverty, underdevelopment, and chronic divisions between rich and poor. Rather than trying to marginalize leaders like Chavez, Correa, Evo Morales of Bolivia, and Christine Kirchner of Argentina, the Obama administration should accept the fact that the U.S. is no longer the Northern Colossus that always gets it way. In any case, it is the U.S. currently being marginalized in the region, not its opponents.

Instead of signing silly laws, like "The Countering Iran in the Western Hemisphere Act" (honest to God), the White House should be lobbying for Brazil to become a permanent member of the United Nations Security Council, ending its illegal and immoral blockade of Cuba, and demanding that Britain end support for its colony in the Falkland's or Malvinas. The fact is that Britain can't "own" land almost 9,000 miles from London just because it has a superior navy. Colonialism is over.

And while the administration cannot directly intervene with the U.S. Court of Appeals in the current dispute between Elliot Management, Aurelius Capital Management, and Argentina, the White House should make it clear that it thinks the efforts by these "vulture funds" to cash in on the 2002 Argentine economic crisis are despicable. There is also the very practical matter that if "vulture funds" force Buenos Aires to pay full fare for debts they purchased for 15 cents on the dollar, it will threaten efforts by countries like Greece, Spain, Ireland and Portugal to deal with their creditors. Given that U.S. banks—including the "vultures"—had a hand in creating the crisis in the first place, it is especially incumbent on the American government to stand with the Kirchner government in this matter. And if the Fifth Fleet does get involved, it might consider shelling Elliot's headquarters in the Cayman Islands.

After centuries of colonial exploitation and economic domination by the U.S. and Europe, Latin America is finally coming into its own. It largely weathered the worldwide recession in 2008, and living standards are generally improving throughout the region—dramatically so in the countries Washington describes as "left." These days Latin America's ties are more with the BRICS—Brazil, Russia, India, China and South Africa—than with the U.S., and the region is forging its own international agenda. There is unanimous opposition to the blockade of Cuba, and, in 2010, Brazil and Turkey put forth what is probably the most sensible solution to date on how to end the nuclear crisis with Iran.

Over the next four years the Obama administration has an opportunity to rewrite America's long and shameful record in Latin America and replace it with one built on mutual respect and cooperation. Or it can fall back on shadowy Special Forces, silent subversion, and intolerance of differences. The choice is ours.

Obama Seeks CEOs' Help in Latin America

By Jim Kuhnhenn
Associated Press, April 14, 2012

Declaring that a new environment for cooperation exists in the Americas, President Barack Obama sought to convince U.S. business Saturday that he's serious about expanding trade in Latin America while persuading the region to look northward once again.

Obama dismissed some of the tensions in the region as remnants of the past. He said the discussions and press accounts sometimes make him feel like he is in a "time warp" of "gun boat diplomacy and yanquis and the Cold War and this and that" dating to a time before he was born.

"That's not the world we live in today," he said. "My hope is that we all recognize this enormous opportunity we've got."

But playing the persuader is not an easy task. The U.S. faces trade competition from China, resistance from labor at home, a set of difficult regional issues that could dilute any focus on trade, and now the distraction of Secret Service agents in Cartagena relieved of duty on allegations of misconduct.

The business session was the first ever associated with a Summit of the Americas and it included executives from Wal-Mart Stores Inc., PepsiCo, Yahoo and Caterpillar. Obama was joined on the stage at the forum by host, Colombian President Juan Manuel Santos and Brazilian President Dilma Rousseff.

He complimented the governments of Colombia and Brazil for their remarkable economic growth, saying that they served as models for success in the region.

"When we look at how we're going to integrate further and take advantage of increased opportunity in the future it's very important for us to not ignore how important it is to have a clean, transparent, open government that is working on behalf of its people," he said.

While U.S. exports in dollar amounts have increased in the Americas, its share of the market has declined over the past decade. China, in particular, is surpassing the U.S as a trading partner with Brazil, Chile, and Peru.

In the United States, labor is restive over a trade deal with Colombia that is awaiting final certification. The Colombian government has worked to meet the requirements of a labor rights agreement that was a condition of passage in Congress last year. The question in Cartagena was whether Obama, over the objections of U.S. union leaders, would certify that Colombia successfully has met the terms.

Obama commended the trade deal with Colombia as a "win-win" for both countries, but was silent on its final implementation.

> *Among those pushing Obama to engage further in trade with Latin America is the U.S. Chamber of Commerce. Donohue told business leaders in Colombia that the U.S. is focusing too much on the Asia-Pacific region at the expense of Latin America. He called for more countries from the Americas to join the Trans-Pacific Partnership, which includes Chile and Peru.*

U.S. Chamber of Commerce President Tom Donohue, who was among the attendees, said in an interview Saturday that even if Obama did not take that step while in Cartagena, he would not consider that a setback and predicted final certification probably would come within weeks. He said Obama may not make a major announcement so as not to irritate allies who oppose the deal.

Trade could be eclipsed by other issues: the discussion over Cuba's exclusion from the summit, a call from Latin American countries to consider legalizing drugs to ease the violence associated with narcotrafficking, even Argentina's claims to the British-controlled Falkland Islands.

Adding an embarrassing wrinkle to the visit was Friday's acknowledgment by the Secret Service that agents facing allegations of misconduct for deeds before the president's arrival had been sent home.

On the drug front, Obama flatly declared at the conference that legalizing drugs was not the solution to the drug cartels and the violence that has confronted the region. He said he was open to holding the debate but said strong economies, the rule of law and reduced demand for drugs would better contain the flow of drugs.

Among those pushing Obama to engage further in trade with Latin America is the U.S. Chamber of Commerce. Donohue told business leaders in Colombia that the U.S. is focusing too much on the Asia-Pacific region at the expense of Latin America. He called for more countries from the Americas to join the Trans-Pacific Partnership, which includes Chile and Peru.

"When people think about trans-Pacific they're all thinking about Asia," Donohue said in the interview. "The reason I raised that is to put focus on the bigger question: 'Where are we going to put our assets? Where are we going to put our energy?'"

Donohue is pressing for a trade deal with Brazil, South America's largest economy and one with growing global influence. But he acknowledged that there is no appetite in the United States to initiate such a step before the November elections.

Obama, in answers to questions submitted by Latin American journalists before leaving for Cartagena, said the U.S. exports three times more to Latin America than to China. He said 60 percent of Latin America's exports to the United States are manufactured goods, whereas 87 percent of Latin America's exports to China were commodities.

"We believe that economic partnerships can't just be about nations extracting another's resources," he said.

The U.S. relationship with Argentina is increasingly contentious. U.S. companies complain that Argentina is erecting sizable barriers to U.S. exports. The Obama administration has bristled at the behavior and some in Washington wonder whether Argentina will remain in the Group of 20 large and emerging world economies.

Those issues could likely come up when Obama meets with Argentina's president, Cristina Fernandez, on the sidelines of the summit.

Remarks by President Obama at CEO Summit of the Americas

By President Barack H. Obama
Whitehouse.gov, April 14, 2011

President Obama: Well, first of all, I want to thank President Santos and the people of Colombia for the extraordinary hospitality in the beautiful city of Cartagena. We're having a wonderful time. And usually when I take these summit trips, part of my job is to scout out where I may want to bring Michelle back later for vacation. So we'll make sure to come back sometime in the near future. (Applause.)

I want to acknowledge Luis Moreno of IDB, as well as Luis Villegas of the National Business Association of Colombia, for helping to set this up, and everybody who's participating.

As President Rousseff indicated, obviously we've gone through some very challenging times. These last three years have been as difficult for the world economy as anything that we've seen in our lifetimes. And it is both a result of globalization and it is also a result of shifts in technology. The days when we could think of each of our economies in isolation, those days are long gone. What happens in Wall Street has an impact in Rio. What happens in Bogota has an impact in Beijing.

And so I think the challenge for all of our countries, and certainly the challenge for this hemisphere, is how do we make sure that that globalization and that integration is benefiting a broad base of people, that economic growth is sustainable and robust, and that it is also giving opportunity to a growing, wider circle of people, and giving businesses opportunities to thrive and create new products and new services and enjoy this global marketplace.

Now, I think the good news is this hemisphere is very well positioned in this global economy. It is remarkable to see the changes that have been taking place in a relatively short period of time in Latin and Central America and in the Caribbean. When you look at the extraordinary growth that's taken place in Brazil, first under President Lula and now under President Rousseff, when you think about the enormous progress that's been made here in Colombia under President Santos and his predecessor, what you see is that a lot of the old arguments on the left and the right no longer apply.

And what people are asking is, what works? How do we think in practical terms about delivering prosperity, training our people so that they can compete in the global economy? How do we create rule of law that allows businesses to invest with some sense of security and transparency? How do we invest in science and technology? How do we make sure that we have open and free trade at the same time as we're making sure that the benefits of free trade are distributed both between nations but also within nations?

And the good news is I think that, through various international organizations and organizations here within the hemisphere, we've seen enormous progress. Trade between the United States and Latin, Central—South America, Central America and the Caribbean has expanded 46 percent since I came into office—46 percent.

Before I came to Cartagena, I stopped in Tampa, Florida, which is the largest port in Florida. And they are booming and expanding. And the reason is, is because of the enormous expansion of trade and commerce with this region. It's creating jobs in Florida, and it's creating jobs in Colombia, and it's creating jobs in Brazil and throughout the region. Businesses are seeing that if they have an outstanding product or an outstanding service, they don't have to restrict themselves to one market, they now have a regional market and ultimately a global market in which they can sell their goods and succeed.

A couple of things that I think will help further facilitate this productive integration: Number one, the free trade agreement that we've negotiated between Colombia and the United States is an example of a free trade agreement that benefits both sides. It's a win-win. It has high standards—(applause)—it's a high-standards agreement. It's not a race to the bottom, but rather it says each country is abiding by everything from strong rules around labor and the environment to intellectual property protection. And so I have confidence that as we implement this plan, what we're going to see is extraordinary opportunities for both U.S. and Colombian businesses.

So trade agreements of the sort that we have negotiated, thanks to the leadership of President Santos and his administration, I think point the way to the future.

In addition, I think there is the capacity for us to cooperate on problems that all countries face, and I'll take just one example—the issue of energy. All of us recognize that if we're going to continue to grow our economies effectively, then we're going to have to adapt to the fact that fossil fuels are a finite resource and demand is going up much faster than supply. There are also, obviously, significant environmental concerns that we have to deal with. So for us to cooperate on something like joint electrification and electric grid integration, so that a country like Brazil, that is doing outstanding work in biofuels or hydro-energy, has the ability to export that energy but also teach best practices to countries within the region, create new markets for clean energy throughout the region—which benefits those customers who need electricity but also benefit those countries that are top producers of energy—that's another example of the kind of progress that we can make together.

On the education front, every country in the region recognizes that if we're going to compete with Asia, if we're going to compete with Europe, we've got to up our game. We have to make sure that we've got the best-trained workers in the world, we've got the best education system in the world. And so the work that President Rousseff and I are doing together to try to significantly expand educational exchanges and send young people who are studying science and engineering and computer science to the United States to study if they're Brazilian, down to Brazil to study best practices in clean energy in Brazil—there's enormous opportunity for us to work together to train our young people so that this hemisphere is filled with outstanding entrepreneurs and workers, and allows us to compete more effectively.

So there are a number of areas where I think cooperation is proceeding. Sometimes it's not flashy. I think that oftentimes in the press the attention in summits like this ends up focusing on where are the controversies. Sometimes those controversies date back to before I was born. (Laughter.) And sometimes I feel as if in some of these discussions or at least the press reports we're caught in a time warp, going back to the 1950s and gunboat diplomacy and Yanquis and the Cold War, and this and that and the other. That's not the world we live in today.

And my hope is, is that we all recognize this enormous opportunity that we've got. And I know the business leaders who are here today, they understand it; they understand that we're in a new world, and we have to think in new ways.

Last point I want to make—I think when you think about the extraordinary success in Brazil, the success in Colombia, a big piece of that is governance. You can't, I believe, have, over the long term, successful economies if you don't have some basic principles that are being followed: democracy and rule of law, human rights being observed, freedom of expression. And I think—and also personal security, the capacity for people to feel as if they work hard then they're able to achieve, and they have motivation to start a business and to know that their own work will pay off.

And I just want to compliment both Brazil and Colombia, coming from different political traditions, but part of the reason why you've seen sustained growth is governments have worked effectively in each country. And I think that when we look at how we're going to integrate further and take advantage of increased opportunity in the future, it's very important for us not to ignore how important it is to have a clean, transparent, open government that is working on behalf of its people.

And that's important to business as well. The days when a business feels good working in a place where people are being oppressed—ultimately that's an unstable environment for you to do business. You do business well when you know that it's a well-functioning society and that there's a legitimate government in place that is going to be looking out for its people.

So I just want to thank both of my outstanding partners here. They're true leaders in the region. And I can speak, I think, for the United States to say that we've never been more excited about the prospects of working as equal partners with our brothers and sisters in Latin America and the Caribbean, because that's going to be the key to our success. (Applause.)

Mr. Matthews: President Santos, I guess there are some issues in America—we have a very large Hispanic population. Ten percent of our electorate is going to be Hispanic in background. We are the second-largest Spanish-speaking country in the world after Mexico. People have dual languages in the United States, of course, but there is so much Spanish speaking. You have the chance to sit next to President Obama now. Do you want to ask him about the ways you think the United States could help your country in the drug war?

President Obama: Do you want me to respond?

Mr. Matthews: Yes, sir.

President Obama: Well, this is a conversation that I've had with President Santos and others. Just as the world economy is integrated, so, unfortunately, the drug trade is integrated. And we can't look at the issue of supply in Latin America without also looking at the issue of demand in the United States. (Applause.)

And so whether it's working with President Santos or supporting the courageous work that President Calderón is doing in Mexico, I, personally, and my administration and I think the American people understand that the toll of narco-trafficking on the societies of Central America, Caribbean, and parts of South America are brutal, and undermining the capacity of those countries to protect their citizens, and eroding institutions and corrupting institutions in ways that are ultimately bad for everybody.

So this is part of the reason why we've invested, Chris, about $30 billion in prevention programs, drug treatment programs looking at the drug issue not just from a law enforcement and interdiction issue, but also from a public health perspective. This is why we've worked in unprecedented fashion in cooperation with countries like Mexico on not just drugs coming north, but also guns and cash going south.

This is one of the reasons why we have continued to invest in programs like Plan Colombia, but also now are working with Colombia, given their best practices around issues of citizen security, to have not just the United States but Colombia provide technical assistance and training to countries in Central America and the Caribbean in finding ways that they can duplicate some of the success that we've seen in Colombia.

So we're mindful of our responsibilities on this issue. And I think it is entirely legitimate to have a conversation about whether the laws in place are ones that are doing more harm than good in certain places.

I personally, and my administration's position, is that legalization is not the answer; that, in fact, if you think about how it would end up operating, that the capacity of a large-scale drug trade to dominate certain countries if they were allowed to operate legally without any constraint could be just as corrupting if not more corrupting then the status quo.

Nevertheless, I'm a big believer in looking at the evidence, having a debate. I think ultimately what we're going to find is, is that the way to solve this problem is both in the United States, us dealing with demand in a more effective way, but it's also going to be strengthening institutions at home.

You mentioned earlier, the biggest thing that's on everybody's minds—whether it's the United States, Canada, Brazil, Colombia, Jamaica—is, can I find a job that allows me to support my family and allows my children to advance and feel secure. And in those societies where you've got strong institutions, you've got strong business investment, you've got rule of law, you have a law enforcement infrastructure that is sound, and an economy that's growing—that country is going to be like a

> *I think when you think about the extraordinary success in Brazil, the success in Colombia, a big piece of that is governance. You can't, I believe, have, over the long term, successful economies if you don't have some basic principles that are being followed: democracy and rule of law, human rights being observed, freedom of expression.*

healthy body that is more immune than countries that have weak institutions and high unemployment, in which kids see their only future as participating in the drug trade because nobody has actually trained them to get a job with Google, or Pepsi, or start their own small business.

And so I think that it's important for us not to think that if somehow we look at the drug issue in isolation, in the absence of dealing with some of these other challenges—institutional challenges and barriers to growth and opportunity and the capacity for people to climb their way out of poverty, that we're going to be able to solve this problem. The drug issue in this region is, in some ways, a cause, but it's also, in some ways, an effect of some broader and underlying problems. And we as the United States have an obligation not only to get our own house in order but also to help countries in a partnership to try to see if we can move in a better direction. (Applause.)

Mr. Matthews: Mr. President, do you want to respond? I think the question that seems to be apparent here in the last couple of days is, first of all, tremendous enthusiasm, a zeitgeist here that's almost unusual in the world for positive optimism about the development in this part of the world. It's not like it was—just isn't the way it was we grew up with.

The challenge I think you just heard from the President of Brazil was the notion that Latin America is not interested in being our complementary economy anymore—the agricultural end while we do the industrial end; they do the provision of raw materials and we do the finest and highest-level high-tech work. How do we either respond to Brazil's demand, really, to be partners and rivals—they want to use our educational resources, they want to come north to learn how to compete with us—right, Madam President? You want to be equals. You want to learn everything we know, and then take it back and shove it at us, right? (Laughter.) Isn't that it?

Well, anyway, that's the response—I'd ask you for your response. (Laughter.)

President Obama: Chris, I'm not sure you're characterizing what President Rousseff said—(laughter)—but this is what happens when you get some of our U.S. political commentators moderating a panel. (Laughter.) They try to stir up things that may not always be there. (Applause.) And Chris is good at it. He's one of the best. (Laughter.)

But, look, this is already happening. This is already happening. Brazil has changed, Colombia has changed—and we welcome the change. The notion somehow that we see this as a problem is just not the case, because if we've got a strong, growing, prosperous middle class in Latin America, those are new customers for our businesses. (Applause.)

Brazil is growing and that opportunity is broad-based, then suddenly they're interested in buying iPads, and they're interested in buying Boeing airplanes and—(laughter.)

President Rousseff: Boeing—Embraer. (Laughter and applause.)

President Obama: I was just trying to see how she'd respond to that. (Laughter.) But the point is, is that that's a market for us. So we in the United States should welcome not just growth, but broad-based growth, of the sort that President Rousseff described.

I'll give you just—I said I was in Tampa. All those containers that are coming in, they have, in some cases, commodities coming from Latin America, but they also have finished products that are coming in from Latin America. We have commodities that are going into Latin America that we're sending back on those containers, as well as finished products. And so this is a two-way street.

When I came into office, one of my first decisions was to say that the G20 was not a temporary thing to respond to the world economic crisis; this should be the permanent forum for determining and coordinating direction in the world economy. And frankly, there were some folks who were members of the G8 who were upset with me about that determination, but realistically you can't coordinate world economic issues if you don't have China and Brazil and India and South Africa at the table—and Mexico. That's not possible.

So the world has changed. I think the United States and U.S. businesses stand to benefit from those changes. But it does mean that we have to adapt to that competitive environment. And all the advantages that President Rousseff mentioned we have as the United States—its flexibility, our scientific edge, our well-educated workforce, our top universities—those are the things that we continue to have to build and get better at. And that's true for every country here.

Every one of the businesses here are going to be making determinations about where you locate based on the quality of the workforce, how much investment you have to make in training somebody to handle a million-dollar piece of equipment. Do you feel as if your intellectual property is going to be protected? Do you feel as if there's a good infrastructure to be able to get your products to market? And so I think this is a healthy competition that we should be encouraging.

And what I've said at the first summit that I came to, Summit of the Americas that I came to, was we do not believe there are junior partners and senior partners in this situation. We believe there are partners. And Brazil is in many ways ahead of us on something like biofuels; we should learn from them. And if we're going to be trying to mount a regional initiative, let's make sure that Brazil is taking the lead. It doesn't have to be us in every situation.

Now, the flip side is—and I'll close with this—I think in Latin America, part of the change in mentality is also not always looking to the United States as the reason for everything that happens that goes wrong. (Applause.)

I was in an interview—several interviews yesterday. These were actually with Spanish-speaking television stations that have broadcast back in the United States. And the first interviewer said, why hasn't the United States done more to promote democracy in the region, because you've done a lot in the Arab Spring but it seems as if you're not dealing with some of the problems here in Latin America. The next questioner said, why are you being so hard on Cuba and promoting democracy all the time? (Laughter and applause.) That's an example, I think, of some of the challenges we face that are rooted in legitimate historical grievances. But it gets—it becomes a habit.

When it comes to economic integration and exchanges, I am completely sympathetic to the fact that there are challenges around monetary policy in developed and less-developed countries. And Brazil, for example, has seen the Real appreciate in ways that had been hurtful. I would argue a lot of that has to do with the failure of some other countries to engage in rebalancing, not the United States. But having said that, I think there's not a country in Latin America who doesn't want to see the United States grow rapidly because we're your major export market.

And so most of these issues end up being complicated issues. Typically, they involve both actions in the United States as well as actions in the other countries if we're going to optimize the kind of growth and prosperity and broad-based opportunity that both President Santos and President Rousseff have spoken about.

And the United States comes here and says: We're ready to do business. We are open to a partnership. We don't expect to be able to dictate the terms of that partnership, we expect it to be a negotiation based on mutual interest and mutual respect. And I think we're all going to benefit as a consequence of that. (Applause.)

Mr. Matthews: Thank you very much, President Rousseff, President Santos, and my President, President Obama. Thank you. It's been an honor.

Latin America and the United States: Looking Towards 2020

By Sergio Bitar
Inter-American Dialogue, September 7, 2011

Introduction

We are very pleased to offer this policy brief prepared by Sergio Bitar, a long-time member and now non-resident senior fellow of the Inter-American Dialogue. Bitar served as senator as well as minister of energy and mines, education, and public works under three separate administrations in Chile. His forward-looking, nuanced, and constructive perspective about possible partnerships between Latin America and the United States over the next decade deserves to be part of the public debate. We hope that Bitar's views, which do not necessarily represent the opinions of *Dialogue* members or staff, contribute to a more thoughtful consideration of inter-American affairs.

Michael Shifter, President

The ongoing and unprecedented speed of global change demands a new responsibility from Latin American countries: if they are to govern more effectively they must anticipate change and think in the long term.

Across all policy areas—economic, social, technological, political, military, climate change, and immigration—global transformations are increasingly affecting the well-being of nations. Success will come to those best able to prepare for and design long-term strategies. The same holds true for international policy and, in particular, for future relations with the United States.

President Barack Obama's 2011 visit to Brazil, Chile and El Salvador generated both favorable and critical reactions that did not, in my view, adequately capture the magnitude of the changes underway that will shape the future. Nor did they correctly reflect the type of relations between the United States and Latin America that could characterize the coming decade.

This paper discusses four distinct issues: the new global reality that will frame US-Latin America relations, the new approach that could emerge in the United States, the possible paths for Latin America, and potential areas of collaboration between the United States and Latin America.

September 2011: The New Global Reality

Over the last decade, the United States has had to adjust to the relative decline of its global power. Its future influence will be subject to greater economic limitations. Latin America, meanwhile, with the exception of a few countries, has emerged from a decade of good governance in a stronger position. The region generally enters the next decade in favorable circumstances for continued development.

In speeches in the three countries he visited, President Obama recognized the emergence of a new multipolar world. As in Egypt and India and at the 2009 Summit of the Americas in Trinidad and Tobago, he proposed new alliances for the pursuit of global governance and, as a result, new partnerships among countries. Speaking in Santiago to the entire region, Obama used the word *partner* or *partnership* 24 times and repeated a phrase he had said in Trinidad: "There are no senior partners and there are no junior partners, there are only equal partners."

Obama's vision clearly differs from that of his predecessor. While President George W. Bush employed similar terminology, he carried out a markedly unilateral and militaristic policy based on the premise of a hegemonic power, which was divorced from the current reality. The data supporting this new reality are eloquent. The United States has accumulated an unprecedented debt that will limit its ability to wield global influence for many years, particularly in the coming decade. The recent financial crisis deeply shook the US economy and the international financial system, raising questions about the capacity of the United States to properly regulate its banking and financial sectors. The US military is over-extended, fighting wars on three fronts at the same time, and seems uncertain about how to deal with Chinese expansion.

Against this backdrop, the US administration appears to be advancing a new vision, one that maintains that the country will continue to be the leading power—but its power relative to others will decline. This vision recognizes that military muscle alone is not enough to maintain order, spread US values, and advance strategic interests. Instead, it reaffirms that the basis for renewed US power lies in the strengthening of a competitive economy, which is the only way to sustain its global influence.

For such a concept to take hold greater austerity in the US domestic economy will be required and new alliances to regain influence will need to be pursued. That thinking was reflected in President Obama's State of the Union address in January 2011.

Meanwhile, emerging economies keep upsetting the balance of economic power. In a February 2011 talk at the Carnegie Endowment for International Peace in Washington, Indian economist A. Virmani projected that the size of China's economy (measured by per-capita income, adjusted for purchasing power, and multiplied by the population) would overtake that of the United States by 2020, while India and Brazil would surpass Japan and France, respectively, by 2015, and Russia would surpass Germany shortly after 2020.

China keeps growing at a pace that shows no signs of slowing. Its saving rate is more than 40 percent, the world's highest. Its consumption level in recent years has been less than 40 percent of GDP, while Europe's is 60 percent and the United States' exceeds 70 percent.

Its domestic market has a tremendous potential for growth, fueled by the rapid expansion of the middle class. The domestic market and strong public spending enable China to protect itself from the vagaries of external demand and keep growth rates up. That middle class will keep driving demand for commodities and food, along with new goods and services. China's economy is nimble and competitive. In this decade, it risks a slowdown only if growing pressure for a political opening and more freedom and participation prove unmanageable for the ruling Communist Party.

India, likewise, is seeing continued growth that will make it a stronger influence in global and hemispheric affairs. In this context, it is plausible that in coming years Latin America will continue to move towards Asia. After all, Asia's share of new global demand will be greater than those of the advanced economies, and the region will also offer new export markets and investments in Latin America.

The two giants—China and India—will join Brazil, Russia, Indonesia, and Turkey in posting growth rates that exceed those of the developed nations and therefore accounting for a larger share of world GDP.

The world that is taking shape will be multipolar and more interconnected and interdependent than ever before. The United States will be its largest shareholder, though a minority one—and it will have to come to terms with these new circumstances.[1] Latin America, for its part, faces a new window of opportunity that it should take advantage of. It is well positioned for a forward push to pursue substantive reforms in the coming decade. The United States cannot underestimate the importance of a region whose current population of 500 million is expected to reach 600 million by 2020.

National differences aside, Latin America's democracies have spread and will continue to deepen. The progress achieved should be viewed in light of the changes underway in the Middle East. For the most part, Latin America has little risk of armed conflict among countries. Its key challenge is to defeat the violence and organized crime that threatens democratic institutions, especially in northern Central America.

Latin American economies have grown and diversified. In recent years their governments' macroeconomic management has been more responsible and effective than that of the developed countries. Most nations have made significant strides in reducing poverty, although serious inequalities remain.

Speaking at the Center for Strategic and International Studies on March 18, 2011, Secretary of State Hillary Clinton emphasized just how important Latin America has become for the United States. More than 40 percent of US exports go to the region; the United States sells more to Chile and Colombia than to Russia; and Brazil is a global power with a growing economy and deepening democracy that will play a greater role in the energy field. Clinton underlined that geography was an important factor to maintain and improve the close link between the United States and Mexico and Central America, to work jointly with new initiatives to address serious crime and drug issues.

New US Approaches

"A National Strategic Narrative," a recent report by two active service US military officers writing under the pseudonym Mr. Y, reflects the new argument to maintain US global influence.[2] There is confusion over and disagreements about how to address the new situation.

Since the fall of the USSR, the United States no longer faces the kind of enemy that would help define a national security strategy to order priorities. Although the Japanese challenge in the 1990s surprised many, it had neither the size nor the military might to cause concern. China, a large, highly competitive economy with global reach in all areas, poses a different kind of challenge.

The United States' unquestionable military power can only be used under very specific circumstances. Moreover, it is very costly to be the world's policeman. To remain competitive and sustainable, the United States will have to shift its efforts toward innovation and domestic investment in order to exert global influence and finance its technological and military superiority.

The wide range of powers that is emerging—by region and issue—requires flexible and diverse alliances that are underpinned by economic and technological capacities and credible values.

Economic thinking about development has also been changing. Even the World Bank, an institution that has traditionally embraced the economic logic espoused by the so-called Washington Consensus, has shifted its emphasis. Speaking in 2011 at the Peterson Institute for International Economics, World Bank President Robert Zoellick said that a market economy and sound macroeconomic management are not enough for development. He said the criteria to select and implement programs and projects should not only include economic aspects, but social (poverty reduction) and political (citizen participation) dimensions as well. Also critical are institutional reforms that foster accountability and transparency.

These ideas will gain an influence in Latin America if they are consistent and repeated enough. Indeed, citizens armed with new interactive communication technologies will increasingly challenge control exercised by ruling Latin American elites, demanding greater openness and participation.

As communications technology grows by leaps and bounds, the United States is also experiencing greater exposure to foreign issues. International problems once far removed from the average US citizen now have a direct impact and are increasingly the subjects of domestic debate.

Conservative sectors tend to see the expansion of other countries as a threat and react either by clamoring for hardline policies or urging isolation. Liberals with ties to organized labor, on the other hand, demand stricter labor and environmental standards in free-trade agreements and insist that they be closely monitored. It is likely that future US-Latin America relations may be more subject to US domestic interests and pressures than in the past.

Latin America should closely follow the evolution of global economic and political developments, including what happens in the United States and Chinese behavior. Relations with the United States will take place in a global, not a hemispheric, context.

Latin American Paths

Future US-Latin America relations will hinge on development strategies and goals proposed by countries in the region. The driving forces of the future will depend on internal factors—areas of specialization and people's aspirations—and on global processes of change that each country will have to adapt to and take advantage of. Setting a long-range strategy and defining priorities are the principal tasks facing each Latin American nation. Only then will it be possible to clearly identify and pursue areas of collaboration.

Latin America's strategic thinking is poor. Short-term views have usually prevailed over longer-term visions that help set ambitious goals and objectives and seek internal pacts to achieve results.

> *For the most part, Latin America has little risk of armed conflict among countries. Its key challenge is to defeat the violence and organized crime that threatens democratic institutions, especially in northern Central America.*

When one compares Latin America's development with those of successful Asian countries, what stands out are the economic and social weaknesses that slow the region's growth: inequality, low productivity, low savings rates, ideology, lack of ambition, and absence of a vision for development. Asian experts' analysis of the future of Latin America is instructive.[3] High levels of violence in the region are also striking.

Still, the current decade is promising for Latin America. External factors will provide more markets, better prices, and foreign investment. The economic and political situation in most countries is more solid than in the past. It is time to move decisively on fundamental reforms.

Will Latin America be able to avoid the so-called "middle-income trap"? Various countries are able to reach per capita incomes of between $10,000 and $15,000 (measured by purchasing power parity), yet few have gone beyond that range to achieve higher levels. Brazil seems to be the only case going in this direction.

What Is Needed?

One of the most important decisions for Latin America is how best to take advantage of the favorable circumstances. It is crucial to manage intelligently the expansion of export income from natural resources. Current favorable circumstances—the product of high mineral, fuel, and food prices, abundant capital flows to the region, and a recovering global economy—present twin risks: complacency and the populist temptation.

Both can bring undesired effects. Mismanagement of the economy, excessive consumerism, and unchecked fiscal expansion may lead to overheating, inflation, and then a contraction. On the other hand, squandering available resources instead of making productive and social investments can weaken the future economic foundation, prevent increases in productivity, and discourage necessary export specialization in new products.

Two guidelines are essential to pursue a course that avoids both risks. The first is to apply an economic policy that protects the domestic economy from frequent global volatility (e.g., stabilization funds financed by export revenues, disincentives to short-term or speculative capital). In mismanaged economies, abrupt variations in foreign exchange can harm the productive capacity in alternative export sectors (i.e., Dutch disease) or delay the upgrade of services that are crucial to increase productivity.

The second guideline involves using export revenues to invest in the renovation and specialization of the productive structure. To do this well will call for going beyond the false dilemma between the export of commodities vs. goods and services. Instead, it is vital to act on *both* those fronts. Since the outlook for global growth means rising demand for minerals, energy, and food supplies, producer countries have no other option but to boost productivity, incorporating high technology and offering greater value-added. Such a comparative advantage should be used as leverage to open up opportunities for new areas of specialization, expert training, and technological research.

The combination of policies will vary depending on the country, as seen in the cases of Mexico and Brazil. Mexico, which is more closely tied to the US economy and other developed countries and exports fewer natural resources, will have a more limited space for growth than Brazil in coming years. As a recent Inter-American Development Bank (IADB) report[4] notes, Brazil will grow faster because it sells less to industrialized countries and has larger mineral, energy, and food products available for export to Asia.

Still, nothing is predetermined. It is clear that the future will be decided by the changes pursued by each nation. Mexico could undertake reforms and introduce incentives to increase its oil and agricultural output, both in high demand globally. It could also improve its connections with the US economy, which might yet exceed recovery expectations.

Essential Priorities for Latin America

Which policies and international agreements could be most fruitful in helping countries both specialize in high-tech natural resource production while at the same time diversify into more sophisticated sectors?

Education and infrastructure are two priority areas for development—and Latin America can avail itself of foreign assistance in both. In education, some countries need to guarantee K–12 coverage, and all of them need to improve quality. These are domestic tasks, but foreign support can help narrow the gap in areas such as graduate studies and technological research. President Obama's proposal to increase the number of US graduate students in Latin America to 100,000—and also increase the number of Latin Americans studying in the United States by the same number—can play a key role in launching ambitious initiatives of cooperation.

Infrastructure is the second major challenge. It is estimated that Latin America will need US$1 trillion for infrastructure improvements in the coming decade. In addition to fiscal resources, better infrastructure will require growing support from the IADB, CAF, and other international financial institutions, along with private contributions through concessions or international businesses. China could become an even more relevant actor in the region should it decide to complement its search for commodities and food with investments in infrastructure and other industries.

Energy is another critical area. The United States will need to secure supplier arrangements with Latin American oil producers, while Latin America will need markets, along with investment and innovation in biofuels and renewable energy, especially solar. On renewal energy and environmental questions, it would be fruitful to pursue technology transfers and joint research initiatives.

The intense relationship with Asia will increase the importance of the South Pacific and will demand better infrastructure and services. The Trans-Pacific partnership should provide Latin American APEC members with new opportunities for coordination with the rest of the region and the United States.

Though each country's path will be different, there are shared priorities. These include: education, science and technology, infrastructure, productivity, specialization, social inclusion, equal opportunity, strengthening of democratic institutions, and citizen participation.

Education and infrastructure will provide the human and physical capital. Better services and new technologies will help increase productivity. And an emphasis on renewable energy will increase exports in more environmentally friendly ways. The strongest performers will be those that make a big bet on changing production structures to achieve the green economy of the future and that forge Korean-style public-private partnerships.

The task ahead is complex. Neither good macroeconomic policies nor growth alone are sufficient. Absent greater equality, protection, and social inclusion, success will remain elusive. Sustainable growth is not possible in countries marked by inequalities in income and power and that lack national unity and self-confidence. Greater social mobility, an emphasis on merit, and equal opportunity are preconditions for tackling ambitious challenges and avoiding the middle-income trap. This task will demand tax reforms that generate resources to provide public goods that will increase national well-being and productivity, which go hand-in-hand.

In the new stage of Latin America's development, strengthening institutions and broadening citizen participation are other prerequisites for success. Although our democracies are marked by periodic elections, it is now crucial to expand citizen participation, enlarge the role of civil society, and guarantee transparency in government. In some South American nations, democratically elected executives bent on staying in power have attempted to subordinate independent institutions. In Central America and Mexico, organized crime undermines the governments and the democratic system. This scourge is draining national energies; defeating it is a collective task. Installing a democracy and living in peace is considerably harder than implementing sound economic policy. And without democratic institutions, economic policy is not sustainable.

Active involvement in global governance should also be a priority for Latin American countries, especially medium-sized and smaller ones. In a multipolar world, it makes sense for Latin America to support multilateralism and participate more actively in global governance. In the coming years, Latin America should seek a larger presence in the G-20, the International Monetary Fund, the World Bank, and the United Nations. Unlike larger countries, each of the small and medium-sized countries will not be able on their own to influence the international issues that concern them. Joint action to reform multilateral agencies is, therefore, crucial to the defense of their national interests.

Each country will have to reinforce its strategic thinking and look at the medium term to identify the vital reforms that improve the well-being of its citizens.

New Opportunities for US-Latin America Relations: Which Partnerships?

To prepare new partnerships it is important to have in mind the three processes already reviewed: prevailing global trends, US government policies and the status of the US economy, and priorities that Latin American governments are ready to carry out.

The United States faces years of constraints. It will have to devote greater resources to preserving the competitive and technological edge that is critical to maintaining its influence.

It is likely that Latin America—especially South America—will continue to multiply its exchanges with Asia over the next five years. Rates of investment and the expansion of the middle class in China, India, and other middle-income countries will drive global growth through expanded domestic consumption. Latin America will account for a larger share of the demand for products than industrialized countries.

In this global context, the United States will be closely following events in Latin America—as a market, an energy supplier, and a region with which it shares problems and opportunities. Most US attention will focus on Mexico and Brazil, albeit for different reasons and with different emphases. Mexican markets, oil resources, and migrants have a strong impact in the United States. Mexico and the United States need to work closely together in combating drugs and organized crime. Brazil will draw high levels of US attention because of its rising global role, expanding market, industrial progress, and the production of oil, food and biofuels.

Immigration will continue to be necessary for the United States to sustain its growth. Negative aspects of immigration tend to grab the spotlight, but the fact remains that Latin American immigrants make a major contribution to the US economy. A recent report[5] projects that the US population will increase from 310 million in 2010 to 370 million in 2030, half of it as a result of immigration. This would make the United States the only industrialized country to have population growth through 2030.

Leaving aside Brazil and Mexico—whose size will make them increasingly important actors—the rest of the countries should cooperate and coordinate with one another more effectively to have some influence on global political and economic trends. The expanding role of Brazil and Mexico is guaranteed by their sheer size. But smaller Latin American countries must seek closer cooperation and coordination to enhance their influence. Each will take the initiative and seek mutually beneficial arrangements with the United States. As a start, three areas are worth pursuing: democracy strengthening; energy and climate change; and education, science, and technology.

Democracy Strengthening

a) In Central America, collaboration could bolster the fight against organized crime, improve citizen security, and strengthen democratic institutions. The United States has proposed a Central America Citizen Security Partnership. High levels of drug consumption and arms sales to countries south of the border give the United States a special responsibility in this regard. Mexico and Colombia can also make an important contribution, while South America can cooperate in security, crime investigation, police training, and other initiatives.

b) South American nations should get more involved in providing assistance to Haiti.

c) The region should also offer support to help facilitate a transition to democracy in Cuba. Despite the steps taken by the Obama administration regarding visits and remittances, the ineffective US embargo continues with no end in sight. For Latin Americans, it will be important to have conditions in place for a peaceful transition when Cuban leadership changes. It is helpful to encourage some processes underway in Cuba, such as the release of political prisoners, improved freedom of expression, and economic reforms, which could pave the way for a democratic opening.

Energy and Climate Change

Although President Obama has spoken about an Energy and Climate Partnership of the Americas, its content, priorities, goals, and resources remain unclear.

a) There are opportunities for collaboration in developing renewable energy sources, especially solar, and assisting with nuclear plant safety and ethanol, cleaner coal, and natural gas research.

b) Partnership with the United States could also help Latin America reduce CO_2 emissions, protect tropical and temperate forests, and safeguard glaciers and water resources. Latin America abounds in natural resources and must take measures to protect them.

c) Climate change and increasing concentration of the population will intensify the impact of natural disasters. Emergency preparedness requires effective institutions, first responder training, equipment acquisition, public education, and improved land use and construction standards. Latin American countries can take the initiative in these areas.

Education, Science, and Technology

Education, science, and technology help increase productivity and drive growth. Collaboration in these areas could focus on goods and services, with an emphasis on the use of information and communications technology. Latin American countries should propose innovative initiatives and explore areas of potential agreement, including:

a) President Obama's only quantitative proposal was to increase the number of US graduate students studying in Latin America to 100,000 and the number of Latin Americans studying in the United States to 100,000. To date, Asia has taken better advantage than Latin America of the academic excellence offered by US universities. New proposals designed to stimulate and fund these exchanges are needed. Chile's 2008 *Becas Chile* student aid program is a good example with much potential.

b) Joint research in areas of importance to Latin America should be expanded. These include renewable energy, especially solar, biotechnology, and collaboration between Latin American and US businesses and research centers. A Rand Corporation report[6] identifies 16 technology applications that will change living conditions in this decade and notes that some Latin American countries will be able to adopt them if they carry out certain policies and make a sustained effort. And it is important to remember that proficiency in English is an essential tool in a knowledge-based society.

c) With respect to trade, the United States should move to eliminate barriers and open its market to Latin American products, especially foods. If WTO talks remain deadlocked, free trade agreements between the United States and Latin America should be expanded. There are serious political obstacles given the concern that such an approach would result in less employment in the United States. A more open global economy helps small and medium-sized countries whose development depends on exporting goods and services with increasing value-added.

The 24 references to "partner" and "partnership" in President Obama's Santiago speech should not remain empty talk. While some may interpret Obama's logic of partnership as a sign of disinterest, I believe it reflects the new reality within which the United States will have to function.

It falls to all Latin Americans to take a more active role in pursuing opportunities and demanding that the United States make a firm commitment to its proposed new partnerships.

Are Latin Americans prepared for this? Is there enough will in the United States to seek such partnerships? It is worth making a serious effort to see if this can work.

Notes

1. See Bruce Jones, "Largest Minority Shareholder in Global Order," Policy Paper 25 (Washington, DC: Brookings, March 2011).

2. Mr. Y, "A National Strategic Narrative" (Washington, DC: Woodrow Wilson Center for International Scholars, 2011).

3. See Harinder Kohli, "Vision Latin America 2040" and Homi Kharas, "Latin America, Is Average Good Enough?" in *Latin America 2040: Breaking Away from Complacency* (Sage Publications, 2010).

4. Alejandro Izquierdo and Ernesto Calvi, "One Region, Two Speeds" (Washington, DC: IADB, March 2011).

5. Nicholas Eberstadt, "World Population Prospects and the Global Economic Outlook: The Shape of Things to Come," AEI Working Paper Series, No. 5 (Washington, DC: American Enterprise Institute, February 2011).

6. Richard Silberglitt, Philip S. Antón, David R. Howell, and Anny Wong, "The Global Technology Revolution 2020, In-Depth Analyses" (RAND Corporation, 2006).

2

NAFTA Twenty Years Later

A truck crosses the border between Mexico and the United States in Nuevo Laredo, Mexico, Friday, October 21, 2011.

Assessing NAFTA

In 1994, the United States, Canada, and Mexico entered into a continental trade deal, agreeing to eliminate virtually all tariffs and restrictions on the exchange of goods between them. The North American Free Trade Agreement (NAFTA) created the world's largest free-trade zone and ushered in a new era of regional economic liberalization.

For the developed economies of the United States and Canada, NAFTA introduced new market opportunities and lower production costs. For Mexico, NAFTA created opportunities for economic development by bringing American and Canadian businesses into the country. Mexican officials hoped the deal would level the playing field between Mexico and its neighbors to the north.

After twenty years, NAFTA remains in place. Government officials, policy analysts, economists, and social scientists are now reflecting on the last two decades, examining the trade deal's effects on the people and economies of North America. These effects have been significant for Mexico in particular. As part of the agreement, the country made significant changes to its infrastructure and economic policies. In addition to the treaty's economic impacts, experts are also examining the social implications of the treaty—namely, NAFTA's relevance to public health issues, the environment, and poverty alleviation.

Mexico's Adaptations

Prior to the 1990s, Mexico heavily regulated many of its industries in order to protect them from international competitors. The Compañía Nacional de Subsistencias Populares (National Company of Popular Subsistence, CONASUPO) served as government buying agent, guaranteeing that Mexican agricultural products were purchased at a consistent price threshold. When it entered into NAFTA, Mexico began to phase out government-sponsored agricultural enterprises, including CONASUPO, and the country's agricultural sector was disengaged from government pricing programs.

In addition to eliminating most controls on pricing, Mexico undertook an important constitutional change: in 1991, it approved an amendment to its constitution regarding land use. Previously, indigenous populations who had gained land during the Mexican Revolution in the early twentieth century were prohibited from selling, renting, or otherwise redistributing those lands. The aim of the provision was to insure land access to poor people. The 1991 amendment eliminated this land use provision, enabling increased access to Mexican land for industrial agriculture and promoting private investment and credit for Mexican farmers.

Furthermore, Mexico (like the United States and Canada) eliminated most tariffs and trade restrictions on imports and exports. Because NAFTA resulted in significantly different pricing structures for various products, the United States, Mexico, and Canada needed to agree upon a set of pricing guidelines. For Mexico, this aspect of NAFTA was gradual—the elimination of tax regimes occurred over time. As a result, the country was slow to realize many of the financial benefits of NAFTA.

Economists and Mexican officials anticipated that the trade deal would be a boon for the country's labor force. To be sure, a large number of American businesses opened factories in Mexico City and along the US-Mexico border. Transportation corridors between American and Mexican facilities and cities expanded, creating job opportunities across a number of sectors. However, outside of Mexico's northern states and the greater Mexico City area, NAFTA's impact has been felt less, and in southern Mexican states such as Oaxaca, poverty levels remain high.

Public Health and Environmental Issues

There is a debate over whether or not the trade relationships established by NAFTA will foster an increase or decrease in attention to public health and environmental protection. During the early years of NAFTA, scholars looked at data regarding greenhouse gas emissions for evidence. Some theorized Mexico would lower its environmental standards in order to facilitate greater output from its factories and manufacturing facilities. Other believed that NAFTA would bring Mexico into line with the environmental standards of the United States and Canada. In recent years, a clearer picture of Mexico's greenhouse gas emissions has emerged. According to scientists, the country's greenhouse gas emissions have increased as a result of its manufacturing output. At the same time, however, Mexico's industrial efficiency is improving at a modest rate, making production more efficient and reducing the emission of certain types of air pollution.

While experts are correlating data on greenhouse gas emissions with NAFTA, they are still gathering information about environmental pollution from Mexican manufacturing facilities. Of particular interest are Mexican "maquiladoras," or manufacturing facilities located along the US-Mexican border. These factories receive American parts and supplies through relaxed trade restrictions and export finished products worldwide. A large number of these facilities are operated by American subsidiaries. Maquiladoras have been in operation since the 1960s, but their numbers have increased significantly since the passage of NAFTA. The number of Mexicans employed by maquiladoras has increased significantly since the early 1990s.

Although maquiladoras have provided job opportunities in the northern states of Mexico, they have been criticized for paying low wages and disregarding employee safety standards. Maquiladoras have also been accused of maintaining poor waste management standards. An estimated 1.3 million workers are employed by approximately three thousand maquiladoras along the US-Mexico border. A considerable number of those workers are unaware of the potential dangers posed by their workplace. In a 1998 survey of maquiladora workers, more than 50 percent of respondents said they had never been made aware of any potential workplace hazards. Twenty percent of survey respondents also reported a work-related illness.

Meanwhile, water and air quality remain low throughout the border region. Although these conditions violate Mexican law and NAFTA protocols, there have been few improvements. It has been theorized that the only factor lowering pollution rates in the region was reduced output caused by the global recession of 2007–10.

The Socioeconomic Effects of NAFTA

NAFTA initiated significant changes in Mexico's land use regulations. Previously, the constitution prohibited poor Mexicans from selling or otherwise reallocating their own lands. The assumption was that the country's indigenous population would permanently lose their land and livelihood if permitted to enter into private land arrangements. Although the land use amendment has fostered private investment and economic development in previously underdeveloped regions, it has also raised alarms among sociologists and advocates for the poor.

A 2012 study concluded that the amendment reflected an institutionalized prejudice among Mexicans against the country's indigenous populations. According to the study, supporters of the amendment wrongly believed that poor indigenous populations would adjust quickly to the new land use agreement and relocate to areas where jobs were available. Indeed, migration among Mexico's poor population has become more common as the country has developed economically. However, prior to the land use amendment, internal migration in Mexico occurred more slowly under the influences of the pre-NAFTA domestic economy. In the era of NAFTA, migration patterns respond to the ever-changing demands of a globalized economy. The mass migration of rural populations to urban areas has caused an increase in the establishment of slums around Mexico City.

Additionally, critics argue that NAFTA has encouraged the entrenchment of industrialized agriculture in Mexico. They argue that the land use amendment has taken land from indigenous people and put it under the control of Western-based corporations who have little regard for its long-term sustainability and whether or not the products produced on the land are used to meet local demand for foodstuffs. Meanwhile, the lack of domestically produced foodstuffs and the international price of corn has caused increases in tortilla prices, a staple food among Mexico's poor populations.

The mass migration of Mexicans also has important implications for the United States and Canada. The issue of illegal immigration has sparked a contentious debate in America. While some argue that the United States should tighten its immigration policy and border security, others argue that migrants benefit the economy by performing jobs that American citizens do not want.

In a 2010 paper, Emilio Viano of American University asks another question: should NAFTA promote the movement of people across Canadian, Mexican, and United States borders in the same manner it promotes the cross-border flow of commodities and products? Looking back on twenty years of NAFTA, Viano's question is a valid one. As NAFTA's signatories look to update certain provisions of the treaty in the twenty-first century, it is likely that this question will be a major part of the discussion.

NAFTA's Lessons and Implications for Free Trade Agreements

By creating the largest free-trade zone in the world, NAFTA signaled a new era of global trade and inspired other nations to enter into similar regional trade agreements. In many ways, NAFTA has been a success. It has fostered increased trade and cooperation among the United States, Canada, and Mexico. In 2009, the Carnegie Endowment for International Peace sponsored a study of NAFTA, offering a number of suggestions for modifications to the agreement. Many of the foundation's recommendations involve the health and well-being of workers, environmental and waste management standards, and the promotion of a level economic playing field among signatories. The latter recommendation, according to the study, entails the introduction of development programs targeting rural development, education, environmental protection, and job creation.

From Mexico's perspective, NAFTA has largely met the expectations the country identified when it signed the agreement. According to a recent Congressional Research Service report, NAFTA helped stabilized the Mexican economy, promoted economic development in a number of regions, and fostered foreign investment in Mexico. Significant challenges remain regarding poverty, worker health and safety, and the environment. For this reason, many experts argue that the next stage of NAFTA should feature a focus on these issues in an attempt to ensure the equitable benefits of free trade agreements for their respective participants well into the future.

In Our Opinion: NAFTA's Success Shows Importance of Free Trade

Deseret News, August 15, 2012

A couple of myths regarding free trade agreements seem to persist. One is that they cost jobs here in the United States. The other is that trade deficits are necessarily always bad.

Both are worth considering this year as the United States, Canada and Mexico mark the 20th anniversary of the signing of the North American Free Trade Agreement, which took effect two years later, in 1994. The evidence is clear that NAFTA has been good for all three countries, but that's not the story some people like to spread.

Has it cost jobs? In some sectors of the U.S. economy, yes. But the premise behind free trade is that each nation can provide some items more cheaply, and with better quality, than the others. The result is cheaper goods for all, freeing up more money for investment in other sectors of the economy.

When it comes to understanding the benefits of global trade, clothing provides a perfect example. Americans of modest means today can afford many more outfits than their ancestors of even 50 years ago, and with much better quality. And yet, few of the clothes they wear were manufactured in this country. NAFTA provides similar benefits on a tighter geographic scale.

In a similar way, trade deficits can bring an influx of foreign capital and investment to the United States that helps create jobs. Daniel Griswold of the Cato Institute—"a think tank dedicated to the principles of individual liberty, limited government, free markets and peace," according to its website—wrote in an essay last year that an examination of the evidence has "found that civilian employment in the past 30 years has actually grown quite a bit faster during periods of rising trade deficits compared to periods of declining deficits."

Griswold found that during the first five years of NAFTA, "the U.S. economy added a net 15 million new jobs, including 700,000 manufacturing jobs." Using 2010 figures, he found that, despite recessions, the U.S. economy employed 20 million more workers than it did before NAFTA.

NAFTA has helped the economies of all three nations. Trade among them tripled during the first 14 years, according to the Office of the U.S. Trade Representative. Contrary to frequent criticisms, the three partners have negotiated agreements that provide for effective domestic labor laws and working conditions. They also

> *Contrary to frequent criticisms, the three partners have negotiated agreements that provide for effective domestic labor laws and working conditions. They also have cooperated on environmental rules. And the manufacturing base has expanded in all three nations.*

have cooperated on environmental rules. And the manufacturing base has expanded in all three nations.

NAFTA does have shortcomings, but these involve ways in which it has yet to be fully implemented. Harold L. Sirkin, senior partner of The Boston Consulting Group, wrote recently that the three countries have failed to fully integrate their economies and become more cooperative in areas where they don't need to be quite as competitive. Canada's strengths include natural resources and energy, the United States is a leader in technology and higher education, and Mexico has an abundant supply of inexpensive labor and natural resources of its own.

Free trade doesn't solve all ills. Mexico's political turmoil and its perpetual problem with corruption in official institutions continue to stifle employment and living standards. Its problems with organized crime and the drug trade have brought tourism nearly to an end while making it virtually impossible in some regions to conduct commerce. Those are serious problems keeping the Mexican people from enjoying the full fruits of their labors, as are various American efforts to punish cross-border immigration.

But NAFTA's nearly two-decade record is one of overall success, signalling hope for the future.

After Some Sluggish Years, NAFTA Creates Border Boomtowns

By Monica Ortiz Uribe
Fronteras, October 22, 2012

Texas border cities are showing signs of prosperity 20 years after the signing of the North American Free Trade Agreement.

The situation was just the opposite in the years after North America opened its doors to free trade. Manufacturing jobs in the Southwest declined by an average of 4 percent, according to the U.S. Bureau of Labor Statistics. Nationally those jobs dropped by nearly 6 percent.

Along the U.S.-Mexico border the decrease in manufacturing was particularly devastating to the city of El Paso, which for 40 years relied heavily on the garment industry. In the 1950s El Paso began building a reputation as America's Blue Jean Capital.

The city marketed itself as the place where an ample Latino workforce could sew a pair of Wranglers for cheap. Some 50,000 El Pasoans worked in manufacturing, half of them in apparel. But beginning in the 1990s those jobs started to disappear. Some went to Mexico while others went to Central America and Asia. El Paso was suddenly faced with an identity crisis.

"The community went into shock," said El Paso City Councilman Steve Ortega.

Ortega is one of a handful of young leaders who came of age during the city's slow and painful post-NAFTA transformation.

"In 1998 there was a community summit that was called together by business and political leadership," he said. "The question was 'What is El Paso going to do?' And at that time the idea was, 'Let's start to focus on our location as a positive.'"

So El Paso decided to befriend its enemy. Instead of cursing the job-snatching factories across the border, the goal became to service them. That meant starting companies that could provide services like logistics, transportation, accounting and company management. Over the last 20 years those service sectors and others have matured and multiplied, ultimately helping boost the economy. Today, one out of every four new jobs created in El Paso is credited to cross-border trade.

An example of such a company is Secure Origins, founded six years ago. Its business is to monitor the transportation of goods across the U.S.-Mexico border using GPS and computer technology. Through this monitoring they aim to prevent contraband, like narcotics, from mixing with the cargo.

The company was founded in El Paso by a local entrepreneur with a history in computer software. Its chief of operations, John Rippee, joined the company after serving as a helicopter pilot in the U.S Army.

"I think there's probably more promise and opportunity here than you've ever seen in the history of the region," Rippee said. "That's why I'm here."

The young company demonstrated its promise to the state of Texas which, in 2007, awarded it a $2 million grant to expand operations. Earlier this month the city of El Paso contracted Secure Origins for $195,000 to start a program meant to expedite commercial truck traffic at the port of entry.

"We have $80 billion dollars of trade every single year coming through in this particular region," Rippee said. "If we could increase that 10 percent, that's billions of dollars that are coming back across our borders. Those are more jobs, that's increased quality of life."

Secure Origins hires and develops engineering students from the local university. The company is housed together with other emerging tech companies in an old garment factory. It's the kind of industry turnaround that's advancing the economy even in the face of a national recession.

A study by the Federal Reserve Bank of Dallas released this summer shows that in the last decade per-capita income in Texas border cities has been rising faster than the national average. The study attributes two-thirds of that growth to cross-border trade. California is experiencing similar growth while Arizona and New Mexico are just waking up the economic opportunities of trade with Mexico.

"It's a good transition overall for the economy," said Roberto Coronado, who co-authored the study. "Service related jobs typically come with higher wages, higher standards of living and that's exactly what we find in our analysis."

There's still a ways to go. Border cities still rank below the national average for per-capita income. In 2010, per-capita income in El Paso was $28,698, or 30 percent lower than the national average of $41,560. The good news, according to the Dallas study, is that in the past 10 years El Paso has managed to narrow the gap by 10 points.

In order to continue making positive gains, Coronado says cities like El Paso must work on improving their educational institutions and city infrastructure. The U.S.-Mexico border is also home to some of the poorest zip codes in the nation.

But the proof of new prosperity is undeniable. In 2009 a medical school opened in El Paso. The city recently signed a deal to host a Triple A baseball team and El Pasoans are even excited about soon getting their first IMAX theatre.

Meanwhile dozens of locally owned restaurants, bars and cafes have flourished in the hands of young entrepreneurs like Raul Gonzalez, also known as Chef Rulis. On a recent weekday at lunch, his place was packed.

> *In 2010, per-capita income in El Paso was $28,698, or 30 percent lower than the national average of $41,560. The good news, according to the Dallas study, is that in the past 10 years El Paso has managed to narrow the gap by 10 points.*

"You can come here and you'll have musicians and artists sitting next to bankers and lawyers sitting next to health care workers," Gonzalez said.

Four and a half years ago Gonzalez left his banking job in Houston. Opening his own hometown restaurant has always been his dream.

"People are proud of their local establishments," he said. "And we are getting people to be proud of the city, which is important because the people are what make the city cool."

And that's a pride long overdue.

Last Great Interstate: A NAFTA Highway Fraught with Controversy

By Terri Hall
Examiner, December 18, 2012

With the end of 2012 marking the 20th anniversary of NAFTA, it's instructive to take a fresh look at the book that chronicles that battle over the last interstate highway—a NAFTA superhighway—yet to be built: *Interstate 69: The Unfinished History of the Last Great American Highway* by Matt Dellinger.

Dellinger credits David Graham, grandson of a railroad magnate and son of an auto manufacturer in Southern Indiana whose family farm and businesses made them legendary in their small community for decades, with the idea of building an interstate highway connecting Evansville with Indianapolis. That little idea that started over breakfast with some of Graham's influential friends grew into a NAFTA superhighway concept in short order. Absent federal funding, an interstate through southwest Indiana was a non-starter, but connect that idea to a larger intercontinental highway connecting the busiest trade crossings in Canada with those in Mexico, and now you've got six other states and a plethora of economic interests joining Indiana in the quest for not only funding, but also a whole new trade corridor that will transform North America.

The book tells the story of I-69 through Dellinger's travels on the proposed route, meandering through each of the seven states the NAFTA highway would traverse and telling the personal stories of landowners versus the special interests advocating for the highway, of dying cities and towns desperate for economic development and jobs the road could bring against the backdrop of the reality that a road can also bypass and kill thriving towns and change the face of communities forever—whether for good or bad. Dellinger also tells the plight of politicians stuck in the middle, who when push comes to shove, usually side with special interests and even grant the backers special favors.

Knowing highways can make or break a community and even a state, through facilitating commerce or providing seamless travel between major cities which can attract major employers, the author captures the tension between the project's cheerleaders and detractors, and often the urban versus rural divide. To the big business interests pushing I-69, the small towns and farms in the path of this NAFTA trade corridor are just green fields to be paved over for the "greater good"—casualties in the name of "progress."

Since the U.S. Supreme Court Kelo decision, property rights have been trumped by economic development. Though the concept of I-69 pre-dates Kelo, Kelo is key in understanding the threat of I-69 to property rights across America. Dellinger documents the plight of Indiana and Texas landowners in their quest to quash I-69 through their respective states. In both cases, farmers preferred achieving I-69 through upgrading existing highways rather than cutting through large new swaths of farm and ranch land.

Cronyism from day one

The book opens in 1990 around the breakfast table at the home of David Graham in Washington, Indiana. David invited two friends, David Cox, with the Daviess County Growth Council, and Jo Arthur, with the Southern Indiana Development Corporation, to meet David Reed, who was conducting an economic development study for the Hudson Institute on the potential for development in southern rural Indiana. Reed was staying with Graham, which was no coincidence since Graham knew the CEO of the Hudson Institute, Mitch Daniels, since 1976. Daniels later became Indiana's Governor and pushed road privatization, tolling, and, of course, I-69.

Graham brought up the idea of the Southwestern Indiana Regional Highway Coalition to build an interstate connecting Indianapolis with Evansville, but it was Reed who directed Graham and his cohorts to explore an even bigger idea—to connect it to NAFTA in a multi-state effort to open up an international trade corridor from the border crossings in Michigan to Brownsville and Laredo, Texas. Reed later published his report making the case for I-69 to spur NAFTA trade and rural economic growth.

Graham, following in his father's footsteps—Robert Graham once served as director of the National Automobile Chamber of Commerce who represented the auto industry on the original Pan American Highway Committee—then took his idea on the road, selling it to the other six states, primarily to Chamber of Commerce groups, and eventually establishing a Midcontinent Highway Coalition to lobby for I-69 in D.C., with oil and gas guy John Caruthers of Shreveport hired to run it.

With the help of Congressman Frank McCloskey, a rough map of I-69 made its way into the federal highway bill known as ISTEA in 1991 with his last minute amendment inserting high priority corridors 18 (from Indianapolis to Memphis, TN, via Evansville) and 20 (from Laredo, Texas, to Texarkana) and then amending the reach of corridor 18 (from Shreveport to Houston) to connect with corridor 20, even before all seven states' Departments of Transportation were even briefed on the concept.

The Coalition eventually hired some big guns, Carolina Mederos of Patton & Boggs (founded by the son of Hale Boggs, creator of the highway trust fund) in 1995, and in 1996, Randy Delay, brother of Houston-area Congressman Tom Delay (and House Majority Whip at the time), to lobby Congress. Greater Houston Partnership, Houston's Chamber of Commerce led by none other than Kenneth Lay also Chairman of Enron, paid an extra $100,000 to hire Delay. They delivered.

NAFTA highway I-69 is born

Mederos, former Department of Transportation executive turned lobbyist, managed to further define the route of I-69, particularly corridor 18, in the 1995 National Highway Designation Act. The Coalition wanted specifics on the route between Memphis and Shreveport and determined it would traverse through both Mississippi (at Trent Lott's insistence) and Arkansas. Texas Senator Kay Bailey Hutchison ensured corridor 18 would extend beyond Houston to the Rio Grand Valley and designated corridors 18 and 20 as future parts of the interstate highway system.

Mederos knew there was no longer an interstate highway program to fund I-69 so she and Delay decided to create a whole new program as part of the federal highway bill known as TEA-21 in 1998, just to "find" some funding for I-69. She called it the "National Corridor Planning and Development Program" and the "Coordinated Border Infrastructure Program," arguing the original interstate system primarily built east-west highways, and with the advent of NAFTA and the north-south trade patterns and manufacturing and population moving south, it justified new highways—particularly I-69.

TEA-21 officially designated corridors 18 and 20 Interstate-69 and extended the corridor to capture the existing I-69 in Michigan in northern Indiana as well as I-94 Port Huron, Detroit, and Chicago to take in the Ambassador Bridge and Detroit-Windsor tunnel crossings to bolster the trade argument. On the southern end, I-69 splits three ways with a leg going to Laredo, Brownsville, and McAllen. So now I-69 officially extended from Canada to Mexico. Together the northern and southern border crossings account for half the truck traffic that crosses both borders. The bill also snagged $140 million in funding over five years—I-69 eventually receiving $70 million of it.

Indiana insurrection

With the legislative groundwork laid, Dellinger delves into the birth of the opposition to I-69 in the same place it all started—Indiana. Even Indiana's State Museum and its Hall of Transportation describe the inherit resistance to privatization. Dellinger describes the railroad age in Indiana and how private railroad operators extorted money from travelers via tollhouses that blocked free passage, and they had the power to "decide which towns thrive and which ones decline."

Once again, the Graham family played a role in Indiana's transportation history when David's grandfather Ziba started a street car system that eventually branched out to interurban rail lines. By 1910, Ziba's children were building trucks and paved roads were gaining ground. The rise of the bus replaced rail, and eventually the auto replaced both around 1950.

Before Indianans could blink, their Governor Mitch Daniels began to push privatization yet again and bought into the foreign-owned toll road idea that caught fire in Texas. Daniels eventually sold the Indiana Toll Road to Spain-based Cintra and Australian-based Macquarie for 75 years. The toll rates doubled, the financial footing of the private consortium now teetering toward insolvency, and the unpopularity of public private partnerships (P3s) have ensued.

Thomas and Sandra Tokarski live on a wooded 35 acres in Stanford, Indiana, just southwest of Bloomington, IN, right in the path of I-69. Here the battle between urban and rural would take root. They didn't see the need for the highway, and neither did the federally-funded Donahue study published in 1990. But the Indiana Department of Transportation (INDOT) still pursued it, forcing the Tokarskis to take on the battle against I-69.

They meticulously picked apart every feasibility study they could get their hands on, and began by writing to their politicians, pleading for facts and sanity to reign over the false hope of economic

In another ironic twist, the former mayor of Dyersburg, TN, opined that a textile mill in town closed down due to NAFTA. Their 1,200 workers, even in a right to work state, couldn't "compete" with China and Mexico. Yet now he wants a NAFTA superhighway plowing through his community so more jobs can be shipped out of Tennessee.

development. They promised environmentalists, fiscal hawks, and farmers and ranchers would all rise up against the project, and they were right.

They organized their neighbors and formed Citizens for Appropriate Rural Roads or CARR, but got more roadblocks and abusive government. In 1995, the Tokarskis filed a federal lawsuit under the National Environmental Policy Act (NEPA) citing INDOT's failure to consider all viable alternatives—primarily the upgrade to existing roads instead of the new corridor route. The Environmental Protection Agency agreed and forced INDOT to do a supplemental environmental impact statement to consider all the impacts. Ultimately, this only bought more time to fight it politically, which they lost when the consultant hired by INDOT to do the new study was hopelessly biased in favor of the new terrain route since it was a company that also did business with INDOT—classic conflict of interest. Consequently, the consultant advanced the new terrain route.

At the same time, Daniels was pushing road privatization and initially proposed a P3 for I-69, but later found it wasn't toll viable enough for a private deal, so he proposed not only the new terrain route, but to fund it using some of the whopping $3.85 billion up-front payment from the sale of the Indiana Toll Road to build I-69 as a freeway. It's no coincidence that the route chosen directly benefited David Graham, the highway's father, who was close to Daniels. Indeed, later the state altered the route again to give the Graham family land on all four corners in Washington, Indiana where it intersects US 50.

Ultimately, the Tokarskis lost again when the first two and half miles of I-69 from Evansville was built in 2008. They'd battle for 20 years, and yet still live under the threat of I-69 running through their serene property near Bloomington. Ironically, Graham ended up leaving Indiana for Florida shortly after, not unlike Pfizer pulling out of New London, CT, after eminent domain destroyed Suzette Kelo's home for what was supposed to be a Pfizer facility. In both instances, the instigators did untold damage to property rights in the name of economic development, and then took off before the original project they lobbied for was completed.

Desperation drives other states

Unlike Indiana, the central states of Kentucky, Mississippi, Arkansas, Tennessee, and Louisiana were desperate to get I-69 running through their states. The promise of economic development and the revival of dying towns losing their young people to bigger cities and their aging populations helped them become the corridor's biggest cheerleaders.

Tennessee actually broke ground on the first segment of I-69 using a pass-through financing deal (where a county issues the debt and the state pays them back for it) and didn't do it as a toll road. Perhaps the opposition didn't come through these states since I-69 mostly involved upgrading existing roads.

In another ironic twist, the former mayor of Dyersburg, TN, opined that a textile mill in town closed down due to NAFTA. Their 1,200 workers, even in a right to work state, couldn't "compete" with China and Mexico. Yet now he wants a NAFTA superhighway plowing through his community so more jobs can be shipped out of Tennessee. The same could be said of Michigan. No state has been more adversely impacted by NAFTA and the wholesale shift of jobs out of the U.S. by the auto industry, but it, too, wants to see I-69 complete the decimation.

Texas for sale

In Texas, Governor Rick Perry is cut from the same cloth as Daniels—the more privatization the better. In fact, his economic development office put the "For Sale" sign out with an official ad campaign. His transportation department (TxDOT) pimped out Texas infrastructure overseas seeking foreign ownership first from France, but eventually Spain.

Perry's grand Trans Texas Corridor (TTC) plan—a 4,000 mile network of multimodal foreign-owned toll projects across the state using P3s—included four major north-south international trade corridors, one of which was I-69. It would have confiscated over 500,000 acres of private property, most of it through the agricultural food basket of Texas.

Like the Tokarskis, ordinary Texans in the path of the TTC, like David and Linda Stall, Hank Gilbert, and an unexpected coalition of groups including TURF, ranging from environmentalists, property rights advocates, and anti-tax conservatives, all rose up to halt the biggest land grab in Texas history. They not only worked through the NEPA process, they worked their state legislature in a Texas-sized revolt that reaped a moratorium on P3s in 2007. But Perry managed to weaken the final bill to grandfather in portions of the TTC.

By 2011, TURF saw it through to get the repeal of the Trans Texas Corridor from state statute, but 15 segments of road can still fall under a P3—again, thanks to Perry and his highway department's lobbying of local politicians. Though Dellinger tries to paint some of the TTC's detractors in a negative light for their concerns over the TTC facilitating a North American integration, his book fully makes the case that it's true.

Economic development at what cost?

The bottom line is: the promise of economic development is a crap shoot at best. No one has a crystal ball that can deliver a winning formula ensuring all parties end up with greater prosperity or quality of life. Quality of life, after all, is as individual as each human being. Some people are going to get hurt, and others will prosper at the expense of those parties. The way government works, it's the government picking the winners and losers based on cronyism, so facts, fairness, and reason get smothered by the economic interests of the well-connected.

One thing is certain, facilitating international trade erodes our national sovereignty through deeper economic integration with Canada and Mexico and relaxing border crossings, and it hurts American workers and communities whose jobs are being shipped overseas or wages depressed to stay "competitive" with third world countries. With the risks so heavily outweighing the benefits, I-69 as it was initially envisioned is best left as unfinished business of the "breakfast club" where it all began.

The Failures of NAFTA

By Catie Duckworth
Council on Hemispheric Affairs, June 19, 2012

On December 8, 1993, a triumphant President Bill Clinton signed the North American Free Trade Association (NAFTA) bill into law. Reflecting popular sentiment, he praised this monumental economic treaty by stating, "I believe we have made a decision now that will permit us to create an economic order in the world that will promote more growth, more equality, better preservation of the environment, and a greater possibility of world peace." Initially, NAFTA supporters promised a plethora of benefits for the countries of North America. American proponents promised that NAFTA would create more jobs reflecting higher wages in the United States, while also reducing the U.S. trade deficit with Mexico and Canada. Mexican leaders claimed that the bill had the potential to create a sizable and revitalized middle class in Mexico by raising wages and strengthening living conditions for its impoverished citizens. Mexican President Carlos Salinas, whose administration had been tarnished by charges of corruption, proclaimed that NAFTA would, at long last, enable Mexico to join the developed world. Likewise, leaders from both countries pitched NAFTA as a solution to illegal migration across the U.S.-Mexico border; with more and better-paying jobs, as well as cheaper goods in Mexico, the United States would no longer be an attractive land of opportunity. Regrettably, the majority of these promises never materialized. The limited benefits that have resulted from NAFTA have been overshadowed by its numerous failures, which have both negatively affected the United States and greatly harmed Mexico, especially in the agricultural sector.

Failures for the United States

In 1992, Gary Hufbauer, a NAFTA enthusiast from the Institute of International Economics, predicted that "NAFTA will generate a $7 to $9 billion [USD] surplus that would ensure the net creation of 170,000 jobs in the U.S. economy the first year." However, quite the opposite occurred; the U.S. trade deficit with both Mexico and Canada increased, costing the United States an estimated 150,000 jobs in 1994 alone. According to the United States Census Bureau, while the United States actually had a trade surplus with Mexico of approximately $1 billion USD in both 1993 and 1994, by 2007 the growing trade deficit with Mexico had reached an all-time high, at $74 billion USD. Although U.S. exports to Mexico did increase slightly under NAFTA, the U.S. encountered the new problem of "revolving door exports." Most U.S. exports to Mexico have consisted of mechanical parts, which are used to assemble goods in Mexican factories that are then imported back into the United States for cheap, a process known as the *maquiladora* system. Such exports have doubled since the implementation of NAFTA, leading only to more imports from Mexico and a deepening trade deficit.

> ... *Mexican living conditions have consistently declined since NAFTA's advent. In the pact's first five years, real wages in Mexico fell by 20 percent, and workers in the manufacturing sector now earn about a fourth of their pre-NAFTA wages.*

The combination of increased imports from Mexico and a growing trade deficit have led to job losses, mostly in high-wage, non-college-educated manufacturing positions, in all 50 U.S. states and the District of Colombia. When these displaced American workers later re-enter the job market, they find difficulty securing new jobs and often have to settle for markedly lower wages. As of March 2011, the United States has lost approximately 700,000 jobs due to disruptions in supply chains brought about by NAFTA.

Failures for Mexico

Although NAFTA has been detrimental for the United States, the free trade agreement has been far worse for Mexico. While proponents touted NAFTA as ostensibly a beneficial social policy, the income gap in Mexico has in fact widened since NAFTA's implementation, with this development creating even more poverty in a country already afflicted with the concentration of wealth in too few hands. The poverty rate in Mexico rose from 45.6 percent in 1994 to 50.3 percent in 2000, and the number continues to climb. In 2010, the World Bank reported the most recent poverty rate in Mexico at 51.3 percent.

Perhaps the most devastating blow dealt by NAFTA to the Mexican economy was the near destruction of Mexico's agricultural sector, in which 2 million farm workers lost their jobs and 8 million small-scale farmers were forced to sell their land at disastrously low prices, or desert it, due to sharply declining food prices. Importantly, the U.S. government subsidizes many domestically produced agricultural products, allowing the products to be sold to Mexico at prices 30 percent below the cost of production. Thus, after NAFTA's inauguration, U.S. agricultural exports crowded out Mexican agriculture produce, and the United States became the main food supplier of Mexico. In one case, U.S. corn exports, by maintaining subsidized prices, have all but rendered Mexican corn cultivation obsolete and non-competitive. Corn, or maize, had been one of the main crops and an integral part of the identity of the Mexican people since pre-Columbian days, but due to subsidized U.S. agricultural products, this tradition has all but come to an end. Thus, NAFTA has not only negatively impacted Mexico's economy, but also altered its national identity by infringing on ancestral traditions.

Due to the decline in the competitiveness of Mexican agricultural products, the rural population has been pushed from the countryside into the cities to seek employment in the booming manufacturing sector, one of the many paradoxical consequences of NAFTA. Many American corporations took advantage of this plethora of cheap labor and constructed factories along the U.S.-Mexico border, creating the *maquiladora* system. While these factories, or *maquilas*, created 1.3 million jobs in the export-manufacturing sector, they still were not able to counterbalance jobs lost in the agricultural sector, and it was not long before foreign competition threatened these newly created jobs. Since 2001, one third of all NAFTA-created manufacturing jobs in Mexico have disappeared as North American corporations continue to offshore operations to China, where manufacturing wages are about an eighth of those in Mexico. Although NAFTA is not the only cause of the economic distress Mexico has faced in the past decade, the economic pact failed to generate a Mexican economy capable of competing in a global market, thus negating what little economic benefit it brought Mexico.

Moreover, even with the creation of new manufacturing jobs, Mexican living conditions have consistently declined since NAFTA's advent. In the pact's first five years, real wages in Mexico fell by 20 percent, and workers in the manufacturing sector now earn about a fourth of their pre-NAFTA wages. Additionally, the prices of most goods in Mexico have significantly increased. The cost of tortillas, which represent 75 percent of the daily caloric intake for Mexico's poor, increased by 571 percent in the first six years of NAFTA, rendering meager wages even more insufficient than before NAFTA's implementation and making it increasingly difficult for families to meet basic needs. Wage disparities between Americans and Mexicans have also widened. In 1994, Mexicans earned 23 percent of what Americans earned overall; by 2006, the differential had dropped to 12 percent. With this wage reduction, the lower class in Mexico has expanded, pushing more poverty-stricken individuals into areas that were already troubled by inadequate housing, healthcare, and public safety, and generating further problems for the Mexican state, such as drug violence and urban sprawl.

The Immigration Problem

In an argument that helped push the bill through the U.S. Congress, Janet Reno, attorney general during the Clinton administration, proclaimed that NAFTA would decrease illegal immigration by two-thirds in six years. However, this too was a hollow promise. Prior to 1994, illegal immigration across the U.S.-Mexico border was declining, but eight years after NAFTA's enactment, this trend had reversed, resulting in a 61 percent increase. In 1995, there were 2.5 million illegal Mexican immigrants in the United States; by 2006, there were more than 20 million, two-thirds of whom came to the country after the implementation of NAFTA in 1994.

Every year, some 500,000 Mexicans risk their lives to cross the border because they can no longer make a living in the destroyed Mexican manufacturing and agricultural sectors. Proponents of NAFTA promised the Mexican people a decent living, but 18 years later more and more Mexicans have little choice but to leave

Mexico for the United States each year, resulting in growing concerns in the United States over these trends. Americans' concerns about losing their jobs to "illegals," especially since the economic crisis of 2008, have become a dominant part of American political dialogue. However, there exists another, less acknowledged discussion—one that understands that the presence of illegal immigrants is partially beneficial to the U.S. economy. Because of the abundance of undocumented workers, American farmers can pay wages that are a fraction of the $10 an hour they are required to pay legal U.S. residents. While this is certainly a nefarious practice, the American public derives much benefit from it: If these farms employed only legal residents, prices on American goods would skyrocket. For example, it is estimated that orange juice would cost upwards of $20 per gallon if only documented workers picked oranges on Florida's orange farms. The U.S. government has increased spending on border control without taking into account these various factors.

Overall, neither the United States nor Mexico has seen the benefits promised from NAFTA, but Mexico should be most disappointed. The writers of the bill failed to provide equitable stipulations for labor conditions, environmental protection, or investment regulations. Laborers on both sides of the border saw their collective bargaining powers diminish after NAFTA. Mexico, the United States, and Canada must transform NAFTA from a "free" trade agreement to a "fair" trade agreement through revisions that create jobs instead of destroying them, protect workers, and create an environment that allows Mexicans to stay in their home country and earn a living wage.

NAFTA: Birth of a Free Trade World

By Devin Browne and Jill Replogle
Fronteras, September 4, 2012

When Luis de la Calle first traveled with Mexico's then-president, Carlos Salinas de Gortari, to Washington, D.C., to propose a free trade agreement between the two nations, Mexico's economy was still relatively tiny—just 4 percent the size of the U.S. economy.

Like all pacts of free trade, the North American Free Trade Agreement (NAFTA) would eliminate essentially all tariffs and special protections each country provided its farmers and workers, even though agriculture and manufacturing in the U.S. were significantly more industrialized, and thus more efficient, than those same sectors were in Mexico.

Yet de la Calle and Mexico's other top trade negotiators were sure free trade was in their country's best interest.

It was 1990. Mexico was just emerging from what is now known as the country's "Década Perdida" or "Lost Decade" of deep financial crisis.

"Not very dissimilar to the crisis Greece or Spain are going through right now," de la Calle said.

After a petroleum boom in the 1970s, the market settled and Mexico struggled to find economic stability. The ensuing ten years were marked by a plummeting peso, record-high inflation, and immense national debt. These are the conditions in which NAFTA started to gain traction.

"In a way," de la Calle said, "NAFTA is the child of the 1980s crisis."

Mexico owed money—a lot of it—to the World Bank, to private banks, and to other countries. Officials decided the only way out was to completely restructure Mexico's economy.

"In order to address the debt crisis and pay back the debt, Mexico needed to export," said Kathleen Schwartzman, an economic sociologist at the University of Arizona. "As a condition of that, it had to begin liberalizing the economy."

Under the direction of President Miguel de la Madrid, and later Salinas de Gortari, Mexico lowered its tariffs, joined the General Agreement on Tariffs and Trade (GATT), the precursor to the World Trade Organization, and rewrote its laws to allow foreigners to own businesses and invest more freely in the country.

This was a dramatic shift for Mexico. Since the administration of President Lázaro Cárdenas in the 1930s, the country had been focused on protecting its own farmers and its own industries. Consumers mostly bought Mexican products, and people in the countryside grew their own corn for making tortillas.

But the 1980s debt crisis left Mexico in a financial wreck and exposed its vulnerabilities in the global economy. Its leaders decided to change course. They started looking for countries that might want to invest in Mexico.

Originally, the U.S. wasn't Mexico's first choice to become its top trading partner. To explain this, de la Calle quotes an oft-repeated line attributed to former Mexican dictator Porfirio Díaz: "Poor Mexico, so far from God and so close to the United States."

In a 1992 debate with President George Bush Sr. and presidential candidate Bill Clinton, independent candidate Ross Perot famously suggested NAFTA would create "a giant sucking sound" as jobs moved south of the border.

"Which is another way of saying 'So close to the U.S. and so far away from Europe,'" de la Calle said.

But unfortunately for Mexico, Europe was busy. The Berlin Wall had recently fallen, opening up a huge adjacent market for Western European products and investment.

That left the U.S. as the next best option.

"Mexico was, in a way, very lucky because a bunch of Texans were running the U.S. government," de la Calle said.

The Secretary of Commerce (Robert Mosbacher), the Secretary of State (James Baker), President George Bush Sr.—all Texans who have a long history of doing business with Mexico.

Plus, free trade was becoming an increasingly popular concept. More than 120 countries were in the process of forming the World Trade Organization.

And the U.S.—starting first with Canada, and then with Mexico—wanted to sell its goods to everyone in the western hemisphere.

U.S. officials promised NAFTA would stem the tide of Mexicans coming across the border to look for work. It would also ensure that the U.S. remained a superpower in a globalizing world.

"It was the most far reaching agreement that anyone on the face of the globe had negotiated up to that time," said Carla Hills, the U.S. Trade Representative under the first President Bush.

Of course, some groups opposed NAFTA vigorously. American labor was worried U.S. manufacturers would move their operations, and jobs, south of the border, where employees were cheaper and environmental standards lower. Environmentalists worried about the same thing.

In a 1992 debate with President George Bush Sr. and presidential candidate Bill Clinton, independent candidate Ross Perot famously suggested NAFTA would create "a giant sucking sound" as jobs moved south of the border.

Mexican manufacturers feared they wouldn't be able to compete. And subsistence farmers in southern Mexico prepared for an uprising to defend their corn and bean fields from American agribusiness.

Critics on both sides of the border predicted fallout over one point in particular: NAFTA would allow money and goods to flow freely across the border, but not labor.

"It would not have permitted the trade agreement to be negotiated had we had an immigration chapter," Hills said.

Politicians from the U.S., Mexico and Canada signed off on NAFTA in late 1992, creating the template for a free trade world.

Remarks at the Center for Strategic and International Studies (CSIS) on Latin America

By Hillary Rodham Clinton
US Department of State, March 18, 2011

Secretary Clinton: (Applause.) Thank you. Oh, thank you very much. Thank you. Thank you. Thank you. Thank you. It is a delight to be back at CSIS and have this opportunity to speak with you. I want to thank Mack for his introduction. Always ask a long-time friend to introduce you because then you're guaranteed, at least if he doesn't provide embarrassing detail, to have a positive prelude.

I can think of no one more fitting than Mack to have provided that opening because he is a long-time champion of U.S. engagement in Latin America and did an excellent job as my husband's envoy during the Clinton Administration.

My thanks also to John Hamre, Andrew Schwartz, CSIS for your generosity in hosting us this afternoon. As an institution that is focused on not just the day-to-day policy, but also on the deeper forces and dynamics that shape it, this is an ideal place to discuss what I see as one of the central strategic opportunities for the United States today.

Now, obviously, there is a lot going on around the world and much that demands our urgent attention from the historic changes in the Middle East and North Africa where I just was yesterday to the tragedy unfolding in Japan. But as I often say, we have to deal with both the urgent and the important at the same time. And with President Obama departing for Brasilia in just a few hours, now is a good time to turn our attention from the urgent events of the day and consider another important part of the world.

The President's trip coincides with the anniversary of a major milestone in hemispheric relations. Fifty years ago, President Kennedy launched the Alliance for Progress, pledging that the United States would join with Latin American leaders to address head-on a development challenge that was, as he put it, staggering in its dimensions. He understood that our failure to tackle poverty and inequality in Latin America could tear the social fabric and undercut democracy's prospects throughout the hemisphere. President Kennedy announced the alliance here in Washington to an audience of Latin American ambassadors at the White House. President Obama will mark this anniversary in Latin America. And I think that is fitting.

Too few Americans have noticed that something remarkable has been happening

---

in the region. Now, there are, of course, plenty of challenges and they often hog the headlines—transnational crime, continuing inequality and poverty, inadequate education and so on. Now, those are challenges that apply in many cases, including in our own country.

But the real story of Latin America today runs in a very different direction. It is a story of political transition and a broad commitment to democratic development, a story of pragmatic leaders who helped turn a once-troubled region into an area of dynamic 21st century economies and societies, a story of active new players on the global stage.

Now in the coming days, President Obama will visit three countries—Brazil, Chile, and El Salvador—each is living this story in unique ways. The President will build on the pledge he made at the Summit of the Americas early in his presidency to work as "equal partners" in a "new chapter of engagement" based on "mutual respect and common interests and shared values." He and the three leaders hosting him will show, in word and deed, how much such a partnership can accomplish.

But I want to focus on why this partnership matters to us—what this story means for the United States: For our economic interests, as we rebuild our economy and renew our competitiveness for a new time; for our security and global strategic interests, as we design a 21st century architecture of cooperation with the help of like-minded partners; for our core values, as we promote democracy and human rights around the world; and for our society and our culture as the growing connections between our peoples make us all more vital and innovative. Now during the past two years, I've had the opportunity, as Mack said, to travel the hemisphere and meet with presidents and foreign ministers, journalists and CEOs, activists and entrepreneurs.

Last summer, *The Washington Post* noted that I had visited 17 countries in Latin America and the Caribbean during my first 18 months in office. Apparently, that was more than any other Secretary of State in that period, and I'm proud to hold that record. But what really matters is the common purpose behind these trips and President Obama's—bolstering our current partnerships in Latin America and highlighting the remarkable opportunities we have to accomplish even more together.

So let's start with economic opportunity. This is the challenge on everyone's mind today, and with very good reason. There are still too many Americans out of work. And our recovery from the financial crisis is far from complete.

In this year's State of the Union address, President Obama laid out an agenda for how we will emerge from the crisis stronger than before, how America will win the future. And I share President Obama's optimism. But as certain as we are of the goal, it is not something that America can accomplish alone. Enhancing our competitiveness, accelerating innovation, achieving energy security, and expanding our exports—all of these require robust engagement with Latin America.

It's not only the developing economies of Asia that are aiding the global recovery today. It is also the economies of our neighbors. Brazil, with nearly 8 percent GDP growth last year, is predicted to become the world's fourth- or fifth-largest economy in the coming decades. Peru has also been growing at rates we typically associate with China and India. Chile, Uruguay, and Argentina are close behind, followed by Mexico, Panama, and Colombia. The combined economies of Latin America grew 6 percent last year. This dynamism, coupled with smart public policies promoting broad-based opportunity, led Luis Alberto Moreno, the president of the Inter-American Development Bank, to call this the start of a Latin America decade.

This is good news for the people of Latin America as well as for the United States. Taken as a whole, the Latin American economy is nearly three times the size of India or Russia and not far behind China and Japan. And Latin America has a huge advantage that will serve it well in the coming decades: a young population. If the countries of the region succeed in delivering education for their young people, they will have a significant edge for years to come over other major economies that are starting to feel the strain of an aging population.

The size of the Latin American economy and its young demographics are especially important for the United States, because our economy is tied much more closely to the economies of our neighbors than to those across the oceans. Forty-three percent of all of our exports stay in the Western Hemisphere. We export more than three times as much to Latin America than we do to China. And I want to repeat that, because I don't think there are very many Americans who understand or know that. We export more than three times as much to Latin America than we do to China. We export more to Latin America than to Europe, and more to Chile or Colombia than to Russia.

North America is the largest free trade area in the world. Now, all of these facts point to a very promising trend. Latin America is producing more and more new consumers for U.S. products each year. Tens of millions of people in the region are entering the middle class, more than 30 million in Brazil alone since 2003. At the same time, Latin America is home to dynamic companies, entrepreneurs, and innovators who are purchasing technology and equipment and helping drive competitiveness and innovation in American businesses. The bottom line is that geography matters. It is a comparative advantage to be embraced, and we neglect it at our own peril. Growth in the Latin American market stands to benefit American workers and companies more than growth anywhere else in the world. It is the power of proximity, geographic proximity and also the proximity of our global economic interests and our challenges at home and what it will take to overcome them.

And both our government and our private sector need to direct our efforts to harness that power of proximity. Now, I do understand the concerns of those who worry that globalization and integration will take jobs away from Americans. But I also know that with the right policies we can channel those forces to create more and better jobs for the benefit of American workers.

Look at the American auto industry. It is reviving itself in part by integrating more closely with our neighbors. Assembling a car today involves material inputs and processes that cross borders several times before a finished product rolls off the assembly line. And in the end, our workers are the better for it. Take Embraer, the jet manufacturer and one of Brazil's biggest exporters. The United States accounts for about 65 percent of its sales. But about 70 percent of the parts that it puts into its planes are made in the United States.

Now, these economic relations, therefore, are not zero sum. Ultimately, they do benefit the people of every country involved. That's why it is good news for us that Monterrey, Mexico, is becoming a base for research and development, or that Brazil's agricultural research and investment have helped turn it into one of the world's top food suppliers, or that Petrobras, Brazil's oil company, issued one of the largest stock offerings ever last year, and that Rio will soon host both the World Cup and the Olympics. There's no doubt that when construction and drilling start, American companies will also be there.

Our energy security depends on this hemisphere. The source of one half of our oil imports, Latin America alone accounts for a third of our imported oil, with Mexico our second-biggest supplier. And you probably know that Venezuela is also a major source. But did you know that Colombia is now as well? And Brazil is poised to become one of our top suppliers, thanks to its recent offshore find.

So as we move toward a clean energy economy, Latin America's role will have to grow. And already, we are working on renewable energy technology and resources with Mexico, Brazil, the Caribbean, and across the region, thanks in part to President Obama's leadership in launching the Energy and Climate Partnership of the Americas.

Now, many other players are also recognizing Latin America's potential, and they are making their own inroads, building their own economies, signing their own investment deals and free trade agreements. But that should not worry us. Rather, it should spur us on. President Obama's national export initiative is leveraging every facet of our diplomacy to promote American jobs. As productivity rises, companies need fewer employees to meet their goals. So to create more jobs, we have to expand our existing trade relationships and create new ones. That's why a broad cross-section of businesses, from high-tech companies to heavy equipment manufacturers to the Montana grain growers, all support free trade agreements with Colombia and Panama. They know that opening these markets is essential to our own exports, jobs, and competitiveness.

We're also building a 21st century smart border with Mexico that supports security and competitiveness on both sides. And earlier this month, we took a significant step in finally resolving the longstanding dispute over trucking under NAFTA.

Strengthening our economic relationships has benefits for all the people of the region, but it also has another advantage. It leads to the rise of even more capable partners who can help us accomplish our strategic objectives, from addressing the challenge of climate change to improving security in the region, and that's the second area I want to talk about—the opportunity to partner with Latin America on global strategic issues.

President Obama's visit occurs at a time when there is a growing recognition that the hemisphere stands to gain from greater cooperation premised on shared values, that governments and societies each bring their own capabilities to solving common problems. When we think about addressing the serious challenges of drug

> *The combined economies of Latin America grew 6 percent last year. This dynamism, coupled with smart public policies promoting broad-based opportunity, led Luis Alberto Moreno, the president of the Inter-American Development Bank, to call this the start of a Latin America decade.*

trafficking and criminal violence, for example, countries such as Chile and Colombia have much to share about the process of training effective, accountable police and judges in Central America.

And when it comes to promoting social inclusion, Brazil, Uruguay, and Barbados have set an enviable example. And just as Latin America goes global, building its ties with Europe and Africa, with Asia and the Middle East, so will our relationship. Day to day, it can be as much about how we can work together in the world as about issues particular to our region. As countries step up on the global stage, they will make essential contributions to helping all of us meet some of those most important challenges.

Mexico, for example, made a crucial contribution to the fight against climate change through its remarkable leadership in Cancun last year. Brazil, Mexico, and Argentina in the G-20; Chile and Mexico in the OECD; Chile and Peru in the Trans-Pacific Partnership; and along with Mexico in APEC, these are all helping to build a foundation for balanced global growth, a transparent global economy, and broad-based opportunity. Colombia and Brazil are vital partners this year on the UN Security Council. Uruguay contributes more troops per capita to UN peacekeeping operations than any other country. Costa Rica is working to become the first carbon-neutral nation on earth. We are partnering with Brazil on food security and public health projects in Sub-Saharan Africa. And every country joined to assist Haiti after the earthquake and continues to assist in the reconstruction.

Now as vibrant a picture as the hemisphere presents, it has not yet realized its full global potential. And it is very much in our interest to help our Latin American partners further embrace an active and constructive global role. But let me hasten to add this does not mean that we will always agree, but we will agree much more often than not. And even when we disagree, we will never lose sight of the powerful interests and core values that connect us. And one of our most important, powerful bonds is our commitment to democracy, and that brings me to the third opportunity we have in our engagement in the region.

Latin America has undergone such a profound democratic transformation that it can now be a model and even a mentor for those fighting to create and protect democracy everywhere. Let's not forget that before the Middle East, it was Latin America that people dismissed as arid ground for democracy. We can still recall a time when dictators and strong men dominated the hemisphere. And plenty of Americans thought that friendly autocrats were the best we could ever hope for.

But citizens coming together, asserting their fundamental rights, in the face of autocrats and military governments, overcame the doubts of the world and the challenges of transition to build democracies that deliver results. The very ideals we hope for in Egypt and Tunisia have already taken place in our own hemisphere. This task is not finished, and this hemisphere can do much more to guard against threats and challenges to democracy closer to home. In some countries, insecurity and a lack of opportunity remain real obstacles. In others, democracy is being rolled back rather than strengthened. And Cuba remains a glaring exception to the democratic convergence. That is something that all of us have to face up to and work toward dealing with.

But the overall direction is clear. The region's commitment to democratic development is widespread and strong. And that does give Latin Americans a special role in helping support other nations making the difficult transition to democracy today. In recent weeks, we've seen some promising examples of just that. Veterans of Chile's democratic transition have already visited Cairo to talk about the importance of strong institutions, advancing reconciliation, and ensuring that democracy delivers results. Mexico took the lead in suspending Libya from the Human Rights Council.

And I would add that we in the United States can also learn some things from Latin American democracy as well. Now, one example I particularly like is the encouraging number of female presidents in the region. (Laughter.) And I must say that—(applause)—I am far enough away from my own career in electoral politics that I will not take too much heat for suggesting that these women and societies can teach American voters a thing or two.

And finally, I want to emphasize that all of these opportunities are strengthened by the interdependence of our societies, our cultures, and our peoples. The United States has one of the largest Spanish-speaking populations in the world. Latinos are the fastest growing group in our country today. And we also share a rich heritage from our Caribbean neighbors. More than half of our foreign-born population has roots in Latin America. And these ties have shaped every aspect of our society and culture, and we are the better for it.

I know that immigration and interdependence can bring real challenges, and that they do make a lot of Americans anxious, and that is understandable. But immigration has always been a source of our vitality and innovative spirit. So if we work together to address these challenges, I have no doubt that this will continue to be an enormous advantage for the United States, one that bears directly and crucially on our economic and geopolitical prospects. We cannot afford to surrender that advantage now.

Going forward, all these areas of opportunity will also be a roadmap for our engagement, and President Obama will highlight each of them during his trip. In Brazil, he will announce new economic opportunities and discuss new ways we can work together on our core challenges in energy, innovation, education, and beyond. He will go to Chile to emphasize our fundamental values and shared commitment to democracy. And he will point to the importance of Latin America's broad commitment to democratic development. And in El Salvador, he will show how we can do our part on meeting the shared challenges of security and development in a country that has shown the will to move forward.

Now ultimately, all of these partnerships boil down to this—seizing the phenomenal opportunities we now have in this region: the opportunity to create jobs and drive development; the opportunity to secure democratic progress in our hemisphere and, together, foster it beyond; the opportunity to advance human security in all of its forms, whether acting on our responsibility to address unacceptable levels of violence or unacceptable levels of inequality to promote inclusive growth for everyone.

Now I know that looking for opportunities abroad can sometimes be a tough sell here at home, especially at a time of strained budgets and high unemployment. And I know well how danger, crisis, and catastrophe can take over your week, week after week after week. (Laughter.) But that's why this trip, which some questioned about how could the President go to Latin America on this long-planned trip with everything happening from Japan to the Middle East and North Africa, is being answered in the right way. As the experts here at CSIS will tell you, strategy depends on the ability to look deeper and further than the day to day. And there are so many reasons why this trip at this time is so important.

Just one way of perhaps putting it into context, when I think about why we should invest in our relationships in Latin America, I think about the path that Colombia has traveled over the last years. I remember vividly when my daughter and husband visited in 2000, when Plan Colombia was just beginning. It was a country terrorized by drug traffickers and guerrillas who controlled vast parts of territory and who could strike in any major city. Foreign policy experts, in this city and so many other places, were calling it a failed state.

Ten years later, I traveled to Colombia as Secretary of State. And this time, I walked through the streets of downtown Bogota. I visited a bakery run by former FARC and paramilitary members—and let me tell you, it's not every day that you get to sample the baked goods of former guerrillas. (Laughter.) When I sat down with the foreign minister and then President Uribe, Colombia's security challenges were still very real, but they were only a part of the discussion. We spent more time talking about how Colombia and the United States can work together to take the agenda further, to solve global and regional problems from climate change to partnering in the Security Council to expanding economic growth and about what Columbia could do to help both Central America and Mexico in meeting their own security challenges. We talked about how we could deepen the ties between our societies and advance our shared values, and about what will be achieved when Colombia hosts next year's Summit of the Americas. And we talked about the inclusion and human rights agenda that President Santos is now advancing with extraordinary commitment and results.

So Colombia, in short, had gone from a source of danger to itself and others to a source of inspiration to all of us and to becoming a vital partner in the great debates of our time. Now, the real credit goes to the Colombian people and to the leaders who had to make very hard choices, not just once or twice, but over and over again.

But the United States played an important, some would say an essential role. The money we invested in Plan Colombia over that decade, while significant, is less than we spend in Afghanistan in a single week.

When President Obama returns from Latin America, he will have set the stage for more stories like Colombia's in the years ahead, stories with powerful implications for trade and jobs, for education and innovation, for many advances in human potential that we will be so proud to see and that we will benefit from. And he will have invested in key relationships and delivered a message of partnership throughout the hemisphere. It is a message we must hear at home. These are opportunities we cannot afford to pass up or let them pass us by.

The world is so dynamic right now, events are moving so quickly, people are so connected in ways that could not have even been imagined a decade ago. And what I'm not sure yet that many Americans understand is that if you're not in the mix, if you're not in the arena, if you're not reaching out and building those relationships on an ongoing basis, you will find that others have stepped in to do just that. And there is no part of the world that is more closely linked with who we are as Americans and what kind of future we want for our children than this hemisphere and, in particular, in Latin America.

So I'm excited that in the midst of another unbelievable week in the world, the President is off to a trip that will take him to three important countries and send a message to all the others, and that I had this opportunity to come and discuss with you why we think it is one of the most important long-term commitments that the United States has and must continue to follow through on.

Thank you all very much. (Applause.)

3

After Castro: Cuba's Revolution at Crossroads

The Capitolio in Havana, Cuba, West Indies.

Cuba: An Imminent Thaw?

After more than half a century of trade tension and political posturing, US-Cuba relations have entered a new, post-Castro dynamic. The collapse of the Soviet Union in 1991 meant the loss of Fidel Castro's most significant patron and political ally on the world stage, and the attendant end of the Cold War markedly reduced Cuba's regional influence. Nonetheless, successive American administrations have maintained the US economic embargo on Cuba through the end of the twentieth century and into the twenty-first. Critics argue that the embargo is a policy relic that negatively affects the daily lives of the Cuban people. Others argue that the embargo remains a necessary check on a Cuban regime that continues to commit human rights abuses, most notably the jailing and persecution of political dissidents. Since Castro transferred the responsibilities of the presidency to his brother Raúl in 2008, the US has begun to show some flexibility on the embargo. There have been faint signals that a thaw in US-Cuba relations is possible. In 2011, the administration of President Barack Obama announced the lifting of a travel ban barring American students and church groups from visiting the island.

Castro resigned from the Central Committee of Cuba's Communist Party in April 2011. Although he has continued to publish political treatises and make periodic public appearances, he is no longer the dominant presence on the island that he was in the decades that followed the 1959 revolution. As the international economy has become increasingly globalized and influenced by digital technology, many observers, scholars, and political leaders believe that the Cuban revolution has reached a crossroads: will it hold fast to the ideals and rhetoric of its ailing leader or instead embrace and reenter the world community?

According to a 2011 poll conducted by the Ford Foundation, the Cuban Research Institute, and the Department of Global and Sociocultural Studies at Florida International University, 50 percent of Americans support an end to the US trade embargo on Cuba. The same poll found that 80 percent of Americans believe the embargo has been ineffective. However, there remains a large population of Cuban Americans, including refugees and their relatives, who will back the embargo's termination only after the fall of Cuba's communist regime.

The Embargo and Its Impacts

The United States enacted an arms embargo on Cuba in March 1958 after fighting broke out between Castro's communist rebels and the military regime of Fulgencio Batista. After Castro assumed leadership of Cuba in 1959, he moved to nationalize the country's business enterprises, many of which were subsidiaries of American corporations. He also significantly increased tariffs on American imports. These moves had major financial implications for American interests in Cuba. President

Dwight D. Eisenhower believed that a retaliatory set of sanctions was necessary. In July 1960, America moved to reduce imports of Cuban sugar.

As Cuba's trade relations with the United States broke down, Castro moved to cultivate the country's economic ties with the communist Soviet Union, led at the time by Premier Nikita Khrushchev. In response, President John F. Kennedy initiated several attempts to remove Castro from power. These efforts failed. The most notorious of them was the Bay of Pigs invasion of April 1961, during which a CIA-funded counterrevolutionary army was turned back by Castro's forces. In the summer of 1961, Castro allowed Khrushchev to begin covert installation of Soviet nuclear missile systems in Cuba in an effort to bolster the island's economic and military security. Khrushchev saw the missiles in Cuba as a necessary countermeasure to the presence of American nuclear weapons in Turkey. Cuba's close proximity to the United States afforded the Soviets "first-strike" capability comparable to the one the United States enjoyed. Khrushchev also believed that the presence of missiles in Cuba would distract US-led efforts to keep West Germany out of the Soviet sphere of influence.

The Cuban Missile Crisis began after American intelligence agents discovered the presence of the Soviet nuclear missiles in Cuba in October 1962. The ensuing standoff among the American, Cuban, and Soviet governments and military forces pushed the Cold War to the brink of nuclear conflict. Twelve days of tense military and diplomatic negotiations between the Kennedy administration and Soviet officials resulted in the withdrawal of Russian missiles from Cuba. Khrushchev made the decision to dismantle the Soviet missiles in part because the Kennedy administration agreed to remove its missiles from Turkey, so long as their removal remained unpublicized. Nevertheless, Castro's complicity in the secret installation of Soviet weapons in Cuba ensured that the American trade embargo would continue indefinitely.

The American economic embargo has had a wide-ranging impact on the Cuban economy. Historically, Cuba had relied heavily on US imports, and the embargo cut the island off from its largest trading partner. The absence of American companies in Cuba resulted in fewer jobs and lower tax revenues. Although the Soviet Union provided Cuba with aid, it lacked diverse exports. Without market access to America and its allies, Cuba slid into economic ruin. Cuba's economic turmoil was exacerbated by the fall of the Soviet Union in 1991, which resulted in the end of Soviet aid.

While Cuba maintained a robust health care sector throughout the late twentieth century, its medical infrastructure struggled to innovate in the new millennium. Following the end of the Cold War, American and European pharmaceutical companies flourished and expanded. Cuban doctors and researchers, unable to access new technologies and research, found their country's health care system isolated and in decline. According to the *Annals of Internal Medicine*, the spread of HIV and AIDS in Cuba was exacerbated by its inability to access new medications and testing methods.

The trade embargo has also influenced Cuban society and culture. For decades, daily life in Cuba has subsisted on outmoded appliances, antique automobiles, and meager government handouts. However, the political ramifications of the embargo have been different from those intended by its designers. The American embargo became a scapegoat for Castro's failed socialism. Instead of motivating Cubans to rise up against Castro in the name of democratic government and free market reform, it intensified the adversarial relationship between the United States and Cuba, allowing Castro to leverage anti-American sentiment in order to maintain his hold on power. Although Cuba has seen the introduction of cellphones and some web technologies, it remains in many ways a country frozen in time.

The US Position

In the 1980s, hundreds of thousands of refugees left Cuba and immigrated to the United States—causing considerable social, political, and economic instability in Florida and other states in the American South. Although it was clear that Cuba did not represent an immediate threat to American security, the United States maintained its trade embargo in response to the Castro regime's suppression of political rights and jailing of political dissidents. In 1996, Congress passed the Cuban Liberty and Democratic Solidarity Act (also known as the Helms-Burton Act), which strengthened the embargo and threatened to penalize foreign governments and businesses if they provided the country with goods and services. Meanwhile, the large community of Cuban Americans in Florida continues to apply political pressure in support of the embargo. These groups argue that Castro and his communist regime must be thrown out and replaced with a democratic government.

American officials have repeatedly stated that the Cuban people are not America's enemy. At the start of the twenty-first century, the United States government began to relax some embargo policies. American companies are now allowed to sell agricultural equipment and medical supplies on the Cuban market. According to Texas A&M's AgriLife Extension Service, US exports to Cuba hit a record $711 million in 2008. However, American exports to Cuba decreased significantly in 2010, due to changing commodity prices and changes in Cuban and American trade policy.

A Crossroads for US-Cuban Relations

In 2006, Castro temporarily abdicated his position due to illness, handing leadership duties to his brother, Raúl. The leader of Cuba's revolution had long been suffering from an intestinal condition. Castro's transition out of power became permanent in 2008. After leaving office, he largely disappeared from the spotlight, with few people knowledgeable about his health or whereabouts. Castro occasionally resurfaces at public events and issues statements through Cuba's Central Committee newspaper *Granma*. After his departure from Cuban government, false rumors about his death circulated regularly on the Internet. Despite allegations of poor health, Castro makes occasional television appearances. He appeared on television several times with Venezuelan President Huge Chavez prior to Chavez's death in 2013.

Since his brother's departure, Raúl Castro has taken some modest steps toward economic reform. Although it remains officially communist, Cuba has taken small steps toward a more market-oriented economic system. For example, more Cubans are able to start their own businesses and hire non-family members, and the government has allowed for the limited sale of automobiles.

Although the United States and Cuba have made minor improvements in their diplomatic and economic relations, a number of questions remain as to whether a true warming of US-Cuban relations is possible. There are concerns among the anti-Castro contingent in the United States and Cuba that Raúl Castro's economic reforms are too limited and slow to have any real impact on the Cuban economy. Additionally, economic reforms have not engendered political reforms—Raúl fought alongside his brother during the Cuban revolution and remains a staunch communist. The Cuban political elite are not expected to change the country's political landscape in the near future.

The international community has largely disapproved of America's continuation of the trade embargo, decrying the embargo's impact on the Cuban people. Several US government agencies have cited the potential economic benefits of lifting the embargo and others have argued that the embargo is antiquated and useless, given that Cuba does not pose a military or security threat. Critics of the embargo argue that the United States maintains open political and economic relations worldwide with regimes that have been accused of violating human rights and repressing political expression.

Despite the isolation it faces regarding the embargo, the United States has made only minor adjustments to its Cuba policy. American leaders continue to cite Cuba's record on human rights and civil liberties as justification for maintaining the embargo. Meanwhile, the political forces that oppose any change in policy toward Cuba remain strong. Although Fidel Castro is now a shadow of his former self, his brother Raúl is just as dedicated to preserving the Cuban regime and the legacy of the 1959 revolution. Because of domestic political influences, changes in America's Cuba policy are likely to remain incremental and modest.

U.S. Aggression Towards Cuba Continues: Increase in U.S. Support to Counter-Revolutionary Groups

Liberation, August 30, 2012

There is a public perception that the Obama administration has opened up a new era in U.S.-Cuba relations, in which the United States has "reached out" to Cuba by easing the U.S. blockade. In fact, Washington's aggression has not let up at all.

The misconception about a shift to a less aggressive policy—what the corporate media absurdly refers to as a "thawing" in U.S.-Cuba relations—comes from the lifting of two provisions implemented by the Bush administration after the 9/11 attacks. These had severely limited the right of Cubans living in the United States to visit and to send remittances to their families in Cuba.

These provisions were repealed by the Obama administration mainly because they were detested by the vast majority of the Cuban American community. Most still have family back in Cuba, and wish to visit their loved ones.

In this way, the Obama administration was able to curry favor among larger numbers of Cuban American immigrants without abandoning the principal aspects of a bipartisan strategy to overthrow Cuba's social system.

Sanctions Punish Entire Population

The U.S. empire's long-standing strategy is to use scarcity and underdevelopment as a weapon to strangle the Cuban people. That is the essence of the U.S. blockade on Cuba. According to Cuba's calculations, its economic losses from more than 50 years of the blockade total $975 billion.

Economic sanctions against Cuba, which would otherwise expire, must be re-authorized on a yearly basis. For the first three years of his four-year term in office, President Obama has signed the legislation necessary to extend all aspects of the financial and commercial blockade against Cuba (most recently in September 2011) despite the "change in politics" so often trumpeted by the corporate press.

Sections of the U.S. ruling class view the global economic crisis as an opportune moment to intensify the blockade against Cuba. Because socialist Cuba has no choice but to buy and sell commodities in the global capitalist market, the island is greatly affected by the capitalist crisis. This has led to problems of hardship and scarcity that Washington knows it can amplify by tightening the blockade.

On June 12, the U.S. government announced it was imposing a $619 million fine on the Dutch bank ING for facilitating commercial transactions with Cuba. In half a century of economic sanctions, this is the heaviest fine ever handed out by the U.S. Treasury Department's Office of Foreign Assets Control, a body responsible for monitoring and enforcing sanctions against Cuba.

The $619 million fine accounted for half of ING's net profit in the first quarter of 2012. Far from signaling an easing of restrictions against Cuba, the Obama administration's actions are an open and immediate threat to any foreign company or country that chooses to do business with Cuba.

A press release issued by OFAC states that ING is also required to conduct an internal revision of its future operations, policies and practices, and to assure Washington that no "OFAC-sanctioned transactions" are occurring. This exemplifies the coercive power of U.S. finance capital. In order to avoid U.S. sanctions for doing business with Cuba, Dutch-based ING had to agree to open its books to the U.S. Treasury Department for scrutiny!

Financing Internal Subversion

The Obama administration has increased funding—through agencies like the U.S. Agency for International Development, and National Endowment for Democracy—to counterrevolutionary elements inside Cuba to undermine and attack the Revolution.

Using misleading and false terms like promoting "democracy," "human rights" and "freedom of information" inside Cuba, the U.S. government has increased funds by tens of millions of dollars to foment subversive activity. Part of the money is used to bribe Cuban individuals to form opposition groups, who are then instructed by U.S. officials to falsely accuse Cuba of repression.

Encouraging acts of sabotage and terrorism are also on the agenda. The groups are tiny, often numbering less than a handful of persons, but they are magnified by the U.S. government to justify aggression against Cuba.

The funding includes the introduction of sophisticated surveillance and communications equipment into Cuba for the opposition to set up a network, undetectable by Cuba.

The people of the United States are barely aware of these programs, even though taxpayers foot the bill. But one case has made recent headlines: that of Alan Gross, a U.S. employee of Development Alternatives Inc., in turn financed by USAID.

Gross received at least $500,000 and traveled to Cuba several times in 2009. Each time he brought in high-tech equipment, including Internet satellite phones. A breaking story by Desmond Butler of Associated Press on Feb. 13 explained that Gross also brought in "a specialized mobile phone chip that experts say is often used by the Pentagon and the CIA to make satellite signals virtually impossible to track."

Gross was tried and convicted for "undermining the integrity and independence of Cuba." He received a 15-year sentence. The White House has demanded his unilateral release. Cuba says it would favor a prisoner exchange on humanitarian grounds between the Cuban Five, political prisoners unjustly held in the United

> *Sections of the U.S. ruling class view the global economic crisis as an opportune moment to intensify the blockade against Cuba. Because socialist Cuba has no choice but to buy and sell commodities in the global capitalist market, the island is greatly affected by the capitalist crisis.*

States for almost 14 years, and Gross. But the Obama administration has refused, instead using Gross's case to justify its ongoing hostility.

The electronic plots continue. As recently as June 28, USAID announced a program for organizations that can establish "digital democracy" inside Cuba through technological means, for a total of $18 million in the next three years.

The government and people are not sitting idly by. Cuba's security and vigilant population have helped unmask some of these operations, dealing a blow to Washington's aims.

One example is Raúl Capote, a young Cuban professor who was recruited in 2005 by the U.S. Interests Section in Havana, an operating base for the CIA. He revealed his real identity as a double agent for Cuba two years ago, and has since written numerous exposés of the sinister attempts by the United States to create divisions within Cuban society, focusing on youth, Black Cubans, LGBT people, intellectuals and artists—in short, divide-and-conquer.

U.S. Government Employs Right-Wing Terrorists

A historic outgrowth of the U.S. ruling class's drive to overturn the Cuban Revolution is the nurturing of an extreme right-wing anti-Cuba terrorist network in Miami, a network the Obama administration allows to operate as freely as all past administrations.

In the run-up to the United States' failed land invasion of Cuba in 1961, known as the Bay of Pigs invasion, the CIA recruited thousands of members of Cuba's former ruling class and Batista henchmen. It armed them, trained them and attempted to fashion them into an anti-communist paramilitary force.

With the disastrous U.S. defeat at the Bay of Pigs, the consolidation of Cuba's revolution and its alliance with the Soviet Union, imperialist hopes of bringing down the revolution militarily were postponed indefinitely.

But the counterrevolutionaries based in Miami did not simply vanish. They increasingly turned toward committing acts of terrorism against Cubans and anyone within reach who sympathized with the revolution, or advocated for a normalization of relations with Cuba.

In one example, during an eight-year period beginning in 1975, Omega 7, one organization of terrorists among many, was responsible for up to 50 bombings and two assassinations carried out in New York City, Washington, D.C., and Miami.

Although the U.S. government may at times contain or restrict the activities of the Miami terrorist network, the U.S. government has always allowed them to exist and operate with impunity.

On April 27, after years without such incidents, the Miami terrorists bombed a Miami charter company specializing in flights to Cuba.

Airline Brokers Co. provided air travel for 340 Cuban-Americans who flew from South Florida to Cuba for Pope Benedict XVI's visit at the end of March. This simple act of charter service brought terrorist threats and finally a firebombing. "We had to have armed security guard around my house for about a month," said business owner Vivian Mannerud. "There were many, many threats ... other threats with a suspicious package in my car and so on," she added. Weeks after the incident the FBI claims to have no suspects.

It is important to remember that part of Cuba is currently occupied by the U.S. military. Guantanamo Bay Naval Base, which has been run by the U.S. military since 1898, has thousands of soldiers and a massive arsenal on Cuban soil.

Stand with the Cuban Revolution!

Raúl Capote explained Cuba's resistance in a recent interview by Aday del Sol Reyes: "The enemy will never stop trying to destroy the Revolution. Why? Because Cuba is an example too powerful and Cuban revolutionaries are by far the most active dissidents within this world of global capitalist power, because we are managers and promoters of a culture that is a deadly opponent of capitalist culture ... because we ended half a century of absolute dominion of the empire over the land and we sow hope in the land of a possible better world."

It is the duty of socialists and revolutionaries to help bring Cuba's truth to the people of the United States, and stand with Cuba against the relentless onslaught of the U.S. empire.

U.S.-Cuba Policy: Ending 50 Years of Failure

By Colonel Lawrence B. Wilkerson, USA (Ret)
US Senate Committee on Finance, December 11, 2007

Thank you, Chairman Baucus, Ranking Minority Member Grassley and members of the committee, for the opportunity to testify today on U.S. policy with respect to Cuba.

For almost half a century, U.S. policy with respect to Cuba has failed—miserably.

The latest indicator of this failed policy is that while our President talks of transforming the regime in Cuba, he is apparently unaware that Cuba has already undergone regime change and the Cuban people have accepted it and await, with no small degree of excitement, what their new national leader, Raul Castro, using the existing ministries, bureaucracy, and legislature, will do—particularly with respect to reshaping the island's economy.

Other countries, too, await this reshaping, having carefully positioned themselves to take advantage of the changes as they occur . . . No place in Cuba is more indicative of this burgeoning change—and the poised positions of other countries—than *Habana Vieja*, or Old Havana, the portion of the capital city that simply exhales the long ago past. It is stunning what the Cubans are doing, with the help of foreign investors, in restoring this part of Havana. Like the city planners in Marseilles, France, the Cubans are not driving people from their homes by renovating living quarters and putting them out of the financial reach of their previous occupants; *they are renovating them and then bringing back in their original occupants.* As a result, the city center is not simply beautiful, it is full of life and vitality, children and families. Our own city planners could learn from these efforts.

Yet, while we have significant relations on almost every level with Communist countries 10,000 miles away such as China and Vietnam, we have almost no relations with the 11 million souls on an island 90 miles off our southern coast where all this dynamism is beginning to show.

Cubans on the island are energetic, capable, hard-working people—we have not stolen all of the island's talent through the machinations of our half-century of failed policy, though I must admit we have tried mightily to do so.

Because of our failed Cuba policy, we miss valuable opportunities to share Cuba's rapidly growing store of knowledge and expertise in, for example, how to deliver high quality healthcare to deeply impoverished areas. Moreover, we are missing opportunities to explore mutual interests in vaccine development, to share in Cuba's extraordinary wealth of experience in combating hurricanes and the floods that often accompany them, to explore together Cuba's continental shelf for fossil fuels, and to sell our agricultural products in a more cost-effective and profitable way to an island population that needs these products and would benefit greatly from the shortened transits and thus reduced expenses.

When I was in Cuba in March of this year, I had dinner with Ricardo Alarcón, the President of Cuba's National Assembly—their legislature, as you know. He told me that Cuba would much prefer that a western oil company, such as Exxon Mobil or Royal Dutch Shell, help Cuba with its offshore oil exploration and recovery efforts. But, he said, it was not to be. So, Cuba is moving on, as *el coloso del norte*—the colossus of the north, the U.S.—becomes increasingly irrelevant to Cuba's future.

We also, because of our failed policy, miss a range of broader opportunities to cooperate in the development in Cuba of a robust infrastructure for a growing tourist trade as well as to assist the Cubans more generally as they reshape their economy—an opportunity almost no other country with the resources and the interest, including Israel, is missing. In fact, it strikes me as particularly ironic that the country that consistently casts its vote with our very lonely vote in the United Nations when the U.S. embargo comes up, is doing business in Cuba nonetheless. Tel Aviv's leaders are smart, unlike their counterparts in Washington.

The Economist recently reported that after two years of negotiations, plans are moving forward for Dubai Ports World, a partly state-owned company in the United Arab Emirates, to invest $250 million (US) in converting the now-decaying port in Mariel, which is west of Havana, into a modern container facility. Mariel appeals to international port operators because of its proximity to the United States. As we all know, American ports are close to capacity and environmental restrictions make any big expansion of existing terminals extremely difficult if not downright impossible. If you are thinking ahead—as many other countries in the world are doing—Mariel, which is expected to be functional by 2012, would be an *entrepot par excellence*.

And there is still much more to what we as a country are missing with regard to Cuba because there is the prospect of an exciting opportunity lying across the Straits of Florida. There is an opening to a brand new approach to all of Latin America—a region of the world that the U.S. needs to address in a far more successful way than it has in the last few decades.

One of our own cities has become in almost every significant respect the capital of that region. One need only examine the aviation routes that begin, end and crisscross in Miami to understand how important this new development is; or, consider the fact that our own public schools and armed forces will transform in the next 20–30 years , as projections show that public school populations will be over 50% non-Caucasian in that time and that the enlisted ranks of the military, now dominated by the African-American minority, will soon be dominated by a Hispanic minority.

Mr. Chairman, we ignore our backyard to our increasing disadvantage. It is time we stopped doing so. From unprecedented levels of immigration, to the constant flow of illicit drugs, to throwbacks to the *caudillo* past such as Hugo Chavez, to

governments even today still based on the power of five percent of their people instead of ninety-five percent of their people, Latin America projects perils ahead as
surely as it projects promise. It's the promise we need to enhance and expand and,
in so doing, avoid the peril. And we need to do it with more than the largely lip service of the past; *we need to do it with real actions in the real world*.

In 1924, a very wise American made an astute observation about his own country. Irving Babbitt—who, incidentally, was a true conservative in the Edmund Burke
mold and not one of these so-called neo-conservatives who are actually Trotskyites
in English-speaking camouflage—said: "If the American thus regards himself as an
idealist at the same time that the foreigner looks on him as a dollar-chaser, the ex-
planation may be due partly to the fact that the American judges himself by the way
he feels, whereas the foreigner judges him by what he does."

We need—in some instances, desperately—to change that perception because,
right or wrong, it is swiftly becoming a reality in the minds of billions.

There is an opening to do that with respect to Latin America and to do it quickly
and effectively.

A *rapprochement* with Cuba would create the same opening in Latin America
that a final settlement of the Israeli-Palestinian situation would create in the Middle
East. I am not sufficiently naïve to believe that either development would meet all
regional challenges or solve all problems, but both would be a dramatic and effective start. Both would give America a decisive leg-up on regaining some of the pres-
tige and power we have squandered in the past seven years.

Mr. Chairman, I am not an expert on agricultural goods, finances, petroleum
exploration and recovery, urban development, or healthcare. I am a soldier of three
decades-plus and a sometimes diplomat who, in four years with Colin Powell at the
U.S. State Department, saw vividly how my country has imbalanced dangerously
the elements of its national power.

I am also a strategist, educated as such in one of the finest institutions America
has for such education, the U.S. Naval War College at Newport, Rhode Island.

Strategists look at the long-term. We try as best as possible to see where the
world is going and why, and then design ways to use all the elements of America's
power in order to further and protect our interests as we move forward.

As Secretary of Defense Robert Gates recently stated in the Landon Lecture at
Kansas State University, "One of the most important lessons of the wars in Iraq and
Afghanistan is that military success is not sufficient to win."

I am not certain where Mr. Gates gained his knowledge with regard to this lesson, but I can tell you that I gained my certain knowledge of this incontrovertible
truth about military power in Newport in 1981.

In fact, I learned there a much deeper truth that is just as incontrovertible: military power is the least likely instrument of national power to be successful if you
decide to use it.

A corollary truth with great relevance to Cuba is that sanctions, embargoes,
closing embassies and withdrawing ambassadors, the silent treatment, branding
other countries as evil and advocating and supporting regime change—all of these

methods, even if actually backed by strong military power and the threat to use it, rarely work and, even when they appear to do so, the results they produce are usually negative and even when they are positive, are almost never long-lasting.

Let's examine just two of the extremely negative impacts of our almost half-century of failure vis-à-vis Cuba:

First, for almost half a century U.S policy has sought to end the revolution of Fidel Castro, Cuba's dictator. What that policy has accomplished instead is to keep Fidel Castro's revolution alive and well. Vicki Huddleston, a visiting scholar at the Brookings Institution and a former chief of the United States Interests Section in Cuba, gave new clarity to this reality in a recent op-ed in *The Washington Post*. Here's the gist of what she said:

> President Bush yesterday [24 October 2007] made a case for bringing democracy to Cuba. Yet by telling the Cuban people not to expect help from the U.S. until they have made Cuba free, and by refusing to make any substantive change to U.S. policy, he is actually forestalling democratization...

> We...won't see meaningful movement toward democracy without changes to the U.S.'s rigid travel restrictions. These prevent the person-to-person contact and exchange of ideas that could build support for democracy and competition within Cuba.

> At the same time, the U.S. provides a safety valve that allows the most disillusioned Cubans and their families to escape rather than press for change at home. Bush was joined by many Cuban-born, could-have-been-reformers at the State Department yesterday, including Commerce Secretary Carlos Gutierrez and former Sen. Mel Martinez, Rep. Ileana Ros-Lehtinen and Rep. Lincoln Diaz-Balart of Florida...

Fidel Castro has outmaneuvered two Bush administrations and a total of nine American presidents. By continuing hard-line policies, President Bush is making it more likely that the Castro family will be in power on the 50th anniversary of the Cuban Revolution on Jan. 1, 2009.

The president said our goal in Cuba is democracy. But it should be both democracy and stability. No one—most of all the Cuban people—wants bloodshed or a humanitarian disaster. To encourage democratization and a peaceful transition, the U.S. must start a dialogue with both the people of Cuba and their government.

In his speech, Bush said the Cuban government "isolates its people from the hope that freedom brings, and traps them in a system that has failed them." By maintaining the status quo, the U.S. government is just reinforcing that isolation.

My hat is off to Ms. Huddleston for speaking the truth—and the truth is that our failed Cuba policy is just as responsible for keeping Castro in power as Castro himself, perhaps more so. Even Cuban dissidents realize this: "Instead of encouraging the changes that at this moment are debated within the [Cuban] government, changes that are possible though not certain, [Washington] reinforces the sectors that don't want any reform ... It seems there is a Holy Alliance between those who—in Cuba and the U.S.—don't want anything to change." These words

> *A rapprochement with Cuba would create the same opening in Latin America that a final settlement of the Israeli-Palestinian situation would create in the Middle East. I am not sufficiently naïve to believe that either development would meet all regional challenges or solve all problems, but both would be a dramatic and effective start.*

are from Oscar Espinosa Chepe, Cuban economist and former prisoner.

The U.S. has reconciled with the Communist governments in China and Vietnam. We support dictators throughout Central Asia under the strategic mantra of "contact and influence is better than isolation." We talked to the Communist Soviet Union for the duration of the Cold War. But we cannot bring ourselves to deal with Havana and have maintained that failed policy for almost half a century. It is simply absurd to continue to do so.

Second, let's examine what I believe to be the most dramatic change in Cuban policy that has taken place since the Soviet Union disappeared from Cuba's calculus—a change which we have utterly ignored.

The export of revolution at the behest of the Soviets has been transformed into the export of healthcare at the behest of the Cuban people. When I visited Cuba this past March, this was one of the areas of Cuban activity on which I focused—the delivery of first-class healthcare to impoverished people in Cuba, in Venezuela and elsewhere in South and Central America, and increasingly in sub-Saharan Africa. I visited Cuba's medical "contingency brigade," for example, and talked with doctors and other healthcare personnel about the brigade's recent, highly successful tenure in Pakistan following the devastating earthquake there in late 2005.

The passion in the doctors' eyes as they related their experiences in delivering basic healthcare in isolated, extremely cold and snow-covered regions of Pakistan was truly heartwarming. Some of the human interest stories the doctors related brought laughter to us all and served to demonstrate conclusively how deeply these medical personnel had been touched by their almost year-long experience in Pakistan. They were proud to announce that as a result of the good relations thus created, Cuba was asked to open its first-ever embassy in Islamabad. Such effective public diplomacy has become a hallmark of Cuba's medical outreach. I might add that such effective public diplomacy puts to shame our own public diplomacy, particularly in Latin America.

I also visited the Finlay Institute's Center for Research, Development and Production of Human Vaccines—incidentally, one of the places that former Undersecretary of State for International Security Affairs, John Bolton, alleged in 2002 was manufacturing biological weapons. I didn't find any such activity (and we did discover that at best the Institute has a rudimentary Bio-Level III capability and no Bio-Level IV capability—the latter needed if a country is to engage in sophisticated biological agent research and development). It's safe to say that I considered the assessment by the former commander of the U.S. Southern Command, General Charles Wilhelm, as more definitive: "During my three year tenure, from September 1997 until September 2000 at Southern Command, I didn't receive a single report or a single piece of evidence that would have led me to the conclusion that Cuba was in fact developing, producing or weaponizing biological or chemical agents." I knew General Wilhelm when I was Deputy Director of the Marine Corps War College and I know I can trust his views. I knew John Bolton when he was Undersecretary of State. I know I cannot trust his views.

In March of this year, what I did find at the Finlay Institute, for example, was information about its having developed a serogroup B meningococcal vaccine (VA-MENGOC-BC), one that had virtually eliminated that deadly disease among the children of Cuba. Moreover, I discovered that there was a significant incidence of the disease among children in the western U.S., but that due to the embargo on Cuba our doctors and health officials had been unable to avail themselves of this new and very effective (better than an 80% success rate) vaccine.

One of the most dramatic moments for me occurred when I visited one of Cuba's hospitals in Havana and plowed through a waiting room of people from all over the world—poor people who had come to this Cuban hospital largely to have eye surgery of some sort, many to have cataracts removed so their blindness or near-blindness would be eliminated. Speaking to some of them was, again, heartwarming. They all said that they were there because of Cuba's outreach. Again, this is powerful public diplomacy.

We could learn much from how the Cubans deliver healthcare particularly applicable to our rural areas and our inner cities where impoverished people predominate. And in the process, the contact would benefit Cubans. They would be able to study what is strong and robust about the U.S. healthcare system—the high technology components, for example—and at the same time learn that freedom and democracy are pretty good items too.

Mr. Chairman, because I don't consider U.S. leaders as consistently incompetent, I have to ask why some of the policies they produce fail so badly. After all, the embargo on Cuba and its concomitant policies have persisted for almost half a century and through many presidents and Congresses.

And, Mr. Chairman, the policy is recognized publicly as utterly bankrupt. On November 28, for example, the *Providence Journal* made this poignant editorial comment: "The absurdity of U.S. policy toward Cuba becomes ever clearer. Consider that our government does not prohibit U.S. tourists from enjoying the new resorts in North Korea, run by what might be the world's most brutal regime but does ban them from visiting Cuba, a dictatorship much milder than Pyongyang's. The latter, desperate for dollars, lures Westerners with luxury mountain and beach hotels sealed off from its suffering masses. Cameras and other recording devices, by the way, are banned."

When a foreign policy phenomenon such as this occurs—a failing policy yet a continued application of that policy—we must search in different places to find the reasons.

In the case of U.S. Cuba policy the search ends in Dade County, Florida, and similar environs. There, monied interests among certain Cuban-Americans and their supporters have hamstrung any efforts to change the failed policy. Republican or Democrat, presidents and their congresses are too cowed by the prospect of losing the Florida vote to take any ameliorative action. And so this feckless, stupid and failed policy persists. More recently, in terms of national security policy, our necessary focus on the Middle East and south Asia has made us blind to opportunities elsewhere and has cut off any chance of our seeing clearly the excellent opportunity that lies across the Florida Straits.

Mr. Chairman, I believe it is high time we recognized that opportunity and waded right into it.

Thank you for allowing me to testify. I stand ready to answer any questions you may have if I am able to do so.

Cuban Economy Is Still Stagnant Despite Reforms: Cuban National

By Christopher Witrak
Minyanville, December 4, 2012

Nearly 60 years after the Cuban Revolution, much has changed: It's now legal for citizens to own and sell property, start a business, and emigrate (at least to Spain and Ecuador if not the US). This year, Cuba released numerous political prisoners, made it easier for Cubans to travel, and expanded other personal liberties as well as private sector jobs (178 private sector job categories and 350,000 licensed business owners now exist). For the first half of 2012, the island's economic growth was reported to be 2.1%—better than what was seen in the United States. For all of 2012, its been reported that Cuba will grow a total of 3.1%, missing the government's estimate of 3.4%.

As restrictions ease, however, more Cubans are arriving in the US by various measures. The US accepts 20,000 Cubans per year via the immigration lottery; thousands more are accepted under family reunification plans and political asylum. Via the terms of the "1995 wet-foot, dry-foot policy" amendment to the 1966 Cuban Refugee Adjustment Act, any Cuban who shows up in the US is automatically allowed entry without a visa and can apply for residency one year later. In recent years, the number of Cubans availing themselves of the Refugee Act has been between 4,000 and 5,000. Yet last year, the *Miami Herald* estimated that this figure had risen to 7,400 per year while other sources say that number is close to 10,000.

Probably the most perilous way to enter the US is by boat from Cuba. Last month, the *South Florida Sun Sentinel* (via ABC News Univision) reported that the largest number of Cubans has tried to reach the United States this way since the financial crisis began in 2008. The US Coast Guard detained 1,275 Cubans traveling by boat in the 2012 fiscal year ending in September versus just 422 in 2010. Another 97 have been picked up over the past month and a half.

According to many experts, government reforms themselves have emboldened citizens to leave the country. Decree-Law No. 302, which goes into effect on January 14, 2013, modifies Law No. 1312, or "Immigration Law." Among other changes to immigration law, the decree lessens the punishment for those who left the country after 1990 and wish to return to visit the island. Cubans can also travel abroad more easily next year.

Minyanville spoke with a Cuban national who has been in the US about one month to find out more. The individual (identified as "he" for the sake of this article) did not want the specifics of his arrival (which is legal if he leaves shortly) revealed. However, it is well known that Cubans have come to the US through Canada, Mexico, Ecuador (where approximately 100,000 Cubans have settled), and Spain (where thousands of Cubans of Spanish descent have been allowed to move.)

The main reason Cubans are on the move, said our source, is that the local economy is stagnant. "One thing is what [the government] tells you, and another is the truth. The economy really isn't doing better. There are a lot of government programs to help improve the economy, but there are no perceptible results. There is a lot of poverty."

On a side note, Cuban-Americans who had migrated in the 1960s after Castro came to power were present during the interview, and added their own commentary mostly to complain that the source was sugar-coating answers, although it's hard to believe "a lot of poverty" is painting a rosy picture.

Our source verified what Jorge Duany of the Cuban Research Institute at Florida International University said in an interview with ABC/Univision News:

> [The increased number of Cubans leaving is] due to the continuing economic downturn in Cuba, which is leading a large number of people outside of Cuba. Short-term reasons for this rise could be that there are a number of people who are unemployed and looking for a job in the small private sector in Cuba who were laid off by the government and have doubts about future prospects.

Starting a Business: Try Something in Tourism

All citizens are allowed to start a small business in Cuba. Whether or not fellow citizens—many of whom earn $20 per month—can afford the goods and services from these enterprises is a different matter.

Our source explained how one would start a business:

> In order to start a business, you need to acquire a permit from the government, but first you need to give a "contribution" to the government. The government does not question from where you receive the money. It could even be from relatives in the US. You could start a brick-and-mortar business with 10,000 to 15,000 Cuban convertible pesos, which equals $10,000 to $15,000 in Cuba, but many Cubans need money from family members living abroad in order to launch the business. Afterwards, the government does not care if you continue to receive money from outside sources [though it must be in limited amounts] and you conduct your commerce. Business owners also have to pay taxes.

To put this in perspective, a $15,000 fee would be the equivalent of 50+ years' worth of earning for the average citizen.

The government outlawed the US dollar in 2004 after former Cuban President Fidel Castro had legalized its use in 1993. Our source said that when Cubans receive US dollars from family members, they have to pay a 10% fee at banks and convert them to the Cuban convertible peso, informally called *chavito*. The convertible peso has an official 1-to-1 parity with the US dollar, but the conversion fee results in Cubans only receiving 0.90 convertible pesos for every US dollar. The Cuban peso, or national peso, constitutes the other form of official currency used in Cuba. One convertible peso or US dollar equals 25 national pesos.

The interviewee named the restaurant and tourism industries as two sectors doing relatively well when asked which businesses benefited the most from the small business reforms. The interviewee added later, "The best job in Cuba is tourism. The tips alone will allow you to make it."

By all accounts, including the Cuban Oficina Nacional de Estadística e Información, a little over 2.7 million tourists visited the island in 2011, and the number has steadily increased since 2007. The vast majority—more than two million—come from Canada and Europe. US citizens can even get a so-called "people-to-people" license (essentially claiming the trip is educational).

Tourism's pay is so strong that it has attracted individuals from unexpected sectors of the economy. Our source told us about two surgeons who left their positions to become taxi drivers because the tips earned from tourists exceeded their salaries as surgeons. A musician earned significantly more from his tips working at a hotel than a dentist earned from his salary. Many medical professionals only earn 625 national pesos, or $25, per month.

Food: Small Entrepreneurs Have the Edge

Once in Cuba, not surprisingly, tourists need to eat. In this area, the small business owner is at an advantage and many privately run restaurants have done well largely because of their connection to the tourism industry.

According to our source, a Cuban national would have to pay the equivalent of a month's salary or more to eat a single meal at one of these establishments. A meal can cost 4 convertible pesos, and many Cubans only eat at restaurants when relatives from abroad visit and pay for their meals. (The situation was similar with other goods, not just food. Our source talked of living in a town with only one store carrying clothing virtually inaccessible to the average Cuban as purchasers needed convertible pesos to afford them.)

Our source noted that the large, state-owned restaurants cannot compete with the smaller, privately run restaurants, which offer better service and better food. In fact, at least according to an AP report (via Huffington Post), the government may begin renting state-owned restaurants in hopes of improving the quality of the restaurants. The Communist Party newspaper *Granma* published an article in which the Interior Commerce Vice Minister Ada Chavez Oviedo said that a pilot program will begin on December 1 in three of Cuba's fifteen provinces: Artemisa, Villa Clara, and Ciego de Ávila. State-owned restaurants suffer from theft of food by the workers. The renters will be responsible for the maintenance, the repairs, and the utilities of the restaurant. The government has also started similar policies for beauty salons and barber shops.

Our source elaborated on the business structure of a private restaurant:

> Restaurateurs can either grow their own food or purchase food from farmers. All farmland is state owned, and the government only leases pieces of government registered land to individuals such as farmers or restaurants owners. The government calls this *"Uso Frutus Gratis,"* or free use of the fruit of your labor. The land is never yours, though. Plus, a contribution (a sort of tax) from the harvest must be paid to the state for the funding of institutions such as hospitals and schools. [The government may begin experimenting with new land cooperatives.]
>
> Despite the possibility of renting land, most restaurants owners have to purchase produce from farmers in the marketplace. Those who sell food in the marketplace can charge whatever price they want, making their *oferta de mando*, or offer of demand. Problems occur because the lack of a fixed price allows sellers to charge whatever price they wish and constantly change prices. When you go to a market, farmers will begin competing on price, constantly undercutting each other."

Our source's description of the interactions in a local market indicated that market mechanisms may still seem alien to some Cubans.

When asked about any popular restaurants in the country, our source said that no restaurant franchises existed and restaurants varied from city to city. On the topic of available, affordable food, our source called the US "the ceiling of heaven" and frequently referenced the prevalence and proliferation of McDonald's (NYSE:MCD) and Starbucks (NASDAQ:SBUX).

Rationing and the Black Market

Our source reasoned that the government allowed a black market to exist out of fear of civil unrest if the people's basic needs are not met. The government will step in, though, if it believes a person has become reckless or too conspicuous with one's wealth, he said.

The state-run rationing system provides little for the average Cuban. Similar to starting a business, one needs money to acquire anything other than basic necessities. Our source said, "Every head of the household gets a rationing booklet from the government that covers essentials. The book lists what may be collected from the government throughout the year. For example, Cubans may only get one pair of underwear and one pair of shoes per year from the government. However, the shoes may be the wrong size." Frequently, the government will run out of a particular good. The US-Cuba Trade and Economic Council in its "Report for Calendar Year 2011"

The government outlawed the US dollar in 2004 after former Cuban President Fidel Castro had legalized its use in 1993. Our source said that when Cubans receive US dollars from family members, they have to pay a 10% fee at banks and convert them to the Cuban convertible peso, informally called chavito.

states that ration cards are supposed to supply food for 30 days, but may only provide 14 days worth of food.

Ironically, would-be entrepreneurs can find themselves on both sides of the black market with the same business, and our source related the following story:

> One family, which rented a small piece of land, went from living in poverty to operating a registered car dealership. Through working the land and bartering or selling the remainder of harvest after taxes, the family saved enough money to purchase a small car. The car provided access to different markets in different towns because the family members could transport the food and goods, such as heavy bags of rice, to areas that lacked these items. The individual with the car transported food and goods from the interior of the country to the urban areas like Havana and made a killing. Urban residents have a rough time acquiring food from the countryside, though many urban gardens exist in cities like Havana.

The family purchased additional cars with the profit from sales and sold more goods in multiple areas. However, selling food and goods outside of the family's town was illegal, making the family a group of black market dealers.

Eventually the family collected a small fleet of cars and asked the government for permission to become a car dealer. The family registered the business with the government and paid taxes, making the business legitimate again. Entrepreneurs in Cuba constantly walk the line between legal and illegal commerce.

Overall—and despite accusations that he was going easy on Cuba—our source expressed disappointment with the results of the changes Cuban President Raúl Castro has introduced and tremendous disillusionment. While there have been various reforms, many of which were implemented since 2010, it's made little difference day-to-day. Asked if the government was likely to make other major political reforms, the individual simply responded, "No."

Time to End the Cuba Embargo

By Doug Bandow
The National Interest, December 12, 2012

The U.S. government has waged economic war against the Castro regime for half a century. The policy may have been worth a try during the Cold War, but the embargo has failed to liberate the Cuban people. It is time to end sanctions against Havana.

Decades ago the Castro brothers led a revolt against a nasty authoritarian, Fulgencio Batista. After coming to power in 1959, they created a police state, targeted U.S. commerce, nationalized American assets, and allied with the Soviet Union. Although Cuba was but a small island nation, the Cold War magnified its perceived importance.

Washington reduced Cuban sugar import quotas in July 1960. Subsequently U.S. exports were limited, diplomatic ties were severed, travel was restricted, Cuban imports were banned, Havana's American assets were frozen, and almost all travel to Cuba was banned. Washington also pressed its allies to impose sanctions.

These various measures had no evident effect, other than to intensify Cuba's reliance on the Soviet Union. Yet the collapse of the latter nation had no impact on U.S. policy. In 1992, Congress banned American subsidiaries from doing business in Cuba and in 1996, it penalized foreign firms that trafficked in expropriated U.S. property. Executives from such companies even were banned from traveling to America.

On occasion Washington relaxed one aspect or another of the embargo, but in general continued to tighten restrictions, even over Cuban Americans. Enforcement is not easy, but Uncle Sam tries his best. For instance, according to the Government Accountability Office, Customs and Border Protection increased its secondary inspection of passengers arriving from Cuba to reflect an increased risk of embargo violations after the 2004 rule changes, which, among other things, eliminated the allowance for travelers to import a small amount of Cuban products for personal consumption.

Three years ago, President Barack Obama loosened regulations on Cuban Americans, as well as telecommunications between the United States and Cuba. However, the law sharply constrains the president's discretion. Moreover, UN Ambassador Susan Rice said that the embargo will continue until Cuba is free.

It is far past time to end the embargo.

During the Cold War, Cuba offered a potential advanced military outpost for the

Soviet Union. Indeed, that role led to the Cuban missile crisis. With the failure of the U.S.-supported Bay of Pigs invasion, economic pressure appeared to be Washington's best strategy for ousting the Castro dictatorship.

However, the end of the Cold War left Cuba strategically irrelevant. It is a poor country with little ability to harm the United States. The Castro regime might still encourage unrest, but its survival has no measurable impact on any important U.S. interest.

The regime remains a humanitarian travesty, of course. Nor are Cubans the only victims: three years ago the regime jailed a State Department contractor for distributing satellite telephone equipment in Cuba. But Havana is not the only regime to violate human rights. Moreover, experience has long demonstrated that it is virtually impossible for outsiders to force democracy. Washington often has used sanctions and the Office of Foreign Assets Control currently is enforcing around 20 such programs, mostly to little effect.

The policy in Cuba obviously has failed. The regime remains in power. Indeed, it has consistently used the embargo to justify its own mismanagement, blaming poverty on America. Observed Secretary of State Hillary Clinton: "It is my personal belief that the Castros do not want to see an end to the embargo and do not want to see normalization with the United States, because they would lose all of their excuses for what hasn't happened in Cuba in the last 50 years." Similarly, Cuban exile Carlos Saladrigas of the Cuba Study Group argued that keeping the "embargo, maintaining this hostility, all it does is strengthen and embolden the hardliners."

Cuban human rights activists also generally oppose sanctions. A decade ago I (legally) visited Havana, where I met Elizardo Sanchez Santa Cruz, who suffered in communist prisons for eight years. He told me that the "sanctions policy gives the government a good alibi to justify the failure of the totalitarian model in Cuba."

Indeed, it is only by posing as an opponent of Yanqui Imperialism that Fidel Castro has achieved an international reputation. If he had been ignored by Washington, he never would have been anything other than an obscure authoritarian windbag.

Unfortunately, embargo supporters never let reality get in the way of their arguments. In 1994, John Sweeney of the Heritage Foundation declared that "the embargo remains the only effective instrument available to the U.S. government in trying to force the economic and democratic concessions it has been demanding of Castro for over three decades. Maintaining the embargo will help end the Castro regime more quickly." The latter's collapse, he wrote, is more likely in the near term than ever before.

Almost two decades later, Rep. Ileana Ros-Lehtinen, chairwoman of the House Foreign Relations Committee, retains faith in the embargo: "The sanctions on the regime must remain in place and, in fact, should be strengthened, and not be altered." One of the best definitions of insanity is continuing to do the same thing while expecting to achieve different results.

The embargo survives largely because of Florida's political importance. Every presidential candidate wants to win the Sunshine State's electoral votes, and the Cuban American community is a significant voting bloc.

But the political environment is changing. A younger, more liberal generation of Cuban Americans with no memory of life in Cuba is coming to the fore. Said Wayne Smith, a diplomat who served in Havana: "For the first time in years, maybe there is some chance for a change in policy." And there are now many more new young Cuban Americans who support a more sensible approach to Cuba.

Support for the Republican Party also is falling. According to some exit polls Barack Obama narrowly carried the Cuban American community in November, after receiving little more than a third of the vote four years ago. He received 60 percent of the votes of Cuban Americans born in the United States.

Barack Obama increased his votes among Cuban Americans after liberalizing contacts with the island. He also would have won the presidency without Florida, demonstrating that the state may not be essential politically.

Today even the GOP is no longer reliable. For instance, though Republican vice-presidential nominee Paul Ryan has defended the embargo in recent years, that appears to reflect ambition rather than conviction. Over the years he voted at least three times to lift the embargo, explaining: "The embargo doesn't work. It is a failed policy. It was probably justified when the Soviet Union existed and posed a threat through Cuba. I think it's become more of a crutch for Castro to use to repress his people. All the problems he has, he blames the American embargo."

There is essentially no international support for continuing the embargo. For instance, the European Union plans to explore improving relations with Havana. Spain's Deputy Foreign Minister Gonzalo de Benito explained that the EU saw a positive evolution in Cuba. The hope, then, is to move forward in the relationship between the European Union and Cuba.

The administration should move now, before congressmen are focused on the next election. President Obama should propose legislation to drop (or at least significantly loosen) the embargo. He also could use his authority to relax sanctions by, for instance, granting more licenses to visit the island.

Ending the embargo would have obvious economic benefits for both Cubans and Americans. The U.S. International Trade Commission estimates American losses alone from the embargo as much as $1.2 billion annually.

Expanding economic opportunities also might increase pressure within Cuba for further economic reform. So far the regime has taken small steps, but rejected significant change. Moreover, thrusting more Americans into Cuban society could help undermine the ruling system. Despite Fidel Castro's decline, Cuban politics remains largely static. A few human rights

Observed Secretary of State Hillary Clinton: "It is my personal belief that the Castros do not want to see an end to the embargo and do not want to see normalization with the United States, because they would lose all of their excuses for what hasn't happened in Cuba in the last 50 years."

activists have been released, while Raul Castro has used party purges to entrench loyal elites.

Lifting the embargo would be no panacea. Other countries invest in and trade with Cuba to no obvious political impact. And the lack of widespread economic reform makes it easier for the regime rather than the people to collect the benefits of trade, in contrast to China. Still, more U.S. contact would have an impact. Argued trade specialist Dan Griswold, "American tourists would boost the earnings of Cubans who rent rooms, drive taxis, sell art, and operate restaurants in their homes. Those dollars would then find their way to the hundreds of freely priced farmers markets, to carpenters, repairmen, tutors, food venders, and other entrepreneurs."

The Castro dictatorship ultimately will end up in history's dustbin. But it will continue to cause much human hardship along the way.

The Heritage Foundation's John Sweeney complained nearly two decades ago that "the United States must not abandon the Cuban people by relaxing or lifting the trade embargo against the communist regime." But the dead hand of half a century of failed policy is the worst breach of faith with the Cuban people.

Lifting sanctions would be a victory not for Fidel Castro, but for the power of free people to spread liberty. As Griswold argued, "Commercial engagement is the best way to encourage more open societies abroad." Of course, there are no guarantees. But lifting the embargo would have a greater likelihood of success than continuing a policy which has failed. Some day the Cuban people will be free. Allowing more contact with Americans likely would make that day come sooner.

4

Venezuela's Socialist Experiment

Venezuelan president Hugo Chavez in November, 2007.

Venezuela Post Chávez

Since the latter twentieth century, the interdependent relationship between the United States and Venezuela has been marked by periods of negative political rhetoric, reaching a low point under the presidency of Hugo Chávez, who expelled the US ambassador in 2008 and recalled Venezuela's ambassador to the United States. Communication between the two countries has been in the hands of informal representatives since that time.

Two major factors have played a role in this virtual "cold war" between the United States and Venezuela. The first is President Hugo Chávez, who was a firebrand of anti-Americanism until his death in March 2013. Chávez's scathing criticisms of American foreign policy bolstered his popularity among many Venezuelans while triggering a negative response from US officials. The other factor is oil: Venezuela exports large amounts of its vast oil resources to the United States. Despite the political war of words among the two countries' governments, Venezuela's oil continues to flow to the United States without interruption. In 2010, Venezuela exported approximately $26 billion worth of petroleum to America.

Chávez's death will affect the relationship between the United States and Venezuela. In the absence of one of its primary antagonists, some have theorized that US officials may explore an official reconnection with the Venezuelan government. Similarly, the Venezuelan people are contemplating life after Chávez and how his death will affect their country's relationship with one of its largest trading partners.

Hugo Chávez and the US

In 1948, Venezuela's last democratically elected president, Romulo Gallegas, was ousted in a military coup, one that many historians have theorized was staged (or at least supported) by the United States. For the remainder of the twentieth century, Venezuela was controlled by a succession of leaders who favored a strong central government and a state-centered economy over economic liberalism and an open electoral processes. These included Presidents Carlos Delgado Chalbaud (1948–1950), Germán Suárez Flamerich (1950–1952), and Marcos Pérez Jiménez (1953–1958).These regimes were famously corrupt, but maintained power through the vigilance and loyalty of the Venezuelan military. Venezuela's abundant oil resources resulted in strong economic growth throughout the late twentieth century. The government spent generously on social programs and food subsidies. In the 1980s, the Venezuelan government attempted to establish some liberal economic policies in order to counter the worldwide decrease in oil prices. However, these policies failed as the prices of goods continued to increase in relation to the country's per capita income. The economic malaise experienced by Venezuela in the 1990s led to the rise of socialism and Hugo Chávez.

As a young man, Chávez rose through the ranks of the Venezuelan military, earning a university education along the way. After attaining the rank of captain in 1981, he served for a time as a university professor. In the early 1980s, Chávez created a secret organization within the military that was based on the revolutionary political philosophies of the nineteenth-century Venezuelan leaders Simón Bolívar and Ezequiel Zamora. The group was known as the Revolutionary Bolvarian Movement-200 (MBR-200). In 1992, Chávez led MBR-200 in a coup attempt against the administration of President Carlos Andrés Pérez. Chávez was critical of the Pérez government's increasing ties with the International Monetary Fund and the United States. The coup failed and Chávez turned himself over to government authorities. In the belief that it would help quell national unrest, the government allowed Chávez to address the Venezuelan people on national television. He served two years in prison following his televised speech, but his appearance solidified him as the dynamic face of the country's growing socialist movement. President Rafael Caldera freed Chávez in 1994, on the condition that he not return to an active position in the military. Having tried and failed to gain power through the military, Chávez focused instead on his political career. He travelled throughout Latin America, espousing Bolivarian socialism and deriding international institutions. It was during this time that Chávez began his friendship with Cuban leader Fidel Castro. In 1998, Chávez mounted a successful bid for the Venezuelan presidency, espousing the ideals of socialism and railing against the United States and capitalism.

As president, Chávez quickly followed through on his campaign promises to implement a socialist system in Venezuela. He nationalized the country's oil industry and oversaw vast increases in public spending on food, housing, healthcare, and education. Critics argued that Chávez's harnessing of the country's oil revenue resulted in endemic government corruption. Meanwhile, Chávez developed a reputation on the world stage as a strident critic of the United States. When the administration of President George W. Bush deployed troops to Afghanistan following the terrorist attacks of September 11, 2001, Chávez criticized the move as an example of American imperialism. Chávez was equally critical of the American-led invasion of Iraq in March 2003. In 2006, Chávez suggested that the September 11 attacks were not orchestrated by the Islamic fundamentalist organization al-Qaeda but by the American government.

Throughout his presidency, Chávez repeatedly accused the United States of undermining the Venezuelan government and destabilizing Latin America. Often, the primary focus of Chávez's statements was President Bush, whom he referred to as "the devil" during a speech at the United Nations. Chávez's rhetoric resulted in the expulsion of a number of American and Venezuelan diplomats. In 2008, Chávez expelled the American ambassador to Venezuela, accusing him of conspiring against the Venezuelan government. Chávez claimed that he had uncovered a plot by former military officials to overthrow him, and that the ambassador, Patrick Duddy, was involved. Chávez also ordered his ambassador to the United States to return to Venezuela, and vowed that there would be no further diplomatic relations between the two countries until Bush's term ended at the end of 2008.

As president of Venezuela, Chávez emerged as a regional leader for like-minded "revolutionary" Latin American heads of state. In addition to his friendship with Cuba's Castro, he also endeared himself to Bolivian President Evo Morales. His revolutionary bombast, combined with massive increases in public spending on infrastructure and social programs, secured his strong support in Venezuela's legislature. A self-styled revolutionary, Chávez established himself as a counterweight to Western influence in Latin America.

The US, Venezuela, and Oil

For all of the political posturing and rhetorical gamesmanship between US officials and Chávez, the war of words did not significantly impact trade between the two countries. Chávez regularly threatened to cut oil exports to the United States, the fourth-largest consumer of Venezuelan oil. However, this threat was never realized. Chávez likely realized that if the United States ceased importing his country's oil, Venezuela's economy would suffer considerably.

In addition to the increases in public spending he achieved through oil exports to the United States, Chávez's political clout remained rooted in his anti-American rhetoric. The acerbic relationship was mutually beneficial. The United States did little to undo its oil trade with Chávez, as heightened instability in the Middle East helped to solidify the country as a major source of oil.

Although Chávez continued to accuse the United States of imperialism and meddling in Venezuela's internal affairs, the United States did not take steps to introduce economic sanctions or implement other punitive measures. The only penalties levied against Chávez's regime involved lower-level diplomatic staff. In contrast to the bold regime of economic sanctions imposed on Cuba by the United States, Venezuelan oil supplies proved too crucial for the Chávez regime to warrant significant diplomatic action.

A Crossroads for US-Venezuelan Relations

In 2011, the Venezuelan government acknowledged that Chávez had been diagnosed with cancer. After Argentine president Cristina Fernández de Kirchner was diagnosed with thyroid cancer soon after the announcement of Chávez's illness, he suggested that the United States might have developed a way to infect Latin American leaders with the disease. Chávez remained in office after his cancer diagnosis, but began to refer regularly to his vice president, Nicolás Maduro, providing him with increased visibility and responsibility. Chávez travelled to Cuba several times to receive treatment for his illness. Over the course of his treatment, he twice declared himself free of cancer and fully cured of the disease. However, rumors about his poor health continued to circulate, and Chávez was rarely seen in public during the run-up to Venezuela's 2012 presidential election. Despite continuing struggles with his health, Chávez was reelected as president in October 2012. An official inauguration ceremony was scheduled for January 2013, but Chávez was unable to attend because he was in Cuba for medical treatment.

Chávez died on March 5, 2013. Power was transferred temporarily to Maduro, who was elected president in a close election held in April. Following Chávez's death, Maduro suggested that his predecessor may have been poisoned by the United States, a charge US officials dismissed out of hand.

In light of Chávez's death, some have suggested that US-Venezuela relations have reached a crossroads. Although no immediate change in the oil trade between the two countries is expected, some industry analysts have speculated that the management of Venezuela's nationalized oil industry may suffer without Chávez as the country's political center of gravity. Oil companies such as ConocoPhillips and ExxonMobil, which were forced to exit Venezuela after failing to reach an agreement with the Chávez regime, may take steps to restart negotiations. Their involvement in the Venezuelan oil sector would help update the country's petroleum industry infrastructure and improve oil exploration efforts.

Although Venezuelans saw large increases in social spending under Chávez, the Venezuelan economy continues to suffer from high levels of corruption and a shortage of basic goods. In addition to threatening the political standing of the new president, these issues may make increased cooperation with the United States more attractive to post-Chávez officials. It is also possible that US officials will use Venezuela's murky political atmosphere to their advantage, working to support the country's pro-democracy opposition and taking the opportunity to more publicly criticize Venezuela's alleged violations of international economic sanctions on Iran.

Thus, significant challenges remain before the United States and Venezuela can move toward more normalized relations. Maduro, who was sworn in as president on April 19, even as a recount of the close electoral vote was agreed to, does not possess the swagger and charm that made Chávez, for better or worse, a force to be reckoned with; nonetheless, Maduro has kept up his predecessor's anti-American rhetoric, blaming the United States for fomenting postelection unrest in Venezuela. Regardless of who leads the country in the near term, Venezuela must address its domestic economic health and political stability before it begins to consider its diplomatic relationship with the United States and the legacy of Chávez.

On the Legacy of Hugo Chávez

By Greg Grandin
The Nation, March 5, 2013

I first met Hugo Chávez in New York City in September 2006, just after his infamous appearance on the floor of the UN General Assembly, where he called George W. Bush the devil. "Yesterday, the devil came here," he said, "Right here. Right here. And it smells of sulfur still today, this table that I am now standing in front of." He then made the sign of the cross, kissed his hand, winked at his audience and looked to the sky. It was vintage Chávez, an outrageous remark leavened with just the right touch of detail (the lingering sulfur!) to make it something more than bombast, cutting through soporific nostrums of diplomatese and drawing fire away from Iran, which was in the cross hairs at that meeting.

The press of course went into high dudgeon, and not just for the obvious reason that it's one thing for opponents in the Middle East to call the United States the Great Satan and another thing for the president of a Latin American country to personally single out its president as Beelzebub, on US soil no less.

I think what really rankled was that Chávez was claiming a privilege that had long belonged to the United States, that is, the right to paint its adversaries not as rational actors but as existential evil. Latin American populists, from Argentina's Juan Perón to, most recently, Chávez, have long served as characters in a story the US tells about itself, reaffirming the maturity of its electorate and the moderation of its political culture. There are at most eleven political prisoners in Venezuela, and that's taking the opposition's broad definition of the term, which includes individuals who worked to overthrow the government in 2002, and yet it is not just the right in this country who regularly compared Chávez to the worst mass murderers and dictators in history. *New Yorker* critic Alex Ross, in an essay published a few years back celebrating the wunderkind Venezuelan conductor of the Los Angeles Philharmonic, Gustavo Dudamel, fretted about enjoying the fruits of Venezuela's much-lauded government-funded system of music training: "Stalin, too, was a great believer in music for the people."

Hugo Chávez was the second of seven children, born in 1954 in the rural village of Sabaneta, in the grassland state of Barinas, to a family of mixed European, Indian and Afro-Venezuelan race. Bart Jones's excellent biography, *Hugo!* nicely captures the improbability of Chávez's rise from dirt-floor poverty—he was sent to live with his grandmother since his parents couldn't feed their children—through the military, where he became involved with left-wing politics, which in Venezuela meant a mix of international socialism and Latin America's long history of revolutionary nationalism. It drew inspiration from well-known figures such as Simón Bolívar, as well as lesser-known insurgents, such as nineteenth-century peasant leader Ezequiel Zamora, in whose army Chávez's great-great-grandfather had served. Born just a few days after the CIA drove reformist Guatemalan president Jacobo Arbenz from office, he was a young military cadet of 19 in September 1973 when he heard Fidel Castro on the radio announce yet another CIA-backed coup, this one toppling Salvador Allende in Chile.

Awash in oil wealth, Venezuela throughout the twentieth century enjoyed its own kind of exceptionalism, avoiding the extremes of left-wing radicalism and homicidal right-wing anticommunism that overtook many of its neighbors. In a way, the country became the anti-Cuba. In 1958, political elites negotiated a pact that maintained the trappings of democratic rule for four decades, as two ideological indistinguishable parties traded the presidency back and forth (sound familiar?). Where the State Department and its allied policy intellectuals isolated and condemned Havana, they celebrated Caracas as the end point of development. Samuel Huntington praised Venezuela as an example of "successful democratization," while another political scientist, writing in the early 1980s, said it represented the "only trail to a democratic future for developing societies…a textbook case of step-by-step progress."

We know now that its institutions were rotting from the inside out. Every sin that Chávez was accused of committing—governing without accountability, marginalizing the opposition, appointing partisan supporters to the judiciary, dominating labor unions, professional organizations and civil society, corruption and using oil revenue to dispense patronage—flourished in a system the United States held up as exemplary.

Petroleum prices began to fall in the mid-1980s. By this point, Venezuela had grown lopsidedly urban, with 16 million of its 19 million citizens living in cities, well over half of them below the poverty line, many in extreme poverty. In Caracas, combustible concentrations of poor people lived cut off from municipal services—such as sanitation and safe drinking water—and hence party and patronage control. The spark came in February 1989, when a recently inaugurated president who had run against the IMF said that he no choice but to submit to its dictates. He announced a plan to abolish food and fuel subsidies, increase gas prices, privatize state industries and cut spending on health care and education.

Three days of rioting and looting spread through the capital, an event that both marked the end of Venezuelan exceptionalism and the beginning of the hemisphere's increasingly focused opposition to neoliberalism. Established parties, unions and government institutions proved entirely incapable of restoring legitimacy in austere times, committed as they were to upholding a profoundly unequal class structure.

Chávez emerged from the ruin, first with a failed putsch in 1992, which landed him in jail but turned him into a folk hero, then in 1998, when he won 56 percent of the vote as a presidential candidate. Inaugurated in 1999, he took office

> *The participatory democracy that took place in barrios, in workplaces and in the countryside over the last fourteen years was a value in itself, even if it doesn't lead to a better world.*

committed to a broad yet vague anti-austerity program, a mild John Kenneth Galbraith–quoting reformer who at first had no power to reform anything. The esteem in which Chávez was held by the majority of Venezuelans, many of them dark-skinned, was matched by the rage he provoked among the country's mostly white political and economic elites. But their maximalist program of opposition—a US-endorsed coup, an oil strike that destroyed the country's economy, a recall election and an oligarch-media propaganda campaign that made Fox News seem like PBS—backfired. By 2005, Chávez had weathered the storm and was in control of the nation's oil, allowing him to embark on an ambitious program of domestic and international transformation: massive social spending at home and "poly-polar equilibrium" abroad, a riff on what Bolívar once called "universal equilibrium," an effort to break up the US's historical monopoly of power in Latin America and force Washington to compete for influence.

Over the last fourteen years, Chávez has submitted himself and his agenda to fourteen national votes, winning thirteen of them by large margins, in polling deemed by Jimmy Carter to be "best in the world" out of the ninety-two elections that he has monitored. (It turns out it isn't that difficult to have transparent elections: voters in Venezuela cast their ballot on a touch pad, which spits out a receipt they can check and then deposit in a box. At the end of the day, random polling stations are picked for "hot audits," to make sure the electronic and paper tallies add up). A case is made that this ballot-box proceduralism isn't democratic, that Chávez dispenses patronage and dominates the media giving him an unfair advantage. But after the last presidential ballot—which Chávez won with the same percentage he did his first election yet with a greatly expanded electorate—even his opponents have admitted, despairingly, that a majority of Venezuelans liked, if not adored, the man.

I'm what they call a useful idiot when it comes to Hugo Chávez, if only because rank-and-file social organizations that to me seem worthy of support in Venezuela continued to support him until the end. My impressionistic sense is that this support breaks down roughly in half, between voters who think their lives and their families' lives are better off because of Chávez's massive expansion of state services, including healthcare and education, despite real problems of crime, corruption, shortages and inflation.

The other half of Chávez's electoral majority is made up of organized citizens involved in one or the other of the country's many grassroots organizations. Chávez's social base was diverse and heterodox, what social scientists in the 1990s began to celebrate as "new social movements," distinct from established trade unions and peasant organizations vertically linked to—and subordinated to—political parties or populist leaders: neighborhood councils; urban and rural homesteaders, feminists, gay and lesbian rights organizations, economic justice activists, environmental co-alitions; breakaway unions and the like. It's these organizations, in Venezuela and elsewhere throughout the region, that have over the last few decades done heroic work in democratizing society, in giving citizens venues to survive the extremes of neoliberalism and to fight against further depredations, turning Latin America into one of the last global bastions of the Enlightenment left.

Chávez's detractors see this mobilized sector of the population much the way Mitt Romney saw 47 percent of the US electorate not as citizens but parasites, moochers sucking on the oil-rent teat. Those who accept that Chávez enjoyed ma-jority support disparaged that support as emotional enthrallment. Voters, wrote one critic, see their own vulnerability in their leader and are entranced. Another talked about Chávez's "magical realist" hold over his followers.

One anecdote alone should be enough to give the lie to the idea that poor Ven-ezuelans voted for Chávez because they were fascinated by the baubles they dangled in front of them. During the 2006 presidential campaign, the signature pledge of Chávez's opponent was to give 3,000,000 poor Venezuelans a black credit card (black as in the color of oil) from which they could withdraw up to $450 in cash a month, which would have drained over $16 billion a year from the national treasury (call it neoliberal populism: give to the poor just enough to bankrupt the government and force the defunding of services). Over the years, there's been a lot of heavy theoreti-cal breathing by US academics about the miasma oil wealth creates in countries like Venezuela, lulling citizens into a dreamlike state that renders them into passive spec-tators. But in this election at least, Venezuelans managed to see through the mist. Chávez won with over 62 percent of the vote.

Let's set aside for a moment the question of whether Chavismo's social-wel-fare programs will endure now that Chávez is gone and shelve the left-wing hope that out of rank-and-file activism a new, sustainable way of organizing society will emerge. The participatory democracy that took place in barrios, in workplaces and in the countryside over the last fourteen years was a value in itself, even if it doesn't lead to a better world.

There's been great work done on the ground by scholars such as Alejandro Velas-co, Sujatha Fernandes, Naomi Schiller and George Ciccariello-Maher on these so-cial movements that, taken together, lead to the conclusion that Venezuela might be the most democratic country in the Western Hemisphere. One study found that organized Chavistas held to "liberal conceptions of democracy and held pluralistic norms," believed in peaceful methods of conflict resolution and worked to ensure that their organizations functioned with high levels of "horizontal or non-hierarchi-cal" democracy. What political scientists would criticize as a hyper dependency on a strongman, Venezuelan activists understand as mutual reliance, as well as an acute awareness of the limits and shortcomings of this reliance.

Over the years, this or that leftist has pronounced themselves "disillusioned" with Chávez, setting out some standard drawn, from theory or history, and then pro-nouncing the Venezuelan leader as falling short. He's a Bonapartist, wrote one. He's no Allende, sighs another. To paraphrase the radical Republican Thaddeus Stevens in *Lincoln,* nothing surprises these critics and therefore they are never surprising. But there are indeed many surprising things about Chavismo in relationship to Latin American history.

First, the military in Latin America is best known for its homicidal right-wing sadists, many of them trained by the United States, in places like the School of the Americas. But the region's armed forces have occasionally thrown up anti-imperialists and economic nationalists. In this sense, Chávez is similar to Argentina's Perón, as well as Guatemala's Colonel Arbenz, Panama's Omar Torrijos and Peru's General Juan Francisco Velasco, who as president between 1968 and 1975 allied Lima with Moscow. But when they weren't being either driven from office (Arbenz) or killed (Torrijos?), these military populists inevitably veered quickly to the right. Within a few years of his 1946 election, Perón was cracking down on unions, going as far as endorsing the overthrow of Arbenz in 1954. In Peru, the radical phase of Peru's military government lasted seven years. Chávez, in contrast, was in office fourteen years, and he never turned nor repressed his base.

Second and related, for decades now social scientists have been telling us that the kind of mobilized regime Venezuela represents is pump-primed for violence, that such governments can only maintain energy through internal repression or external war. But after years of calling the oligarchy squalid traitors, Venezuela has seen remarkably little political repression—certainly less than Nicaragua in the 1980s under the Sandinistas and Cuba today, not to mention the United States.

Oil wealth has much to do with this exceptionalism, as it also did in the elite, top-down democracy that existed prior to Chávez. But so what? Chávez has done what rational actors in the neoliberal interstate order are supposed to do: he's leveraged Venezuela's comparative advantage not just to fund social organizations but give them unprecedented freedom and power.

Chávez was a strongman. He packed the courts, hounded the corporate media, legislated by decree and pretty much did away with any effective system of institutional checks or balances. But I'll be perverse and argue that the biggest problem Venezuela faced during his rule was not that Chávez was authoritarian but that he wasn't authoritarian enough. It wasn't too much control that was the problem but too little.

Chavismo came to power through the ballot following the near total collapse of Venezuela's existing establishment. It enjoyed overwhelming rhetorical and electoral hegemony, but not administrative hegemony. As such, it had to make significant compromises with existing power blocs in the military, the civil and educational bureaucracy and even the outgoing political elite, all of whom were loath to give up their illicit privileges and pleasures. It took near five years before Chávez's government gained control of oil revenues, and then only after a protracted fight that nearly ruined the country.

Once it had access to the money, it opted not to confront these pockets of corruption and power but simply fund parallel institutions, including the social missions that provided healthcare, education and other welfare services being the most famous. This was both a blessing and a curse, the source of Chavismo's strength and weakness.

Prior to Chávez, competition for government power and resources took place largely within the very narrow boundaries of two elite political parties. After Chávez's election, political jockeying took place within "Chavismo." Rather than forming a single-party dictatorship with an interventionist state bureaucracy controlling people's lives, Chavismo has been pretty wide open and chaotic. But it is significantly more inclusive than the old duopoly, comprised of at least five different currents: a new Bolivarian political class, older leftist parties, economic elites, military interests and the social movements mentioned above. Oil money gave Chávez the luxury of acting as a broker between these competing tendencies, allowing each to pursue their interests (sometimes, no doubt, their illicit interests) and deferring confrontations.

The high point of Chávez's international agenda was his relationship with Brazil's Luiz Inácio Lula da Silva, the Latin American leader whom US foreign policy and opinion makers tried to set as Chávez's opposite. Where Chávez was reckless, Lula was moderate. Where Chávez was confrontational, Lula was pragmatic. Lula himself never bought this nonsense, consistently rising to Chávez's defense and endorsing his election.

For a good eight years they worked something like a Laurel and Hardy routine, with Chávez acting the buffoon and Lula the straight man. But each was dependent on the other and each was aware of this dependency. Chávez often stressed the importance of Lula's election in late 2002, just a few months after April's failed coup attempt, which gave him his first real ally of consequence in a region then still dominated by neoliberals. Likewise, the confrontational Chávez made Lula's reformism that much more palatable. Wikileak documents reveal the skill in which Lula's diplomats gently but firmly rebuffed the Bush administration's pressure to isolate Venezuela.

Their inside-outside rope-a-dope was on full display at the November 2005 Summit of the Americas in Argentina, where the United States hoped to lock in its deeply unfair economic advantage with a hemisphere-wide Free Trade Agreement. In the meeting hall, Lula lectured Bush on the hypocrisy of protecting corporate agriculture with subsidies and tariffs even as it pushed Latin America to open its markets. Meanwhile, on the street Chávez led 40,000 protesters promising to "bury" the free trade agreement. The treaty was indeed derailed, and in the years that followed, Venezuela and Brazil, along with other Latin American nations, have presided over a remarkable transformation in hemispheric relations, coming as close as ever to achieving Bolívar's "universal equilibrium."

When I met Chávez in 2006 after his controversial appearance in the UN, it was at a small lunch at the Venezuelan consulate. Danny Glover was there, and he and Chávez talked the possibility of producing a movie on the life of Toussaint L'Ouverture, the former slave who led the Haitian Revolution.

Also present was a friend and activist who works on the issue of debt relief for poor countries. At the time, a proposal to relieve the debt owed to the Inter-American

Development Bank (IADB) by the poorest countries in the Americas had stalled, largely because mid-level bureaucrats from Argentina, Mexico and Brazil opposed the initiative. My friend lobbied Chávez to speak to Lula and Argentina's president Néstor Kirchner, another of the region's leftist leaders, and get them to jump-start the deal.

Chávez asked a number of thoughtful questions, at odds with the provocateur on display on the floor of the General Assembly. Why, he wanted to know, was the Bush administration in favor of the plan? My friend explained that some Treasury officials were libertarians who, if not in favor of debt relief, wouldn't block the deal. "Besides," he said, "they don't give a shit about the IADB." Chávez then asked why Brazil and Argentina were holding things up. Because, my friend said, their representatives to the IADB were functionaries deeply invested in the viability of the bank, and they thought debt abolition a dangerous precedent.

We later got word that Chávez had successfully lobbied Lula and Kirchner to support the deal. In November 2006, the IADB announced it would write off billions of dollars in debt to Nicaragua, Guyana, Honduras and Bolivia (Haiti would later be added to the list).

And so it was that the man routinely compared in the United States to Stalin quietly joined forces with the administration of the man he had just called Satan, helping to make the lives of some of the poorest people in America just a bit more bearable.

Chavez or Not, It's Time to Rethink the U.S.-Venezuela Relationship

By Dane Bryant
World Politics Review, September 28, 2012

Venezuelan President Hugo Chávez will be seeking an unprecedented third 6-year term when voters go to the polls on Oct. 7. But this time, the challenge from opposition candidate Henrique Capriles Radonski is expected to be credible, in what many analysts believe will be Chávez's closest contest since his initial election in 1998.

Capriles was able to unite a historically divided political opposition by winning the February 2012 primary in decisive fashion, taking 62 percent of the popular vote. His victory galvanized a wide spectrum of political parties behind a single opposition candidate for the first time since Chávez took office more than a decade ago. While polling data in Venezuela is considered largely unreliable, the race has tightened of late, with certain polls showing Capriles, the politically moderate former governor of the state of Miranda, edging closer to the incumbent president.

Additionally, Chávez's lengthy fight with cancer, which may or may not be in remission, has prompted further speculation regarding Venezuela's political future. With no named successor in place, analysts have spent the past year handicapping potential replacements should Chávez be forced to retire from public life, either before the election or, in the event of a successful outcome next month, shortly afterward.

Given the spectrum of potential outcomes, the United States must take the long view in determining the appropriate strategy to adopt toward Caracas, regardless of who is president at the start of 2013.

Over the past four years, the Obama administration has been preoccupied, both militarily and diplomatically, with the drawdown in Iraq and Afghanistan and the shifting dynamics of the post–Arab Spring Middle East. More recently, the Asia pivot has become the lodestar of U.S. strategic planning. As a result, Latin America has not received the attention it warrants, at a time when the region is undergoing rapid changes.

Nonetheless, the White House has remained consistent when it comes to Venezuela, stating publicly that it does not consider Chávez's regime a threat to vital U.S. national security interests and identifying bilateral cooperation on issues of mutual interest as the goal of current policy.

> *Instead, the U.S. must refocus its policy on Venezuela to lay out a path for future relations that are free of mutual recrimination while setting clear parameters for American expectations. The two pillars of this policy, upon which all other decisions are based, should be promotion of both democracy and economic growth.*

The Republican establishment has identified the lack of engagement with Latin America as a weak spot in Obama's foreign policy record, in particular criticizing the president for allowing Chávez, an outspoken opponent of American interests, to strengthen his foothold in the region at the expense of the United States. Conservative think tanks repeatedly point to Chávez's anti-American worldview, Venezuela's alliances with Iran, Syria and Cuba, and the provision of safe havens for documented terrorist organizations, such as Colombia's FARC guerrillas, as examples of the grave security risks associated with the status quo.

There is some merit to both sides' views. The Obama administration's stated policy of working with Venezuela on pragmatic issues, such as counternarcotics and trade, has been viable in the short term. But GOP leaders are right to note that deeper involvement is needed to address the legitimate security risks and democratic challenges posed by the current government's policies. In fact, it will take an approach based on elements of both these arguments to bolster U.S. influence in South America's largest oil-producing country.

The risks of a Chávez-led Venezuela are important to recognize, and by downplaying them, the Obama administration has fed the perception that it is indifferent toward both Venezuela's democracy and the United States' positioning in the region. Still, they cannot be the only basis by which the entire relationship is judged, and by focusing their efforts on demonizing Chávez, GOP critics of Obama's policy fuel Chávez's propaganda machine while doing nothing to address the underlying issues that plague Venezuela.

Instead, the U.S. must refocus its policy on Venezuela to lay out a path for future relations that are free of mutual recrimination while setting clear parameters for American expectations. The two pillars of this policy, upon which all other decisions are based, should be promotion of both democracy and economic growth.

Starting with the October elections, the United States must seek to ensure the legitimacy of Venezuela's democratic process. Though Washington will find its options for direct involvement limited, it can lobby Brazil, Colombia and other Western governments with significant financial investment in Venezuela to press Caracas for increased electoral transparency. In particular, foreign election monitors should be allowed to assess the contest and conduct exit polls for independent validation of the results.

But ensuring a free and fair election is only the starting point, for a smooth transition of power could prove to be the next major obstacle if the election does not go Chávez's way. Given the fragility of Venezuela's democracy, some experts have expressed fears of significant political turmoil and the potential for violence in the event of an upset victory for Capriles.

Moreover, even if a Capriles victory does not cause major unrest, any perceived subsequent reversal of Chávez's populist Bolivarian movement could prompt spontaneous violence from Chávez supporters, particularly among government employees and workers for Petroleos de Venezuela (PDVSA), the state-run oil company. "Chavista" social programs, though unable to provide long-term economic development opportunities, enjoy popular support among Venezuela's poor, who have little patience for austerity programs and macroeconomic stabilization.

This is why the second plank of Washington's Venezuela policy must emphasize sustainable economic growth. Regardless of next week's election outcome, any serious response to the challenges that Venezuela poses to U.S. regional interests must address the country's socio-economic inequalities, which Chávez has depended upon for popular support throughout his political career. Solving the widespread social exclusion and poverty that fuel the Bolivarian movement, if only incrementally, will be critical if the United States is to make any inroads in what could be a vital partnership.

For the past decade and a half, the U.S.-Venezuela relationship has been singularly defined by the Chávez obsession—in both Caracas and Washington. After the upcoming election, regardless of whether Chávez wins or loses, it will be time to begin playing a new game in Venezuela.

Hugo Chávez: Man Against the World

By Richard Gott
New Statesman, January 30, 2013

As illness ends Hugo Chávez's rule in Venezuela, what will his legacy be? Richard Gott argues he brought hope to a continent.

An atmosphere of sadness and imminent tragedy has taken over the towns and cities of Venezuela as Hugo Chávez nears death. For so long portrayed in the west as a buffoon or a socialist firebrand, this immensely important political figure has suddenly begun to be treated with dignity and respect.

What is not yet understood is that Chávez, who is suffering from cancer, has been the most significant ruler in Latin America since Fidel Castro seized power in Cuba in January 1959, more than half a century ago. Such extraordinary and charismatic people emerge rarely in history; they leave an imprint that lasts for decades.

I have long been a supporter of Chávez, writing and talking about him since he first emerged as a serious and revolutionary political contender in the middle of the 1990s. He embodied two vibrant traditions from Latin America in the 1960s: the memory of the left-wing guerrilla movements of that period, inspired by Che Guevara and the Cuban Revolution (and, of course, by Castro) and the unusual experience of government by left-wing army officers, notably General Juan Velasco Alvarado in Peru and General Omar Torríjos in Panama. He also embraced the powerful current of left-wing nationalism in Latin America's leftist parties, often repressed during the years of the cold war, but never far from the surface.

Chávez was born in the village of Sabaneta in July 1954, in the wide cattle lands of Barinas State (he is a year younger than Tony Blair). His parents were schoolteachers and members of Copei, the Christian democratic party.

Ambitious to be a baseball player, he joined the army at the age of 17 rather than following his elder brother to study at the University of the Andes in Mérida.

A frustrated intellectual, Chávez became an inspiring history teacher at the Caracas military academy, influencing a generation of young officers with his tales of Venezuelan dissidents from the 19th century, starting with Simón Bolívar. In Venezuela, a country dominated by white European immigrants and overlaid with a thick cultural veneer of American consumerism, he sought to recreate pride in an alternative historical vision of a land peopled by the often-ignored descendants of Native Americans and black slaves.

In 1982, dismayed by the growing decadence and corruption of the civilian politicians, Chávez formed a "Bolivarian revolutionary movement" within the armed forces that started as a political study group and ended up a subversive organization hoping for an appropriate moment to stage a *coup d'état*. This came after 1989, when civil unrest erupted in several cities; the armed forces were called out to suppress it with great violence, killing more than a thousand people.

Chávez and his small band of middle ranking officers then staged a coup in February 1992. It was successful in much of the country but failed in Caracas, where Chávez was in charge of the insurrection. Faced with defeat, he surrendered and appeared briefly on national television to announce that he was giving up, "for now." His implicit promise that he would return another day brought him immediate popularity countrywide, especially in the shanty towns and rural areas.

Chávez represented the hope of profound change in a stagnant and unequal society, and six years later, in 1998, leading an ad hoc party, the "Fifth Republic Movement," he was elected president of Venezuela with 56 percent of the vote. His victory was the result of the electoral implosion of the ruling parties of the previous 40 years, Copei and Democratic Action (affiliated with the Socialist International). The remnants of these two discredited parties have struggled unsuccessfully ever since to create an opposition worthy of the name.

At the end of 1999, after Chávez had been in power for a year, I went to Caracas to interview him and to write a book about him. It was already obvious then that he was the most interesting figure to have emerged in Latin America since the fall of Salvador Allende's government in September 1973, nearly 30 years earlier. We met on a Monday morning on the verandah of his home at La Casona, an official residence in eastern Caracas surrounded by a gorgeous tropical garden. I had often seen him loom large on television, but in person he seemed a size smaller. He had an infectious grin and a capacity to talk non-stop and it was difficult to get a word in.

We sat there alone throughout the morning, with occasional calls for coffee and orange juice, as he ranged over the entire history of Latin America. He emphasized the need to halt and reverse the persistent population drain from country to town in Venezuela.

He was impressed that my researches had taken me all over the country, not just to visit his birthplace in Sabaneta but to the remote settlement of Elorza, on a tributary of the Orinoco close to the Colombian border, to which he had been exiled in the 1980s when the government first got wind of his activities. Elorza was a tiring, 12-hour bus journey south of Barinas.

He invited me to fly with him that week to look at various rural projects, and half the cabinet came with us. Chávez asked questions all the time, prodding his ministers to take a direct interest in what needed to be done. His capacity to enthuse and educate was remarkable and left me and the ministers exhausted by the end of the day.

I have been back to Caracas most years since then and have talked to Chávez many times. He has always been the same, welcoming, keen to talk, and always recognizing me, even in a crowd. Who was this strange Englishman who had taken the trouble to write a book about him? When among civilians, he would single out old women and small children for attention; at a military parade he would talk to the lowest ranks before taking on the top brass. It is this reversal of normal public practice that has made him so special and so loved.

Chávez had great ambitions to improve conditions for Venezuela's poor and to include them in the national debate, but in the first few years he had no very clear idea how to do it. His single most significant political initiative, announced on day one, was to call for a progressive constitution, ratified by referendum (a pattern copied by Bolivia and Ecuador). The aim was to change the rules of the political game and lay the groundwork for a more participative society. With the wind of a popular election result in his sails, the enfeebled opposition could do nothing to stop him.

Chávez understood at an early stage that Venezuela needed to revive OPEC, the organization of oil-producing countries, where unity of outlook was needed in order to secure a regular and respectable rent. He visited several OPEC states that were unpopular in western eyes, including Iran and Iraq under Saddam Hussein, but it was worth the effort and the opprobrium. With Venezuela leading the first efforts in 1998, the price of oil has risen since then from $10 a barrel to over $100 in 2012. This was a significant change, but Chávez also needed to be persuaded by his own petroleum experts to recover government control of Petróleos de Venezuela (PDVSA), the nationalized oil company and the country's chief source of revenue. Under the *ancien régime*, the company had been organized to benefit itself, not to distribute its royalties for the benefit of the people.

Finally, after a lockout by PDVSA in 2002 (preceded by an equally subversive attempt at a military coup), the Chávez government took full control of the oil company, sacked the old management and forced the foreign companies working under contract to increase the royalties they paid.

Huge sums of money were now diverted into organizing wide-ranging social programs at home and buying influence abroad in the Caribbean, notably in Cuba, as well as in other parts of South America. This has been Chávez's lasting legacy, and is the basis of his project to promote "21st-century socialism" in Venezuela and more widely on the continent.

Chávez's rhetoric has been more powerful than his record of achievement. He has recovered the meaning and potential popularity of the word "socialism," after its worldwide collapse following the self-destruction of the Soviet Union in 1991, and has brought a number of important public utilities under state control. Yet even now France has a larger public sector than Venezuela.

Journalistic NGOs and human rights groups complain about what they see as attacks on freedom of the press in Venezuela, usually mentioning in passing the forced closure of a whites-only television channel that would have been shut down much earlier in other parts of the world. Of the huge widening of the media franchise in Venezuela, in the innumerable new community radio stations and alternative TV channels, there is little comment in foreign reports.

Nor do we hear much from western journalists about the changing nature of life in the shanty towns, with the spread of health programs and education opportunities,

> *Chávez understood at an early stage that Venezuela needed to revive OPEC, the organization of oil-producing countries, where unity of outlook was needed in order to secure a regular and respectable rent. He visited several OPEC states that were unpopular in western eyes, including Iran and Iraq under Saddam Hussein, but it was worth the effort and the opprobrium.*

or the recent construction of housing projects, or the experiments with co-operatives and community councils.

Why has Chávez had such a bad press? Several individual journalists are guilty of idleness, ignorance and bad faith. Living cheek by jowl with the opposition population in the upper-class zones of Caracas, they find it difficult not to share the views and prejudices of their neighbours. Yet the poor performance of individuals does not explain why the badmouthing of Chávez has been so prevalent throughout the western world, on the Europe continent and in the United States as well as in Britain. *Le Monde* and *El País, Libération* and *El Mundo* have been just as critical as the reporters of the *Guardian* and *The New York Times*.

Part of the image problem lies with long surviving caricatures of Latin America in the popular memory that have little relevance to the continent today. There is a history of military dictators, with or without the dark glasses, which dates back to the first half of the 20th century and reached its peak in the era of Augusto Pinochet in Chile and Leopoldo Galtieri in Argentina.

The military tradition led to imprisonment and torture, and the dropping of prisoners out of aeroplanes into the sea. In such a context, how is it that Colonel Chávez, a paratrooper in a red beret, has turned out to be such a progressive man?

Elections in Latin America are more often than not flawed. "You won the election, but I won the count" was the usual response of the Somoza family in Nicaragua to an unfavorable result. Yet outside observers have consistently declared Venezuela's elections to be fair, and Chávez is no Pinochet. The Venezuelan armed forces have been restructured to serve the people.

Another problem is that Chávez's reinvention of socialism, as well as his close affection for Fidel Castro, seem old-fashioned to some. Academics who had hoped for a smooth transition to western democratic patterns in Latin America after the downfall of the dictators have also been disappointed by the Venezuelan experience, so different from what they had hoped for or been led to expect. Chávez has fallen foul of most of the left-of-center politicians and intellectuals in Europe, who have remained in thrall to the social-democratic ideology common in the 1990s. They have ignored his appeal for something different to be summoned up in Latin America.

In a world where such people are subservient to the demands of the American empire, it is easy for the rare figure who speaks out against it to be viewed as an idiot or a despot. Chávez has had good reason to oppose the United States: it has tried to overthrow him. Yet it is not just his rejection of Washington's foreign wars that alarms: these have had many opponents in Europe, too. It is his outright hostility to US economic policy, filtered through organizations such as the International Monetary Fund and the World Bank, whose formulas are slavishly adhered to in western Europe, that is considered outlandish.

Chávez's search for a different economic policy, with a powerful role for the state, is thought to be foolish, utopian and destined to fail. Yet with many countries in Europe in a state of economic collapse—largely the result of their long embrace of neoliberal policies—his project for Latin America may soon have wider appeal.

Venezuela and Latin America, and the wider world beyond, now face a future in which Chávez will no longer be physically present. However, he has not only helped to construct and project Venezuela as an interesting and important country for the first time, at ease with itself and its historical heritage, he has reimagined the continent of Latin America with a vision of what might be possible. Long after successive presidents of the United States have disappeared into the obscurity of their presidential archives, the memory of Hugo Chávez will survive in Latin America, along with that of Simón Bolívar and Che Guevara, as an influential leader who promised much but was cut down in his prime.

Chavez's Economics Lesson for Europe

By Richard Gott
The Guardian, May 16, 2012

Some years ago, travelling on the presidential plane of Hugo Chávez of Venezuela with a French friend from *Le Monde Diplomatique*, we were asked what we thought was happening in Europe. Was there any chance of a move to the left? We replied in the depressed and pessimistic tones typical of the early years of the 21st century. Neither in Britain nor France, nor anywhere in the eurozone, did we see much chance of a political breakthrough.

Then maybe, said Chávez with a twinkle, we could come to your assistance, and he recalled the time in 1830 when revolutionary crowds in the streets of Paris had come out waving the cap of Simón Bolívar, the South American liberator from Venezuela who was to die at the end of that year. Fighting for liberty, Latin American style, was held up as the path for Europe to follow.

At the time, I was encouraged but not persuaded by Chávez's optimism. Yet now I think that he was right; it was good to be reminded that Alexis Tsipras, the leader of Greece's radical left party, Syriza, had visited Caracas in 2007 and inquired about the future possibility of receiving cheap Venezuelan oil, much as Cuba and other Caribbean and Central American countries do. There was a brief moment when Ken Livingstone and Chávez conjured up an oil deal between London and Caracas which looked promising until it was rejected by Boris Johnson.

More important than the prospect of cheap oil is the power of example. Chávez has been engaged since the turn of the century, even before, on a project that rejects the neoliberal economics that afflicts Europe and much of the western world. He has been opposed to the recipes of the World Bank and the International Monetary Fund, and has fought hard against the policies of privatization that harmed the social and economic fabric of Latin America and with which the European Union is now threatening to destroy the economy of Greece. Chávez has renationalized the many industries, including oil and gas, that were privatized in the 1990s.

The words and inspiration of Chávez have had an effect beyond Venezuela. They have encouraged Argentina to default on its debt; to reorganize its economy thereafter and to renationalize its oil industry. Chávez has helped Evo Morales of Bolivia to run its oil and gas industry for the benefit of the country rather than its foreign shareholders, and more recently to halt the robbery by Spain of the profits of its electricity company. Above all, he has shown the countries of Latin America that there is an alternative to the single neoliberal message that has been endlessly broadcast for decades, by governments and the media in hock to an outdated ideology.

Now is the time for that alternative message to be heard further afield, to be listened to by voters in Europe. In Latin America, governments following an alternative strategy have been re-elected time and time again, suggesting that it is effective and popular. In Europe, governments of whatever hue that follow the standard neoliberal template seem to fall at the first fence, suggesting that the will of the people is not engaged.

Chávez and his co-religionaries in the new "Bolivarian revolution" have called for "21st-century socialism," not a return to Soviet-style economics or the continuation of the mundane social democratic adaptation of capitalism, but, as the Ecuadorean president Rafael Correa has described it, the re-establishment of national planning by the state "for the development of the majority of the people." Greece has a wonderful chance to change the history of Europe and to throw their caps of Bolívar into the air, as once the Italian carbonari did in Paris all those years ago. Lord Byron, who planned to settle in Bolívar's Venezuela before sailing off to help liberate Greece, named his yacht Bolívar; he would certainly have been pleased with contemporary developments.

Investors Who Think Venezuela's Economy Will Open Up After Chavez Have Another Thing Coming

By Linette Lopez
Business Insider, January 5, 2013

All signs point to the fact that Venezuelan President Hugo Chávez is not long for this world. The last reports of his condition say that his cancer treatment isn't going very well and that he's suffering from complications from a severe lung infection.

So it's time to look at what's coming next. After all, Chavez, who has been President of Venezuela since 1999, has already given his second in command, Nicolas Maduro, and his party, the United Socialist Party of Venezuela (PSUV), their marching orders. A special election is to be held 30 days after Inauguration Day in the likely event that Chavez can't make it.

Maduro would then be the PSUV's candidate, and for some reason this is making investors optimistic. Check out this assessment of the situation from a recent Morgan Stanley report:

> We continue to recommend our long Venezuela vs. Brazil RV trade as investors envisage a more market-friendly policy from the Venezuelan government if M. Chavez were forced to give up power.

And this one Bank of America Merrill Lynch:

> We expect a major FX adjustment early next year which, together with the ongoing spending cuts, is likely to significantly improve the country's fiscal position. A major delay of the adjustment could occur if the government were to significantly postpone calling new elections. In view of yesterday's results, we think this is unlikely. Either the government takes advantage of its electoral strength, calls elections now and implements the adjustment soon thereafter, or Chávez's health improves enough to allow him to take office and Chávez himself implements the adjustment. We thus believe that the risks of a major delay in adjustment are low.

One of the few things that's clear about Venezuela's political system is that most decisions are made behind closed doors. From Venezuela's current political theater though, we can see that Chavez's party is taking great pains to show unity and stress that it wants to follow Chavez's 30-day directive to the letter.

If there is infighting, though, expect chaos as former bus driver and labor activist Maduro's supporters clash with those of military man Diosdado Cabello, according to ABC's Manuel Rueda.

Chaos, of course, has never been good for markets. Not a great scenario.

There's another option. Maduro could lose the special election to Venezuela's opposition party. As Venezuelan journalist Francisco Toro points out, though, that's highly unlikely as Maduro will have Chavez's powerful political machine behind him.

From *The New Republic*:

> Venezuela's long suffering liberal opposition looks on this spectacle with some hope and not a little trepidation. In elections barely two months ago, the opposition was thumped by more than 11 points as an ailing Chávez, barely able to campaign, nonetheless coasted to a third term. To some, Chávez's charisma carried the day. My analysis is less optimistic: That campaign showed the obscene structural advantages a cash-flush petrostate incumbent enjoys in an increasingly autocratic environment where opposition fundraising is badly hobbled by harassment and intimidation against its donors, and all checks on the abuse of official prerogatives for campaign advantage have been hollowed out. While Maduro has none of Chávez's charisma or storied emotional bond with the poor, he would undoubtedly inherit that advantage.

So that's the third option—that these politicians stick to their script, and the people re-elect PSUV.

The question becomes, then, in that event would Maduro institute more market friendly policies? Based on his record the answer to that is simple—no. Maduro has always been a Chavista without wavering, loyal to a fault. Not only that, but if he's elected he will have to build legitimacy for himself (the party's alone may not carry him).

Now how will he do that? Probably not by making the tough decisions that the Venezuelan economy desperately needs, like cutting spending (as the fiscal deficit approaches 20%), cutting the number of public sector jobs, and/or ending oil subsidies for Venezuelans. Those were policies that made Chavez popular. Discontinuing them may not only anger the Venezuelan populace, but also create the perception that Maduro has turned away from their departed leader's philosophy.

Maduro's close relationship with Fidel Castro doesn't help the "opening up the market" theory much either.

That said, there have been reports of overtures to re-open dialogue between Venezuela and the United States. According to *El Universal*, Maduro had a long phone conversation about life-after-Chavez with Roberta S. Jacobson, the top US State Department official in charge of Latin American affairs, on November 21st.

However, *El Universal* also points out that that call could just be a way for Maduro to buy time:

> Maduro, in turn, may be buying time to consolidate his leadership at home. "A hardliner who is very close to Cuba's dictatorship, Maduro may have talked to Jacobson to send a message within the polarized Chavista movement that he's in charge, before any internal power struggle in Venezuela breaks out in the open," the sources added.

Either way, one phone call with the United States certainly does not make Maduro a free market capitalist. Besides, Chavez himself constantly walked the line between bombastically proclaiming his hatred for the U.S., and ensuring that his enemy, and biggest oil importer, never brought sanctions down against Venezuela.

Foreign Affairs' Javier Corrales calls that tight-rope routine "conservative anti-imperialism", and it looks something like this:

> "And that points to a final piece of the Chávez legacy. He wants to be remembered as the most anti-American leader the world has seen since Fidel Castro. In reality, Chávez broke with Fidel's approach to the Yankee empire early on. To be sure, Chávez has enjoyed provoking the Americans, but only to a certain point, and never so much that the United States brought an embargo down on his head. So he has played his anti-Americanism conservatively: he has sided with the anti-imperialist FARC in Colombia, but has also managed to stay on good terms with the Colombian government. He has cooperated with Iran, but has also maintained good relations with the pro-American Saudis. He avoided nuclear weapons . . .
>
> Chávez came to understand that his expensive revolution needed the U.S. oil market and that he couldn't put his access to that market at risk. If he dies soon, he should be remembered as the United States' reliable oil partner—the ultimate seller."

So it's complicated.

All that said, does Venezuela sound like a place that is ready to get its fiscal house in order to you?

5
The Rise of Mexico

© STRINGER/MEXICO/Reuters/Corbis

Technicians work on an engine at the inauguration of Volkswagen's 100th plant worldwide in Silao, Mexico.

The United States and Mexico: Achieving a Balance

In 1994, the United States, Canada, and Mexico entered into one of the landmark trade agreements of the globalized economy, the North American Free Trade Agreement (NAFTA). While Canada is a critical member of this agreement, NAFTA's implications for US-Mexican relations have been a particular subject of analysis by scholars and political leaders alike. The primary reason for this focus is the fact that NAFTA represents an agreement between one of the world's most powerful industrialized economies—the United States—and Mexico, a nation whose economy and infrastructure continues to develop.

Although the United States and Mexico were trading partners long before NAFTA, the trade agreement has highlighted their mutual economic interests. It has also drawn attention to unresolved economic issues between the two countries. NAFTA has changed the relationship between the United States and Mexico. According to many experts, the trade agreement has not only yielded economic benefits for both countries, it has opened the doors for bilateral agreements on security, development, the environment, and criminal justice. While Washington and Mexico City look to take advantage of these new opportunities, they are also looking to resolve latent issues regarding jobs and immigration.

A New Era in US-Mexico Relations

The United States and Mexico developed extensive economic and diplomatic relations long before NAFTA, but the trade agreement served to synthesize this cooperation. For NAFTA's benefits to be realized, however, a number of changes needed to be implemented—most of them in Mexico City. For example, Mexico's price control system, in place to protect many of its agricultural exports, required phasing out in favor of a system influenced by more liberal market forces. In 1991, Mexico modified its constitution, ending a Mexican Revolution–era restriction on the sale of peasant lands, so that private investment on undeveloped land could begin in the name of economic development. Furthermore, Mexico's environmental protection laws required updating in order to comply with those of the United States and Canada.

In the years since NAFTA, the Mexican government has labored to implement economic liberalization and combat corruption. Corruption has long plagued the Mexican economy, particularly the country's oil and construction industries. These efforts have been praised by US officials, who have worked to bring Mexico into other international agreements. In 2012, President Barack Obama invited the administration of then-president Felipe Calderón to join talks for the formation of the

Trans-Pacific Partnership (TPP). If ratified, this trade agreement would connect the growing economies of Brunei, Vietnam, Chile, Malaysia, and Peru with the economies of Singapore, Australia, the United States, and New Zealand. While Mexico is still working to comply with TPP standards related to agricultural trade and intellectual property law, the American invitation to join the talks served to elevate Mexico's regional and international reputation as an economic heavyweight.

In 2012, Mexico elected President Enrique Peña Nieto. During his campaign, Peña Nieto promised that as president, he would implement more economic reform in the country, including continued updates to the energy and telecommunications sectors. Peña Nieto has also pledged to continue the fight against corruption and crime. Peña Nieto has also reached out to his counterpart in the United States, Barack Obama, maintaining the legacy of cooperation between the two countries. Shortly after his inauguration, Peña Nieto joined Obama in Washington to discuss economic cooperation and the issues of immigration and jobs.

Immigration

Critics have argued that NAFTA fails to address the issue of immigration. They argue that while the trade agreement promotes the flow of American and Mexican products across the US-Mexican border, it does not speak to the flow of people across that same border. During the twentieth century, the comparative economic strength of the United States enticed a steady migration of Mexicans northward in search of jobs. Those who take up residence in the United States without obtaining the proper documentation are illegal immigrants whose low incomes, opponents argue, cause them to use public services and resources that result in significant costs to American taxpayers. This school of thought has fostered a political backlash against Mexican immigrants and calls for increased security at the border and enhanced immigration restrictions in states with large immigrant populations, such as Arizona and California.

Although the number of Mexican immigrants entering the United States has decreased between 2005 and 2010, the issue of immigration reform remains a major policy debate in Washington. The United States Congress has been unable to adopt a bipartisan measure to curtail illegal immigration and create a policy platform aimed at dealing with illegal immigrants already living in the United States. As this logjam has persisted, several states have explored adopting their own immigration policies. Given that this issue of immigration falls under federal jurisdiction, these state government moves are highly unorthodox. In the eyes of Mexico's federal government, the actions of Arizona and other states in this regard are also detrimental to ongoing US-Mexican relations. In 2012, Calderón issued a warning to Mexicans traveling to Arizona and filed a statement with the US Supreme Court claiming that Arizona's laws put Mexicans at risk when traveling in the US (fourteen Mexican state governments passed similar statements in protest).

Through the end of 2012, the issue of immigration reform remained intractable, with lawmakers on both sides of the issue unable or unwilling to strike a compromise. Meanwhile, President Peña Nieto has remained more focused on domestic reforms designed to keep Mexico's workers in the country rather than speaking out against the domestic policies of American states. The Pew Hispanic Center reported in November 2012 that the number of Mexicans leaving the United States now outnumbers the number of Mexicans entering the United States. This is no doubt due to Mexico's continued economic growth. In 2012, the Mexican economy grew by approximately 4 percent. Much of this growth is attributed to robust improvement in the country's agricultural sector.

Jobs

Related to the issue of immigration is the debate over migrant workers. Unlike immigrants, who take up permanent residence in the United States, migrants are based in Mexico and cross the border in search of work on a daily or short-term basis. Migrants sometimes cross miles of desert and dangerous terrain, risking attacks from criminal groups and capture and deportation by US border patrol officers. Migrants often seek low-paying jobs as laborers, picking strawberries or harvesting other agricultural products. Some advocates for migrant workers liken these Mexican laborers to Depression-era American migrants. Mexican migrant workers are becoming a challenge for both the United States and Mexico. For Mexico, migrant workers weaken the country's own labor force. In the United States, the presence of illegal workers remains politically contentious.

Social science research has not been entirely successful in quantifying the numbers of migrating workers arriving in the United States from Mexico, or tracking their whereabouts. However, the data available does reveal that a sizable segment of the Mexican population crosses the border in search of higher wages, a fact that the Mexican government takes seriously. After taking office in late 2012, President Peña Nieto moved away from the type of rhetoric used by his predecessors—who protested American laws, regulations, and proposals designed to curtail illegal migration and immigration—and employed a different approach. Peña Nieto began pushing for domestic economic reforms to increase job opportunities and wages for Mexicans living in rural and underdeveloped areas. His initiatives are intended to give would-be migrants an incentive to stay in the country and contribute to the Mexican economy. Recent migration statistics and data related to Mexico's economic growth suggest these efforts may be working.

In the United States, the debate regarding migrant workers continues. There are continued calls to tighten border security on one side, and demonstrations in favor of increased federal recognition of immigrant populations on the other. The Department of Homeland Security has moved to bolster existing border enforcement initiatives. Determining how effective those policies are, however, has been a challenge, as experts have not yet been able to calculate the number of migrants moving across the border. Data related to migration traffic is complex. If the number of migrants captured at a particular border crossing decreases for a time, for example, it is unclear whether this decline is attributable to official deterrents, the migrants using alternate routes, or other factors entirely, such as criminal gang activity. Without an accurate census of the origins and destinations of migrant workers, it is difficult to enhance existing border security programs.

Adding to concerns by anti-immigration activists that Mexican migrants and immigrants are taking American jobs is the notion that, because of NAFTA, more American jobs are moving to Mexico, where business costs are lower. Since the passage of NAFTA, many American manufacturing facilities have been reestablished on the Mexican side of the US-Mexico border. These plants, often referred to as "maquiladoras," import US raw materials that are made by low-wage workers into products for the American market. Critics of Mexican manufacturing operations argue that maquiladoras exploit workers (particularly women) and pay unfairly low wages.

In the early to mid-1990s, the liberalization of trade stemming from NAFTA, coupled with the costs of plant operations, labor, and capital expenditures in the United States, led US business leaders to make the logical choice to save money by moving to Mexico. According to a 2010 study by the University of Utah, however, the number of factories established in Mexico at the time does not paint a completely accurate picture of jobs in the United States. The study's authors argue that while the Mexican unskilled labor pool may have taken jobs away from the unskilled American labor pool, the American skilled labor pool benefited greatly from the increased productivity and lower production costs. As evidence, they point to the increase in the number of jobs at corporate headquarters located in the United States.

In 2013, a number of labor studies, include studies published by the Harvard Business School and the Boston Consulting Group, show that an increasing quantity of American businesses that had previously moved manufacturing facilities to other countries like Mexico were "reshoring"—building plants in the United States. New research theorizes that companies are reshoring in order to improve their public image, responding to tax incentives, and taking advantage of the availability of American labor. This trend reflects the fact that the federal government and state governments are increasingly seeking ways to entice corporations to invest in American operations rather than move overseas. As the global economy continues its slow recovery from the 2008 recession, it is possible that these reshoring trends may continue. In the meantime, the United States and Mexico are likely to remain strong partners as they continue to seek sustained economic growth.

The Ebbing Mexican Wave

Economist, November 24, 2012

From a vantage point on a scrubby hillside south of San Diego, Mike Jiménez, an agent with the United States Border Patrol, gazes across the Mexican frontier into Tijuana. For decades the poor neighborhood of Colonia Libertad, rammed up against the border fence, has served as a base for illicit crossings. From its tin roof-tops scouts peer over to the United States, monitoring the movements of Mr. Jiménez and his colleagues and relaying their positions by mobile phone to migrants as they creep across the border. Mr. Jiménez has little time for the *coyotes* who guide people into the United States. "They don't care about lives, they care about the money they're going to make. If someone twists an ankle or breaks their leg, they leave them behind," he says. On average, one person dies every day trying to cross the 2,000-mile border.

The decades-old game of cat and mouse between Mexican migrants and la Migra, as the American migration authorities are known, has historically been a fairly one-sided contest. About one in ten Mexican citizens, 12 million in total, live in America, half of them illegally. This makes for the biggest immigrant community in the world. (The wider Mexican-American community, including the American-born offspring of immigrants, comes to about 33 million.) After Mexico City, the world's biggest collection of Mexican citizens is found not in Guadalajara or Monterrey but in Los Angeles.

But the Mexican wave has ebbed. Between 1995 and 2000 some 3 million Mexicans moved to the United States, vastly outnumbering the 700,000 or so who returned to Mexico. Yet in 2005–10 the number of newcomers slumped to 1.4 million, whereas that of returners increased to a matching 1.4 million, according to estimates by the Pew Hispanic Center, a Washington, DC, think-tank. It thinks that now there are probably more people departing than arriving. La Migra has noted the same trend. In 2000 the Border Patrol foiled 1.6 million attempts to cross the frontier. Last year the figure was just 286,000, the lowest for 40 years. The world's biggest migration has gone into reverse.

Back and Forth

Mass migration from Mexico to the United States is a fairly recent phenomenon. Only 40 years ago the United States had more immigrants from Canada, Germany and Italy than from Mexico. The Mexican wave swelled in the 1970s and kept growing in the 1980s and 1990s . . . as a rocky Mexican economy propelled more migrants

---

north and a relaxed American immigration policy made it easy for more to settle. In 2000, the peak year, more than 750,000 Mexicans crossed the border.

The flow has gone into reverse because the rewards for going north have diminished and the risks have increased. Mexicans emigrate for jobs, and there are fewer of them available than there used to be. In 2000 unemployment in the United States was around 4%; it is double that now, and almost double Mexico's rate. The construction industry in the United States, in which many migrants toil, has been especially badly hit. Migrants are also missing out because Americans are eating out less, cleaning their own homes and firing their gardeners. Deportations have increased, to about 300,000 a year. But now even those who have been turfed out are lukewarm about going back. In past surveys by Pew, about eight out of ten of them said they would try to return as soon as possible. Now it is six out of ten.

At the same time getting into the United States has become much harder. Crossing from Tijuana into San Diego used to be a matter of dashing over the frontier in a group that was too big for the border agents to stop. These days the San Diego border is a fearsome thing to cross. Two lines of fencing, one topped with razor wire, are monitored by night-vision cameras mounted on towers. Border Patrol agents—more than 21,000 nationwide, making up America's biggest law-enforcement agency—scoot around on quad bikes. There are seismic sensors to detect footsteps and ground-penetrating radar to scan for tunnels. Robots are sent into sewers to check for holes burrowed into the system. Americans caught helping migrants often used to be let off, but now they are usually prosecuted first time around.

Tijuana, which used to be the most popular place for illegal crossings from south to north, has fallen out of favor. In some years in the 1990s half a million Mexicans were apprehended trying to cross into San Diego, nearly half the total caught along the entire border. Last year Mr. Jiménez and his colleagues stopped just 42,000, barely a tenth of the national total. The favorite place to cross now is the Arizona desert, which few people attempted in the past because it involves a 72-hour trudge with scorching days and freezing nights.

Getting into the United States has become dicier still since Mexico's criminal gangs realized that migrants made good extortion targets. "The obstacle course doesn't begin at the border, it begins in northern Mexico," says David Scott Fitzgerald, a migration expert at the University of California at San Diego. His surveys in small Mexican towns have found that whereas the main perceived risk used to be natural hazards—rivers, animals, the desert—these days the biggest worry is gang violence. The fear is well-founded. Mexico's human-rights commission estimates that each year some 20,000 Central and South American migrants are kidnapped while travelling through Mexico. Mass graves discovered in the border state of Tamaulipas in 2010 and 2011 contained nearly 300 bodies.

Meanwhile many rich Mexicans have fled from places that are no longer safe for the conspicuously wealthy. Texan cities such as Brownsville and McAllen have seen an influx of well-to-do Mexicans who live north of the border while continuing to manage their businesses in Matamoros or Monterrey. San Diego neighborhoods such as East Lake are home to many wealthy exiles from Baja California.

Bienvenidos a Tijuana

Nowadays most of those who pass through Tijuana are on their way south. The Instituto Madre Assunta, a shelter for women and child migrants in Tijuana's hilly outskirts, accommodates about 120 people a month, offering board and lodging along with legal advice and internet access. Ten years ago the center dealt almost exclusively with migrants heading north, says Mary Galván, its director. Now virtually all are women who have just left the United States, many of them unwillingly. "Some were taken [to the US] as babies. They arrive in shock—some don't even know the *pueblo* where they used to live," says Ms. Galván.

The women in the shelter have mixed plans. Ángela, in her 40s, is hoping to visit her family in Oaxaca before going back to San Bernadino, California, with the help of a *coyote*. There she had a job in a plastics-recycling plant, earning $250 a week, compared with the paltry 54 pesos ($4.20) a day that she says she would earn in Oaxaca. Rosa, who has lived in the United States for 24 years, is also determined to go back. "I've spent half my life in America. It's so strange to be back. When they say 20 pesos I think 20 dollars," she says. A younger woman who doesn't give her name is planning to return to her home state of Guerrero with her four children. "It's uglier here," she admits. But crossing the border is so difficult these days that she will stay.

The increase in new arrivals has put pressure on the city. About 400 people are deposited there every day. Víctor Clark Alfaro, of the Binational Centre for Human Rights, estimates that about a third come from prisons or are members of gangs. Tattooed, speaking broken Spanish and sporting weird American fashions (enormous trousers currently seem to be in), they find it hard to get work. One willing employer is organized crime, which likes to recruit young men with links to the drug retailers of San Diego

> *Mexico's human-rights commission estimates that each year some 20,000 Central and South American migrants are kidnapped while travelling through Mexico. Mass graves discovered in the border state of Tamaulipas in 2010 and 2011 contained nearly 300 bodies.*

neighborhoods such as Barrio Logan. To ease the pressure on the border, the American authorities have started flying some deported people to Mexico City. The Tijuana government is also trying to move them on. "It's cheaper for the city to pay for a ticket and for them to go back to their places of origin," says Carlos Bustamante, the mayor.

But even the millions of Mexicans who remain abroad are firmly plugged into life back home. Phone calls from the United States to Mexico add up to more hours than to the whole of western Europe. Mexican expats pay little attention to politics at home: only 40,000 bothered to vote in Mexico's presidential election this year, even though if all of them had voted they could easily have changed the result. But they play an active part in their home country's economic life. Last year Mexicans abroad, overwhelmingly in the United States, sent $22.8 billion to their families. Payments from the United States to Mexico make up by far the world's biggest stream of remittances, bringing in more foreign currency than does tourism.

Inflows have not yet returned to the heights of 2007, when they topped $26 billion, but they are recovering. As in other parts of the world, remittances have been surprisingly resilient during the financial crisis, notes Marcelo Giugale of the World Bank. "Migrant workers [in the United States] have enough money to live on, but the people at home need every dollar. So they think, 'I won't do restaurants or movies any more, but I'll keep sending money to *Mamá*'," he says.

Remittances will be boosted by a growing trend for Mexicans in the United States to have their papers in order. According to Pew, between 2007 and 2011 the undocumented Mexican population there fell from 7 million to 6.1 million and the legal population rose from 5.6 million to 5.8 million. Being legally resident improves migrants' potential earnings and entitles them to the same social-security benefits as other workers. (Fiscally, America has done rather well out of illegal immigrants: many of them pay social-security contributions under a false identity, so they cannot claim many of the benefits that they are paying for.) On present trends, by the time this report is published there will be more legal than illegal Mexican immigrants in the United States. That must be good for people on both sides of the border.

Remarks to the Association of American Chambers of Commerce in Latin America

By Jose W. Fernandez
US Department of State, February 7, 2013

Good afternoon. Thank you for the kind introduction. I am thrilled to be here in Miami with you. I know many of you traveled from countries throughout the region, and it is great to see you.

Two weeks ago, I was in Mexico with assistant secretaries from the Departments of Commerce, Treasury, and Transportation, and we had the pleasure of meeting with the AmCham. As the Department makes economics a corner stone of our foreign policy under the Economic Statecraft initiative, I have found that some of the best insights into local economies as well as global trends come from local AmChams.

When I travel in Latin America, I frequently hear concerns about our so-called "pivot" towards Asia and what it means for the region. There is a great deal of misinformation about the pivot, which is better described as a rebalance, particularly the common misperception that it signifies Latin America is less important to the United States than it was in the past. Nothing could be further from the truth. Our relationships with our regional partners running from the Arctic to Tierra del Fuego are more important than ever. Let's look at the numbers. Forty percent of America's exports stay in this hemisphere. We export six times as much to Latin America and Canada as we do to China. We sell more to Colombia than to Russia. Last year, our two-way goods trade with Canada and Latin America totaled more than 1.3 trillion dollars. Our total goods trade with Canada is valued more than twice as much as our goods trade with India. These numbers show the importance of the Western Hemisphere for U.S. trade, but there is more to the relationship than just dry trade statistics.

We are bound by history and common culture. Millions of American families have ties to other countries in the region. The degree of these linkages creates unique opportunities for cooperation that we do not have with any other region.

However, we are not willing to rest on common culture and the current strength of our relationships with partners in the region. We want to broaden and expand our interaction with countries and economies throughout the Hemisphere. We want to reframe the relationships for a changing world. The rebalance to Asia should more accurately include the word "Pacific." We are thinking increasingly of the Americas and Asia as an integrated whole—a broader Pacific with commonalities beyond geographic links. The Asia-Pacific region is central to foreign policy because of the role it plays in powering global economic growth. The Broader Pacific is home to more than half of the world's population, as well as many key economies, a number of our closest allies, and emerging powers.

Although the Pacific is vital, our focus does not mean we plan on ignoring our Latin American and Caribbean partners in the Atlantic. We fully recognize our valuable partners on the Atlantic side—our Caribbean neighbors, Brazil, and others. The Asia-Pacific region isn't the only side where relationships with key partners are changing.

U.S. economic policy in Latin America is vast and multifaceted, and so I will not attempt to address all of it. Instead, I want to touch on seven areas: 1) economic success stories, 2) the emerging middle class, 3) harnessing the power of the diaspora, 4) infrastructure opportunities, 5) improving government finances, 6) working together on a common international agenda, and finally 7) what we at the State Department are doing to help support U.S. business abroad. These are areas where I believe the U.S. can increase engagement and have an impact in the region.

Economic Success Stories

Mexico and Brazil are only two of the economic success stories in Latin America, but they are two where I am most frequently involved. Since I was just in Mexico, I want to focus there. Mexico, a major regional power that is pro-market and actively engages on global economic issues, offers huge possibilities for increased economic cooperation. The United States and Mexico share many similar interests and concerns. It is in both our interest to increase economic integration among the NAFTA partners in order to make our economies more competitive.

President Peña Nieto has made clear that one of his top priorities is economic reform and a more robust Mexican economy. A key element of this is to prioritize the economic side of the U.S.-Mexico relationship. As I already mentioned, when I traveled to Mexico City two weeks ago along with my colleagues we went to engage the new Peña Nieto administration on how we can deepen and elevate our already close cooperation on economic issues. We discussed ways to work together on transportation, regulatory cooperation, and telecommunications. We want to create a 21st Century Border that promotes the efficient flow of legitimate goods. I heard a desire from government officials and the private sector to learn best practices for supporting entrepreneurship. We are looking to establish an Entrepreneurship and Innovation Dialogue for this purpose. Finally, we are seeking opportunities to work together on global issues, such as regional trade and development.

Enormous regional economic growth has produced a strong middle class that forms the basis for continued political and economic reforms, and I'd like to turn to that next.

Middle Class

Strong regional economic growth led by Mexico and others has produced a strong middle class that forms the basis for continued political and economic reforms.

Between 2000 and 2009, 50 million people joined the middle class in Latin America and the Caribbean. This brought the total middle class population in the region to over 165 million or roughly one-third of the population. For the first time in the region's history, there are as many people in the middle class as there are in moderate poverty. As their incomes increase, members of the middle class will demand better government services, better education, more transparency, and less corruption—all areas where the U.S. has engaged in the past. A recent study has shown that, all else being equal, an increase in the proportion of the middle class in a society results in more active social policies on health and education and improvement in the quality of governance regarding democratic participation and corruption. As the demographics of Latin America changes, so too must our policies and priorities change.

An increased demand for quality education offers us the opportunity to promote U.S. universities as a destination for Latin American students as well as joint programs between U.S. and Latin American schools. President Obama's 100,000 Strong in the Americas initiative is expanding opportunities for educational exchanges, including for historically underserved populations to develop a new generation of "Pan-American" business, scientific, and political leaders. As the home of top flight business and Silicon Valley, the U.S. is ideally situated to engage students and the policy makers on entrepreneurship and innovation as engines for economic growth and job creation.

In order to facilitate trade and meet the rising middle classes' desire for U.S. goods and services, we must also focus on regulatory cohesion. One area where we are making progress is the High-Level Regulatory Cooperation Council with Mexico, where we work together to identify specific sectors where we can improve regulatory cooperation. This will make it easier for companies on both sides of the border to sell their goods. Regional regulatory cooperation, where appropriate, presents real opportunities for cost savings to businesses, and greater market access for goods in key markets, such as medical devices. Costa Rica, for example, automatically approves medical devices certified by the U.S. Food and Drug Administration. There may be opportunities to work with other countries to implement a similar program.

Diaspora

Another area of great opportunity is harnessing the power of the diaspora. Latino immigrants around the world sent over $60 billion in remittances back home last year. With the largest Hispanic diaspora population in the world at 52 million, the United States was the source for over $47 billion of those remittances. In Mexico, Central America, and the Caribbean remittances often account for over 10 percent of GDP. There is a broad consensus within the development and NGO communities that remittances represent a significant opportunity to help meet development and economic growth goals. As the World Bank, Inter-American Development Bank, and other development experts have recognized, in an era of fiscal austerity, we cannot afford to ignore the development potential of remittances. We also believe that migrants are highly effective advocates for U.S. products and investments in their home countries. Immigrants are often among the first to be willing to invest in challenging markets, which brings me to the next topic.

Infrastructure

We are also focusing on the tremendous opportunity American companies have in regional infrastructure projects. Virtually every Latin American country has targeted infrastructure as essential for increased economic growth. Brazil, Colombia, Peru, and Mexico have unveiled several billion dollars of water, port, airport, railroad, electric, and roads projects.

Under the second phase of its Growth Acceleration Program, Brazil will spend approximately 470 billion dollars from 2011 to 2014 to develop its energy generation and distribution system, roads, railroads, ports, and airports, as well as stadiums for the 2014 World Cup and the 2016 Olympics. As Brazil grows its middle class and prepares to host these international games, demand for transportation services is likely to overwhelm the country's inadequate infrastructure and framework of antiquated air transport agreements. For this reason, we are working to leverage our new Aviation Partnership Memorandum of Understanding to open opportunities for U.S. firms in the areas of air traffic management, airport infrastructure, equipment and software, and air services technology.

In Colombia, the government has advanced plans to invest roughly $26 billion (nearly four percent of GDP) in infrastructure projects over four years. Only 15 percent of Colombia's roads are paved, and the nation has just 1,000 kilometers of dual-lane divided highways. Colombia has just 900 kilometers of railroad, and river navigation cannot transport goods on a large-scale.

Mexican president Peña Nieto repeatedly stated during his campaign that he wanted to increase investment in infrastructure through public-private partnerships. He has also made it clear that facilitating cross-border trade will be a central focus to his economic agenda. To do this, Mexico will need to carry out a comprehensive review of existing roads, bridges, and interior infrastructure with the aim of reducing traffic bottlenecks and increasing the efficiency of border crossings. Peña Nieto in his inaugural address already announced three new rail projects. One of which, the Transpeninsular Yucatan-Quintana Roo line, is estimated to cost U.S. $850 million. It is unlikely the Mexican government will be able to fund the projects on its own, so they will likely look to develop public-private partnership ventures.

Helping Latin America achieve its infrastructure development objectives will encourage growth, increase regional integration, and create opportunities for the U.S. private sector. The State Department recently created a newsletter that publishes information on multilateral development bank projects, especially in infrastructure. In addition, Brazil and Colombia are both part of a nine country infrastructure initiative we developed in partnership with the Department of Commerce. Through this initiative, we are coordinating U.S. government agencies' efforts around key infrastructure projects in both countries, as well as engagement on broader issues that prevent U.S. companies from entering these markets. This wave of infrastructure development will not only meet the needs of Latin America's new middle class, it will also help create high paying U.S. jobs in areas such as machine tools, engineering, and project management.

Government Finances

Many countries in the region are facing difficulties due to high debt levels. Poor tax administration in Central American and Caribbean countries hampers efforts to finance public investment, improvements in security, and disaster assistance. To address these challenges, President Obama announced the Domestic Finance for Development, or DF4D, initiative during his 2011 trip to El Salvador to engage partner countries on tax administration while also promoting budget transparency and fighting corruption, recognizing that these objectives are mutually reinforcing. Activities under DF4D include working with partner countries to strengthen the political will for reform and providing technical assistance on tax issues to help countries to take ownership of their development agendas. We partnered with Brazil on a DF4D event in Brasilia last year with officials from El Salvador, Honduras, and the Dominican Republic. In Latin America, we have DF4D programs running in El Salvador and Honduras. Building on this initial success, we have plans to expand programming to more countries in the region later this year.

Common International Agenda

One area of great potential in Latin America is the opportunity to partner with countries on common economic agendas. A great example is the Trans-Pacific Partnership. This 21st century trade agreement will bring together developed and developing countries from across the Pacific—from Asia and the Americas—into a single trading community. It will address new cross-cutting issues, such as helping small- and medium-sized enterprises take advantage of international trade. And we are working to ensure that TPP includes protections for worker rights, the environment, and intellectual property. The TPP aims to promote a level playing field so private companies compete in a fair and transparent system. Our hope is that the Trans-Pacific Partnership can serve as the global standard for future trade agreements, and will serve as a platform for broader regional integration.

The OECD also provides an opportunity to advance pro-market policies throughout Latin America. Many countries in the region have used applications to join the OECD or recommendations from various OECD committees as a catalyst for economic reform. Colombia, for example, adopted the OECD

> *Strong regional economic growth led by Mexico and others has produced a strong middle class that forms the basis for continued political and economic reforms. Between 2000 and 2009, 50 million people joined the middle class in Latin America and the Caribbean.*

Investment Codes of Liberalization in November as part of their preparation for their application to join. The OECD is looking to work with countries in the region in a number of areas including fostering innovation, regulatory coherence, and stronger revenue mobilization through tax reform.

Economic Statecraft and Support for U.S. Business

We strongly encourage American companies to take full advantage of opportunities in Latin America. U.S. companies can be some of the best ambassadors for American ideas and values, especially in the areas of transparency and model corporate governance. More importantly, as American companies enter new markets and export more, they create jobs both in the United States and in other countries where they operate.

We are committed to helping our small- and medium-sized businesses take advantage of the great opportunities that exist overseas. In many states, the majority of companies exporting are small- and medium-sized enterprises. We know that it is not always easy for these companies to develop the know-how to break into overseas markets, especially to learn about opportunities abroad and how to take advantage of them. That is why about a year ago, we started a program called Direct Line. This program provides a unique opportunity for American businesses, particularly small- and medium-sized firms, to engage directly via teleconferences and webinars with U.S. ambassadors and foreign government officials overseas. There is always time to ask questions. We recently held one on renewable energy opportunities in Chile with over 100 participants. We held one last week on opportunities in Brazil's port concessions with 80 participants. Our posts throughout the region have hosted calls including Canada, Mexico, Haiti, Honduras, Colombia, and Uruguay. I encourage you to engage with your local embassy and support this effort, especially by sharing information about the program with your contacts here in the United States. Local AmChams are often one of the first sources of information for American companies looking to enter a new market. We view you as our partner in spreading information about trade and investment opportunities. We are also working to help small businesses in the U.S. and overseas get access to expertise and new markets to grow their enterprises.

Conclusion

The United States' relationships with its neighbors in this Hemisphere are as important as ever. We seek new ways to work together to advance our common interests be it trade and investment, development, or harnessing the power of our people. As representatives of American companies working in these countries, you are our partners and advocates in furthering these ties. We need you to identify new markets of opportunity, encourage new American companies to enter your countries, and most of all, to continue to be good corporate citizens.

Thank you.

Immigration Reform and the English Language

By Kevin Drum
Mother Jones, January 29, 2013

Matt Yglesias, after reviewing the evidence about the effect that immigration has on wages—very little, probably—says correctly that "we're stuck in a mostly phony argument about wages that does nothing to ease people's real fears about nationalism and identity." Paul Waldman goes a step further and isolates the real problem: language. "Make them learn English" may be entirely unnecessary, since Mexican immigrants appear to follow exactly the same language path as every other immigrant group, but in political terms "it could be the key to passing immigration reform":

> As a group, Americans have contradictory feelings about immigration....Most Americans acknowledge that we're all descended from immigrants of one kind or another....
> They also appreciate that immigration gives our country vitality, and that immigrants are exactly the kind of hard-working, ambitious strivers that drive our economy and culture forward. But at the same time, many feel threatened when they see the character of their towns and cities change, and nothing embodies that change more than language. When people walk into a store and hear a language being spoken that they don't understand, they suddenly feel like foreigners in their own neighborhood, alienated and insecure. I'm not putting a value judgment on that feeling, but it's undeniable.
>
> So imagine an individual citizen/voter who has those two contradictory feelings. He sincerely wants his country to welcome immigrants, and he thinks that cultural diversity is basically a good thing, but he got a little freaked out last week when he went down to the drug store and felt like he just got transported to Mexico City. He doesn't like feeling alienated, but he also doesn't like that tiny voice inside him that says, "Send them back where they came from!" He knows that voice isn't right, but when he sees signs in other languages or hears other languages spoken, that voice gets a little stronger.
>
> What the "make them learn English" provision says to him is: Don't worry, it's going to be OK. We're going to make sure that this wave of immigrants is woven into the American tapestry just like the prior waves of Irish and Italian and Chinese immigrants. They won't take America over. They'll *become American.*

This is exactly right, and I think we're less than honest if we don't acknowledge that plenty of us lefties feel a bit of this sometimes too. It's human nature. And that gives me an excuse (again!) to link to my second-favorite Chris Hayes piece ever.

It's about John Tanton, the founder of FAIR, the nation's oldest and most influential immigration restriction group. For years, Tanton tried to preach an anti-immigration message based on economic and conservation grounds. But it didn't work. Chris tells us what *did* work:

> Crisscrossing the country, Tanton found little interest in his conservation-based arguments for reduced immigration, but kept hearing the same complaint. "'I tell you what pisses me off,'" Tanton recalls people saying. "'It's going into a ballot box and finding a ballot in a language I can't read.' So it became clear that the language question had a lot more emotional power than the immigration question."
>
> Tanton tried to persuade FAIR to harness this "emotional power," but the board declined. So in 1983, Tanton sent out a fundraising letter on behalf of a new group he created called U.S. English. Typically, Tanton says, direct mail garners a contribution from around 1 percent of recipients. "The very first mailing we ever did for U.S. English got almost a 10 percent return," he says. "That's unheard of." John Tanton had discovered the power of the culture war.
>
> The success of U.S. English taught Tanton a crucial lesson. If the immigration restriction movement was to succeed, it would have to be rooted in an emotional appeal to those who felt that their country, their language, their very identity was under assault. "Feelings," Tanton says in a tone reminiscent of Spock sharing some hard-won insight on human behavior, "trump facts."

Cultural insecurity and language angst are the key issues here. It doesn't matter if they're rational or not. Anything we can do to relieve those anxieties helps the cause of comprehensive immigration reform.

Ambassador Wayne's Remarks
at U.S. Chamber Breakfast

By Ambassador to Mexico, E. Anthony Wayne
Embassy of the United States: Mexico, February 11, 2013

Good morning. First I'd like to welcome the U.S. company representatives visiting Mexico, and I'd like to thank Myron Brilliant and all the Chamber members who are working on the U.S.-Mexico Leadership Initiative to deepen our bilateral economic relationship. I'd also like to thank Guillermo Wolf and AmCham Mexico for their valuable, consistent work to deepen and enrich U.S.-Mexico relations. And let me offer my thanks to my government colleagues for their dedication to and interest in our vital U.S.-Mexico cooperation: Assistant Secretary Camuñez, Assistant Secretary Bersin, and Assistant Secretary Kurland. It is a pleasure to be here with all of you this morning

My colleagues and I will give some brief remarks and then we can have an open discussion about the U.S.-Mexico trade and economic relationship.

President Obama has said that our two countries "are not simply neighbors bound by geography and history. We are, by choice, friends and partners." At the heart of this special relationship are very deep and strong economic ties. Since 1993, prior to NAFTA's implementation, both Mexico's and the United States' GDP have grown 56 percent. Bilateral trade has increased from $99.2 billion in 1993 to $500.1 billion in 2011, that's a fivefold increase.

Mexico is the United States' second-largest export market and third-largest trading partner, while the U.S. is Mexico's number one trading partner. American companies and workers across the country depend on the Mexican market to boost sales and to support American jobs, evidenced by the fact that Mexico is the number one or number two export market for 22 U.S. states. Mexico is also the destination for more U.S. exports than the BRIC countries combined.

The competitiveness of our two countries is closely linked, and improvements in productivity in one nation make a co-manufactured product cheaper and more competitive on the global market. That is to say, growth in Mexico or the United States will boost exports from both countries: when it comes to manufacturing, we are in it together. Mexico also has a growing educated workforce. Two of the top ten universities in Latin America are in Mexico, and Mexico now produces more engineers than Germany or Canada (over 100,000 a year). This talent pool has attracted investment from a number of advanced global manufacturing firms. Mexico's GDP

> *The United States and Mexico have an opportunity to turn a new page. We have a chance to shape perceptions about our two countries—to turn them away from security problems and violence and on to the positive economic story. The Peña Nieto government is putting a high priority on economic growth as a driving factor for Mexico.*

has grown steadily over the last three years while inflation has remained under control, with growth expected to be nearly 4 percent for 2012, higher than in Brazil and the United States.

Mexico has free trade agreements with 44 countries, more than any other country in the world, and their entry into the Trans-Pacific Partnership negotiations provides an invaluable opportunity to build on the foundation of NAFTA. TPP will provide for further deepening economic integration both within North America and between North America and the broader Asia-Pacific region. The agreement represents an entry into a market of 198 million new consumers who purchase approximately $1 trillion of goods annually. It will help link our integrated supply networks to the growing production chains in dynamic Asian markets while helping to protect the preferential access currently enjoyed under NAFTA. The TPP is designed to address the kind of barriers that impede trade and investment in the 21st century—for example, barriers to digital trade, or services investment, or supply chain development. Addressing these will generate real benefits and create real opportunity for all our economies and businesses, regardless of the level of development, sector, or size of enterprise.

The United States and Mexico have an opportunity to turn a new page. We have a chance to shape perceptions about our two countries to turn them away from security problems and violence and on to the positive economic story. The Peña Nieto government is putting a high priority on economic growth as a driving factor for Mexico. The new cabinet, including Foreign Secretary José Antonio Meade, has many with strong economic backgrounds.

Our challenges, such as organized crime, are shared. We acknowledge our co-responsibility with Mexico to fight the scourge of narco-trafficking and its accompanying violence. It is our joint responsibility to control our shared border, and help prevent the flow of illicit goods and people.

Another priority for President Peña Nieto is to make Mexico a more active partner in the region and in the world. In a late January summit among Latin American, Caribbean, and European Union nations in Santiago, Chile, for example, he pledged that Mexico would make regional cooperation a priority of his foreign policy, with free trade and interregional investment as important mechanisms for this collaboration. Many believe that Mexico has great potential to provide regional leadership in Latin America through a pragmatic, practical approach to regional problems. Much of this will come through the economic lens.

Mexico and the United States now face important choices that will impact our future economic prosperity. In Mexico, there is consensus on the need for structural economic reforms. The first significant labor reform in thirty years was passed late last year. In addition, the three major political parties signed an agreement to work together, el Pacto por Mexico, and included a list of 95 initiatives and their timelines. Included on this list are reforms in the fiscal, telecommunications, and education sectors. Energy is a promised area of reform as well. I know that the AmCham Mexico committees have been working diligently with the new administration to influence these reforms.

In addition, we look forward to continuing our work with the Peña Nieto administration on the very practical steps to improve border trade flows: for example, modernizing customs facilities and the infrastructure on both sides of the border to make it truly a 21st century border. Through a series of specific projects we are working to facilitate the secure, efficient, and rapid flow of goods and people while reducing the costs of doing business between our two countries.

We also look forward to further promoting our service exports, such as tourism. 13.5 million Mexicans visited the United States in 2011 and spent over $9 billion. The U.S. government has implemented some new initiatives to make the United States an even more popular tourist destination. The process to get a visa to the United States has been simplified. In Fiscal Year 2012, for the first time this century, Mission Mexico processed more than 2 million visa applications. In addition, Mexican citizens are also eligible to participate in the Global Entry program, enabling them to bypass migration lines when entering the United States. We are also expanding our business visa facilitation program, including AmCham Mexico as one of our partners, to help small businesses get visa appointments more easily and quickly. So there are many successes to celebrate but also much work to be done in furthering our relationship.

Thank you for visiting Mexico on this important mission. I look forward to hearing more about your objectives here and how we may be of assistance in the long and short term. And I will now turn it over to my Washington colleagues for a few short comments from each, before our discussion period. Thank you.

For Returning Migrants, Good News About Mexico's Economy Doesn't Apply

By Monica Ortiz Uribe
KPBS.org, December 31, 2012

Immigration to the United States has slowed in last three years as a result of the economic recession. Some migrants are even choosing to go back home.

In Mexico, the economy is growing, but that growth isn't happening in a sector that offers hope for returning migrants.

Those who go back typically begin their journey at the border. One of the busiest ports of entry is across from south Texas in Nuevo Laredo, Tamaulipas.

During the holiday season Nuevo Laredo's international bridge looks like a never-ending gypsy parade. A motley crew of travelers bunch together at the inspection area on the Mexican side. They carry truckloads of stuff, from bicycles, to lawn mowers, to waist-high bins brimming with clothes and shoes.

Most are going back to Mexico for a long vacation but others, like Ariel Espinoza, are headed back for good. Espinoza owned his own construction business in Florida.

"The construction business started to go down, down, down," he said.

In good times, Espinoza was making $40 an hour but lately his income has dropped to $12 an hour. It wasn't enough to pay his bills or support his family, so he's moving back to his hometown in central Mexico. He's been gone for the last 18 years.

"It's the goal when you move to the United States (to have) a better life, but right now it's hard," he said.

Mexico's economy is growing at a rate of about 4 percent per year, according to the International Monetary Fund. That's faster than Brazil, one of Latin America's strongest economies. But much of Mexico's growth is concentrated in trade and manufacturing, and these aren't industries where low-skilled returning migrants are easily absorbed. That means returnees like Espinoza may face a struggle ahead.

The central state of Zacatecas has one of the highest departing migration rates in Mexico. But in recent years, the tide has turned as people come back.

At a school in the small town of Pastoría, a teacher gives her students a lesson in science. The school recently enrolled 43 new children whose parents have recently moved back from the United States.

Magaly Lopez Ruiz is the mother of three of those children. All were born in the US. The family moved back from Virginia a year ago after her husband got deported. Readjusting to life in Mexico has been difficult.

"My son rebelled when we first move back," she said. "He stopped eating."

In Virginia, Lopez made at least $600 a week cleaning apartments. Now she's unemployed and her husband works in the fields making about $10 a day. Other families at the school are in similar situations, barely making ends meet.

Rodolfo Zamora Garcia, an economist who specializes in immigration, says the good news about the Mexican economy doesn't apply to returning migrants.

"In the absence of economic opportunity in Mexico, the only form of social promotion they know is immigration," he said.

In fact, the Mexico these migrants return to looks very much like the Mexico they left. Half the population is living in poverty. Loans are hard to come by for those who want to start a business and numerous monopolies in everything from milk to telecommunications discourage budding entrepreneurs.

Until those things change, some economists say immigration north will continue.

Back at school in Pastoría, children blow up balloons to play a game of darts at recess. The recently arrived American students sometimes sneak in a few words to each other in English. One of those students, Christopher Acosta, said he doesn't plan to stay here long.

"We're gonna go back," he said. "When we're a little bit more older, like in high school, we're going to leave."

A More Ambitious Agenda: A Report of the Inter-American Dialogue's Commission on Mexico-US Relations

By Carla Hills and Ernesto Zedillo
Inter-American Dialogue, February 13, 2012

Introduction: Mexico-US Relations Today

Mexico and the United States have forged one of the strongest and most productive relationships in the world. No two countries anywhere engage so intensely on a daily basis, cooperate across such a wide and varied spectrum of issues, and affect the economy and society of the other so profoundly. No two sovereign nations are more demographically and economically integrated.

With annual cross-border commerce of some $500 billion, Mexico is now the United States' second largest trading partner. Some analysts project that it will overtake Canada for the No. 1 position within the decade. Sales to Mexico make up two-thirds of all US exports to Latin America. Mexico, in turn, sends 80 percent of its exports to the United States and purchases nearly 60 percent of its imports from its northern neighbor.

Substantial investment, too, flows in both directions. US investments in Mexico have averaged $12 billion annually for the past dozen years, amounting to more than half of all foreign investment in the country, according to the US State Department. In addition, families in the United States send more than $20 billion in remittances to Mexico each year. The North American Free Trade Agreement (NAFTA), which joined the economies of Mexico, the United States, and Canada in 1994, is today the world's largest economic bloc, exceeding, albeit by a small margin, the total output of the 27-member European Union.

Demography also matters. Some 33 million US residents are of Mexican origin. They make up more than 10 percent of the US population, nearly two-thirds of all Latinos, and around 7 percent of American voters. While US political debates tend to spotlight unauthorized immigration, 80 percent of Mexicans in the United States are legal residents. Still, illegal immigration may be the single most troubling issue in US-Mexico relations, although changing migration patterns and the growing influence of Latino voters may offer solutions going forward.

Security has become an area of intense cooperation as Mexico grapples with an ongoing wave of brutal crime and violence. The United States and Mexico may not always agree on policy or strategy, but the extensive collaboration among their police and security agencies is unprecedented.

Indeed, the bilateral agenda has seen cooperation flourish on almost every issue, with more opportunities emerging as mutual interests deepen. Mexico and the United States are consistently finding new ways to complement and reinforce one another in the global marketplace and on matters of regional and international importance. Both governments have made clear a commitment to consolidate and enhance this cooperation to fully leverage their inevitable and accelerating economic and demographic integration.

The US-Mexican Electoral Cycle

Once every 12 years, presidential elections in the United States and Mexico coincide, and the elected leaders of the two countries assume office within two months of one another. Enrique Peña Nieto was inaugurated president of Mexico on December 1, 2012, while Barack Obama started his second term on January 21, 2013. The concurrence provides an opportune moment for the Mexican and US governments to review their relationship and explore what needs to be done to make it more cooperative and productive.

This report intends to (1) encourage the Obama and Peña Nieto administrations to assess opportunities for enhanced cooperation and (2) present ideas for consideration in light of the nations' shared agenda. Although we are aware that the United States and Mexico will confront myriad issues in the coming period, we focus on three high-priority goals:

The first is to reinforce and deepen economic cooperation. That includes increasing the productivity and international competitiveness of both nations, opening opportunities for long-term growth and job creation, and setting the stage for further economic integration. In a world of persistent, widespread economic insecurity, the more the United States and Mexico coordinate and integrate their economies, the more ably they can compete for global markets. Their economic cooperation is more vital than ever as drivers of the global economy falter—as the European financial crisis persists, as China enters a period of slower growth, as Japan remains stalled, and as many emerging markets appear increasingly vulnerable. Among the concrete objectives the two countries should consider are development of a framework to make their shared labor markets more efficient and equitable; formation of a coherent North American energy market (which could help meet the needs of energy-poor Central America); and coordination among the United States, Mexico, and Canada in negotiations toward the Trans-Pacific Partnership (TPP).

Second, practical approaches are needed to manage the complex issues related to immigration. Both governments have acknowledged the economic value of appropriately regulated immigration. US and Mexican policy should be directed toward increasing the role of immigration in economic expansion and job growth in the two countries, ensuring that individual rights of all immigrants are respected, and curtailing violations of immigration laws. Since the US presidential election in

November, these have become attainable goals, endorsed by the White House with good prospects for majority support in the US Congress.

Third, it is critical to identify more effective responses in both countries, to problems of public security, organized crime, and drug trafficking and abuse. President Peña Nieto has made clear that bringing Mexico's violent crime under control is a particularly urgent, high-priority task. For his part, President Obama has acknowledged that the United States shares responsibility for Mexico's drug and crime problems and that complementary efforts are needed to resolve them. Along with US security assistance to Mexico, the two countries should jointly review Washington's policies toward illicit drugs and firearms, both of which have gained considerable attention in recent months.

There is a broad cross-border consensus that these three issues are the most important challenges for Mexico-US relations, both today and for the longer term.

Economic Integration

NAFTA has fundamentally reshaped economic relations between the United States and Mexico. The trilateral free trade arrangement has served as the guiding framework for integration of the two economies over the past 18 years.

US trade with Mexico has flourished, expanding by some 500 percent, or almost twice as fast as US commercial growth with the rest of the world, since the unveiling of NAFTA. Within the next ten years, Mexico could vault ahead of Canada to become the United States' largest trading partner. And the content of Mexican exports to the United States has changed dramatically. Once heavily concentrated in foodstuffs and petroleum products, Mexico's sales to the United States are now mostly manufactured goods. Mexican producers, moreover, are firmly incorporated into US supply chains—to the extent that US-made products make up nearly 40 percent of the inputs for Mexico's exports. Meanwhile, US investment in Mexico has risen even more rapidly than bilateral trade, climbing six times in the past two decades, about the same pace as the growth of Mexican investment in the United States.

NAFTA, however, is not merely a vehicle to expand trade and investment. It is the essential foundation for making the broader US-Mexico relationship more stable and more productive on many fronts. As the world's largest economic bloc, NAFTA can provide its three partners with a reliable economic anchor during volatile periods in the global economy. Many attributed Mexico's sharp economic contraction in 2009, following the global financial crisis, to its close ties to the US economy. They may be right, but those ties also had a great deal to do with Mexico's rapid rebound and steady recovery.

The three NAFTA partners share a common approach to international economic policy. They are all members of the world's key multilateral institutions and forums such as the Group of 20 and the Organization of Economic Cooperation and Development (OECD). Together they have the potential to exert considerable influence in shaping global economic debates.

Despite the NAFTA-sparked expansion of trade and investment between Mexico and the United States, Mexico's economic growth has been sluggish for much of the past two decades. It picked up steam in the past three years, but economic expansion averaged only 2.7 percent annually from 1994 through 2012—about the same as the United States. The income and wage gaps between the two nations remain largely unchanged, even as Mexico's population has become increasingly middle class and poverty rates have fallen. Like Brazil and other Latin American nations, Mexico may be caught in the "middle-income trap." The country is approaching $15,000 in per-capita income annually, as measured in terms of "purchasing power parity" (PPP), but it is not yet growing fast enough to join the world's most developed nations.

There is an array of proposals to strengthen US-Mexico bilateral trade and investment relations which could produce substantial economic gains for both nations. Harmonized regulations and a more integrated North American transportation system would do the most to spur economic progress. Both governments acknowledge the significant benefits promised by these initiatives and some forward movement may be possible, although they are likely to face political resistance in both countries.

It is encouraging that the two countries have begun to negotiate new arrangements, like the TPP, that incorporate issues and sectors missing from NAFTA and other pacts. Among these issues are energy and water management, infrastructure, all forms of transportation, and labor migration. Progress in any of these areas will take time and likely raise political objections. Still, they should form part of any longer-term agenda.

The United States, Mexico, and Canada all participate in the TPP negotiations, providing the best opportunity in some time to reinforce their existing trade arrangement. If agreement is reached, the three will join a new free trade partnership with eight (and potentially more) of the most dynamic economies in Asia and South America. The TPP talks also aim to establish common rules of origin for all participants, which NAFTA lacks. These would lower costs for and facilitate the economic integration of the three NAFTA partners; they would also strengthen the links between Mexican and US production chains for exporting to markets in Asia and South and Central America.

It is not surprising that Mexico, the United States, and Canada are committed to vigorously pursuing TPP negotiations. If they are successful, they would renovate NAFTA, transforming the tripartite agreement into a more agile and streamlined trade and investment regime—with far greater reach than it has today. Should the United States and the European Union initiate negotiations toward a free trade arrangement, as has been proposed, the three NAFTA partners will together need to identify how Mexico and Canada would be involved.

Even more than refurbishing their bilateral trade and investment ties, Mexico and the United States each need to refashion their economies to make them more robust, globally competitive, and mutually supportive. In the past two decades the tightly linked economies have risen and fallen almost in unison. A reformed and thriving US economy will contribute to accelerated growth in Mexico, while a renovated and fast-growing Mexican economy will bolster US economic fortunes.

Mexico's Economy

Among the world's large economies, Mexico is one of the most open. Its financial system stands among the best managed in Latin America, inflation has been kept in check, and exports are booming. Its sales abroad, mostly manufactured goods, are nearly 50 percent higher than those of Brazil, which has an economy nearly twice the size. Mexico has earned wide praise for its imaginative and effective anti-poverty programs. The country's bonds earn investment grade ratings.

Moreover, the Mexican economy has shown particular spark in the past three years. Recovering quickly from a steep 6 percent GDP drop in 2009, Mexico grew 5.5 percent in 2010 and about 4 percent in 2011 and 2012—a substantially stronger performance than that of the United States. Most forecasts project continued solid growth. Some analysts predict that Mexico will outpace Brazil and most other Latin American nations in the coming period.

Still, the Mexican economy has fundamental shortcomings that, unless remedied, will constrain its productivity, job creation, and capacity to compete. Economic analysts tend to concur on what the main problems are and how to fix them. Their diagnoses appear to be shared by President Peña Nieto and his cabinet.

They endorsed the labor law reforms approved by Congress late in 2012, which are intended to make the Mexican labor market more flexible. The reforms are expected to expand employment overall and increase the share of formal sector jobs in the economy. Legislation to open the finances of state and local governments to scrutiny was approved just prior to Peña Nieto taking office as well.

The success of these legislative initiatives sends a strong signal that Mexico's largest political parties, the PRI and the PAN, are prepared to work together to advance a serious agenda of economic reform in the coming year. It is also encouraging that, despite their ideological differences, Mexico's major political parties have signed the Pacto por Mexico pledging support for a broad program of change.

Since his inauguration, Peña Nieto has strongly reaffirmed his commitment to two closely linked policy reforms: improved management of Mexico's fiscal accounts (both taxation and spending) and a restructured energy industry. The changes should boost Mexico's productivity and growth while elevating the quality of government services. However, both must be achieved for either to work effectively.

Expanding the number of taxpayers and collecting more taxes will be a central focus of fiscal reform. Mexico's annual revenues (including federal, state, and local taxes) are among the lowest of the world's middle and upper income nations. To be sure, tax collection is supplemented by claims on the profits of state oil company PEMEX, but those obligations leave the industry short of the capital it requires for investment. An overhaul of tax policy is urgently needed if public expenditures are to be increased and their composition improved. The country badly lags in critical areas, including infrastructure, education, public security, and social services.

The Peña Nieto government has correctly emphasized the importance of restructuring the oil industry and, more broadly, the country's energy sector. Petroleum has been a mainstay of Mexico's economy for decades. Today it contributes nearly 8 percent of the country's GDP, 15 percent of export income, and one-third of government revenues. Oil production and exports have been stable since 2009, although at a level some 25 percent below their 2004 peak. During the Calderón administration, new fields were discovered and reserves increased steadily. However, these untapped deposits are both expensive and technologically difficult to exploit.

Mexico is also estimated to have the world's fourth largest deposits of shale gas and oil. This offers enormous potential for export and the prospect of sharply reduced fuel and electricity costs for Mexico's fast-growing manufacturing sector. However, no serious efforts have surfaced so far to develop the shale deposits. PEMEX has assigned them low priority and the Mexican Constitution forbids private investment in energy exploration and production.

The Peña Nieto government wants to promote the reform needed to remove the most burdensome restrictions on PEMEX's operations and to allow private participation in hydrocarbon exploration and production. If it succeeds, Mexico would gain access to the capital and know-how needed to assure the country's place as a major oil producer.

A far-reaching overhaul of the energy sector would produce the largest payoff. But it will likely be politically difficult to accomplish in the short run. Still, much would be gained from modest reforms aimed at opening the way for shale gas exploitation and the transformation of PEMEX into a modern, internationally competitive state enterprise.

The new government has highlighted the need to promote greater competition throughout the economy. More competitive markets will reduce prices, stimulate innovation in technology and marketing, and encourage the emergence of new firms and entrepreneurs. The question is clear: What should be done to curtail the monopoly practices that pervade key areas of the economy sizable new investments in education at all levels and to dilute corporate and labor influence over public decisions, which contribute to inefficiencies, higher costs, and poor service? In addition, pervasive informality in the economy keeps tax revenues lower than they should be, suppresses wages, and rewards illegal behavior. Regulatory reform, better enforcement of the law, and a redirection of social programs that have inadvertently created incentives to informal firms and workers are needed.

Finally, the new government has already turned its attention to education reform, making clear its concern that Mexico's economic progress will be retarded unless the country substantially upgrades its schools and universities and develops a robust capacity for technology and innovation.

According to the World Economic Forum assessment of educational standards, Mexico ranks the lowest in the world—122 out of the 139 countries measured. Mexico has succeeded in expanding enrollment so that some 90 percent of young people complete ninth grade, but less than 40 percent of Mexicans finish high school and fewer still pursue post-secondary education.

Unless there is a sustained commitment to improved quality at schools and universities and greater investment in scientific and technical research, Mexico will pay a high price in terms of economic growth and stability. Without a more highly trained workforce and an expanded capacity to innovate and adapt, there is little prospect for the country to raise productivity in its manufacturing and service sectors, to bring down its elevated rates of informality, and to reduce its pervasive poverty and inequality.

The Peña Nieto government will have to make sizable new investments in education at all levels and sustain a focus on teacher and school quality. The US and Mexican governments should substantially expand cross-border exchange programs for students, professors, and researchers. Both countries would benefit.

The US Economy

Like Mexico, the United States faces critical economic problems that require sustained national attention. The main challenge in the coming period will be to bring about more robust growth in order to create jobs, reduce the unacceptably high unemployment rate, and generate greater confidence among investors, business owners, and consumers. The United States also must tackle vital, longer-term issues, such as curbing its annual fiscal deficit (which, in 2012, was roughly 10 percent of GDP) and reversing the growth of US debt.

Other key tasks before the United States include renovation or replacement of deteriorated infrastructure—in transportation, energy, water, and telecommunications—and improvements in the educational system. Bitter partisan differences that make it difficult to reach common ground stand as a roadblock to sensibly addressing these challenges. Yet some progress is occurring. Contentious budget and debt battles remain, but the so-called fiscal cliff has been avoided for the time being. And the US economy continues to advance, albeit haltingly, while unemployment figures improve, the housing sector recovers, and energy production booms.

Economic reforms are vital for greater productivity and prosperity in both Mexico and the United States. They are also essential to a stronger economic partnership between the two countries. That partnership—based on geographic proximity, demographic bonds, supply chain integration, and NAFTA's clear and certain rules—bolsters exports, economic growth, and new job opportunities on both sides of the border, and it raises the global competitiveness of the two nations.

Immigration

No country has sent more of its people to the United States than Mexico. One of every 10 Mexican citizens now lives in the United States, and more than 10 percent of the US population is of Mexican origin. Among foreign-born residents in the United States, one-quarter are from Mexico, as are 40 percent of non-US citizens and 60 percent of unauthorized residents.

In light of these numbers, it is hardly surprising that immigration is a central issue in both the United States and Mexico—although viewed through very different lenses. US citizens tend to see the main problem as the large number of undocumented immigrants, Mexican or otherwise, and continuing flows of unauthorized migrants. Americans, rightly or wrongly, fear that undocumented immigrants compete with them for jobs, bring down wages, increase financial burdens on schools and social welfare programs, and contribute to crime rates. Mexicans have different concerns, led by how their compatriots are treated in the United States, what their rights are and should be, and how the US government deals with the 6 to 7 million undocumented Mexicans within its border. It is no wonder that, for decades, immigration to the United States has been an unsettling factor in US-Mexico relations.

Missing from the debate has been an appreciation of the enormous economic contribution of Mexican immigrants, including many who arrived illegally, to both the US and Mexican economies. More than half of US population growth in recent years has been due to immigration. Migrants fill crucial jobs. They represent a significant percentage of younger workers and new entrants to the US labor force, and their presence improves the age profile of the workforce, boosting US capacity for growth and helping to sustain the US Social Security system. It is estimated that Mexican immigrants, who have accounted for 30 percent of all immigrants annually for the past decade or so, contribute roughly 4 percent a year to US GDP. Last year those immigrants remitted to their home country more than $20 billion, equivalent to nearly half the value of Mexico's oil exports.

Reform could multiply the benefits of immigration. A new policy driven largely by economic demand would open opportunities for millions of now unauthorized residents and be a boon for both economies.

Migration from Mexico to the United States has sharply declined in the past few years. The numbers of people entering the United States are now about the same as those leaving. The weak US job market and Mexico's rapidly expanding economy are partly responsible for this shift. Even more important, however, are the changing demographics in Mexico, where birth rates have stabilized at low levels, population growth is shrinking, and education levels are improving—all of which have eased pressures for migration. Reduced Mexican immigration coupled with an economic rebound in the United States, particularly if it does not stimulate new out-migration from Mexico, have improved prospects for progress on US immigration legislation and policies. There is also post-US election recognition of the growing influence of Latino voters.

While there are legal and political reasons for the United States to continue to pursue effective border and employer enforcement, a sensible US immigration reform package requires two other crucial elements.

- The first is an expanded and predictable temporary labor program that meets US market needs for both professional and low-income workers. Allowing a larger flow of legal, registered migrants would reduce unauthorized immigration and encourage circular, rather than one-way, migration patterns.

- The second and most contentious provision would grant legal status to unauthorized migrants currently living in the United States, perhaps including the opportunity to earn permanent residency status and citizenship. This so-called amnesty provision was the subject of rancorous exchanges during the Republican primary debates in the 2012 US presidential campaign, and it will require sensitive management. But with nearly 12 million undocumented immigrants in the United States (of which over half are Mexican), it surely must be part of any reform. Like a temporary worker program, a well-designed and implemented amnesty initiative could hugely benefit both the US and Mexican economies. Providing law-abiding Mexican migrants to the United States with the opportunity to lawfully hold jobs, apply for training and education grants, and secure loans and aid to educate their children would lead to higher wages and household incomes. These, in turn, would lift tax payments to local, state, and federal governments, increase remittances sent to Mexico, and secure a more highly skilled US workforce.

Prior to last year's presidential election, there was little prospect that such far-reaching legislation could gain approval in the politically divided US Congress. In 2007, the Senate roundly rejected a similar package of immigration reforms proposed by President George W. Bush and supported by then-Senators Obama, John McCain, and Edward Kennedy. More recently, Washington's immigration reform efforts had shifted toward a piecemeal approach.

The decisive impact of the Latino vote on the US presidential election, however, has dramatically increased the chances for a comprehensive reshaping of immigration policy. President Obama has put immigration reform at the top of his second-term legislative agenda. The unprecedented turnout of Latino voters and the fact that their numbers will be substantially larger in subsequent elections has not escaped the notice of either political party. For the first time in decades, Republicans and Democrats alike have strong incentives to tackle immigration.

While a general reform of US immigration legislation is needed and long overdue, there are also compelling arguments for the United States and Mexico to consider establishing a special bilateral arrangement governing their cross-border migration flows. Mexico, after all, is the only developing country with a US border, and Mexican migrants have long made up nearly half of all immigrants to the United States. Moreover, the two countries have important stakes, both political and economic, in a predictable, regulated migration stream. A special bilateral migration agreement merits consideration by both countries.

Security and Drugs

Mexico's continuing wave of crime and violence, fueled by drug trafficking and largely carried out by organized criminal enterprises, may be the most harrowing test of all for the two new governments.

Not long after taking office in December 2006, President Calderón launched a full-scale battle, involving the country's armed forces, against organized crime. During his six-year term, violence claimed upward of 60,000 Mexican lives. Although violence has subsided in some areas, it is uncertain whether the improvements can be sustained.

Criminal violence is a daunting problem for Mexico. The elevated levels of brutality and bloodletting leave Mexicans insecure. By discouraging tourism and investment, both domestic and foreign, and raising the costs of doing business, the violence has taken a serious (though difficult to measure) toll on the Mexican economy.

It has also weakened citizens' confidence in their government and poses a continuing danger to the rule of law and institutional stability. Bringing Mexico's many criminal syndicates under control and curbing the violence associated with them is an urgent priority for the Peña Nieto presidency and vital for the administration's success.

> *The [Peña Nieto] government has already turned its attention to education reform, making clear that Mexico's economic progress requires it.*

So far, the United States has been little affected by Mexico's wave of violence and crime. It has not produced a spillover of criminal activity at the border or increased violence or drug use in the United States. But US officials are appropriately concerned about the expanding power and cruelty of the crime syndicates, and the damage and disruption they are causing in a neighboring country so closely tied to the United States. The principal danger for the United States comes from the impact that crime and violence may have on Mexico's economy, its governing institutions, and its citizens' respect for the law. A debilitated Mexican state and economy would carry an enormous cost for the United States. The spread of Mexican criminal enterprises into the weaker and more vulnerable countries of Central America and the Caribbean is also a concern for both the United States and Mexico.

Many Mexicans blame their crime problems on the United States. They see the US appetite for drugs as the principal source of revenue for criminal organizations and as the driver for much of the violence in Mexico. Even though the United States has been aiding Mexico in the battle against the syndicates, many in both nations consider the US commitment half-hearted at best. In particular, there is concern that the US government is not doing nearly enough to reduce the huge demand for illicit drugs at home or to curb the flow of money and guns to Mexico.

The Obama administration has not shied away from recognizing that the United States bears significant responsibility for Mexico's crime and drug problems and should help to address them. For the past five years, the United States has provided financial aid, equipment, intelligence, and technical support to Mexico through the Merida Initiative. However, the assistance has remained modest (particularly relative to earlier such aid to Colombia) and serious questions have emerged about the initiative's objectives, design, and implementation. US security assistance to Mexico needs to be systematically reviewed by the two countries to determine its effectiveness and what changes are needed.

Despite President Obama's pledges to step up efforts to reduce US drug consumption and better control weapons smuggling into Mexico, not much has been accomplished on those fronts. Only very modest increases in budget resources have been directed to drug prevention and treatment programs. Several programs, particularly those to rehabilitate already incarcerated drug users who are the biggest consumers, have particularly promising track records and merit greater financing for scaled up programs.

To be sure, the US Constitution, as recently interpreted by the US Supreme Court, severely limits restrictions on gun sales and ownership. Congress, too, has been a virtually impassable barrier to new controls on firearms. The December 2012 massacre of 20 school children and six educators in Connecticut sparked a national debate on gun regulation, but it is too early to predict whether major changes in US laws will result. Still, it should be noted that, with few exceptions, the weapons destined for Mexico are transported illegally. Many experts believe that flow could be diminished through vigorous enforcement of existing laws against cross-border arms smuggling.

This is the right time to reassess the Merida Initiative, reinforce efforts to shrink US drug use, and stop the flood of weapons into Mexico. In the end, however, the task of controlling the violence and subduing criminal organizations will mostly fall to Mexico itself. The country will have to commit to a costly, long-term effort and continue to produce the lion's share of the resources to finance it. There are no quick or certain solutions to Mexico's crime and violence problems. They have to be addressed on many fronts. The central task will be to build respect for the rule of law and curb corruption across all Mexican institutions, public and private.

President Peña Nieto has made clear that he plans to continue Mexico's struggle against criminal organizations but with some shifts in the strategy. His plans emphasize reducing violence and the protection of citizen safety, while giving less attention to the interdiction of illegal drug shipments or directly attacking the criminal organizations and their kingpins. On its face, this is an appealing approach, which would respond to the public's overriding concern. However, there are questions as to whether it is possible to design, successfully implement, and sustain a strategy targeted on curtailing violence, and how it will affect the strength of Mexico's criminal syndicates. Still, given the rising dissatisfaction in Mexico with current anti-crime efforts, it is encouraging that the new government is reassessing its approach to public security, examining alternative policies, looking at relevant experiences elsewhere, and seeking more effective strategies.

Peña Nieto has also called for the creation of an elite federal police force of some 30,000 to 40,000 men and women, which would sharply reduce the role of Mexico's military in the anti-crime campaign. This is an important and reassuring step. Troop deployment for public security is not a sustainable approach.

In a country the size of Mexico, a national police force will have to be complemented by appropriately vetted and trained local and state forces, which have to date performed poorly in most areas of the country. Yet a strengthened police force is only one essential element in the anti-crime effort. Mexico has improved its judicial proceedings, but there remain multiple problems that must be addressed to assure fair and timely trials. The prison system needs an overhaul to meet minimal standards of decent treatment and to avoid the specter of prisons that are run by their inmates and serve as command posts for criminal activity.

Drug Policy

Drug policy has come under intense scrutiny across Latin America since the 2009 publication of the report of the Latin America Commission on Drugs and Democracy, a panel that was chaired by three former presidents: Fernando Henrique Cardoso of Brazil, César Gaviria of Colombia, and Ernesto Zedillo of Mexico. (Zedillo is also co-chair of the group responsible for this report.) That document concluded that prevailing drug policies had largely failed and new approaches were essential.

More recently, a number of governments in the region, including that of Calderón, publicly called for changes in regional anti-drug strategies. Most Latin American countries are prepared to consider alternatives that would move beyond the "war-on-drugs" mindset and deal with drugs mainly as a public health issue rather than a crime problem. A few leaders are considering policies that would legalize and regulate the production, sale, and use of marijuana, the least addictive and least harmful drug, and create a less restrictive and less punitive approach to other, more dangerous and destructive drugs, like heroin or cocaine. An Organization of American States (OAS) study on alternative drug strategies, mandated by last year's Summit of the Americas in Cartagena, should establish a basis for further exploration of the issues involved.

The Obama administration has expressed a willingness to discuss alternative policies, declaring that the United States is no longer fighting a "war on drugs." Although the administration has not yet seriously pursued other options, election-day referendums legalizing marijuana use in two states signaled a clear shift in US public attitudes and could set the stage for national reconsideration of drug policy. Under the circumstances, it would make sense for both Obama and Peña Nieto to begin careful joint exploration of the options, including a study on the likely consumption, health, and crime consequences in both countries that might come from legalizing marijuana.

Regardless of the choices Mexico and the United States make, it is important to recognize that it will take considerable time to improve Mexico's security situation. Colombia has been the most successful country in battling drug criminals and reducing threats to the safety and security of its citizens, but it took many years and a huge expenditure of resources to post those gains. And Colombia remains one of the most violent countries in Latin America.

Solid sustained growth, reduced rates of poverty and inequality, and expanded education and employment opportunities are vital to progress on the security front. And progress on security is crucial to advancing those other critical objectives.

Natural Partners

Mexico and the United States are more closely tied to one another than any other sovereign nations in the world, and the pace of their economic and demographic integration is accelerating. For both, sustained cooperation on an array of bilateral, regional, and global issues is essential. They have no choice: No other country affects the lives of US citizens more than Mexico, and none affects the lives of Mexicans more than the United States. No two countries have more to gain from pursuing closer and more robust ties.

A continued reinforcement and expansion of bilateral economic relations is fundamental for both countries. Much still must be done to improve cross-border access to markets, investment capital, technology, human resources, and energy supplies. Even with its current economic problems, the United States' $16 trillion economy is a vital destination for Mexican products and a critical source of capital and technology. And there is room for it to contribute even more to Mexico's economic performance. For its part, the rising Mexican economy, which some experts predict will emerge as the world's fifth largest by mid-century, will inevitably become more and more central to the United States' economic future.

The United States and Mexico would also benefit from working harder and smarter to resolve their differences and to address some crucial shared problems. Immigration and public security are the central priorities for the coming period.

And the two nations should cooperate more on global and regional matters. Challenges to democracy and human rights in Latin America and beyond, growing security problems in Central America, reintegration of Cuba into hemispheric affairs, reform of multilateral organizations, development of new trade partnerships world-wide, and problems of nuclear non-proliferation and climate change are among the many issues that deeply concern both countries. Although, on many of these matters, the United States and Mexico will disagree, they are, nonetheless, natural partners on all of them.

Highlighting the US-Mexico Economic Relationship

By Jose W. Fernandez
US Department of State, January 18, 2013

MODERATOR: Welcome to the Washington Foreign Press Center. Today we are pleased to welcome Jose Fernandez, who is the Assistant Secretary of State for Economic and Business Affairs, who will discuss the U.S.-Mexico economic relationship in advance of participating in a delegation from the U.S. Government that will visit Mexico City to discuss strengthening the U.S.-Mexico bilateral economic relationship.

With that, I will turn it over to Assistant Secretary Fernandez.

ASSISTANT SECRETARY FERNANDEZ: Well, thank you. It's good to see all of you. All of you are from publications that I have read many times in my professional career, so thank you.

As you just heard, I am honored that I'll be going to Mexico next week as part of a delegation that's going to be joined by three other of my colleagues: Susan Kurland from the Department of Transportation—all four of us are assistant secretaries; Susan Kurland from the Department of Transportation; Charles Collyns from the Treasury Department; and Michael Camunez from the Commerce Department.

And the reason for this is that we think that we are in Latin America and also and—but especially with Mexico as well, we are at a unique point in our relationship with Latin America. It's what President Obama and Secretary Clinton have called a moment of opportunity. And this was recognized by President Pena Nieto when he was here, because one of the things that he talked about was focusing on economic reforms and the need to try and increase economic integration among NAFTA partners, not just to—because it's good to do but also to make NAFTA much more competitive on a global basis.

And this is something that we wholeheartedly endorse. We very much endorse his call—President Pena Nieto's call to make economic, trade, investment issues real core components of a bilateral relationship. And if there is anything that we can communicate as part of this trip, it's exactly that point. We have heeded the call. We understand the call. We share the call for turning our economic relations in what is already a wonderful relationship with Mexico a core component.

And I think that this places the economics at the center, clear evidence that we put economics together with the other issues that we deal with Mexico at the center of our relationship. And we really look forward to working with our colleagues and friends in the Mexican cabinet as well as with Mexican business leaders, because we will be meeting with the private sector as well in Mexico, in order to continue to talk about strengthening or deepening our economic relations.

And one of the—as we try and—that was—we speak about increasing economic relations, we have to keep in mind how good, how vibrant, the economic relations already are, right? We have 400 and—I'm going to get this number wrong—$462 billion a year of trade between our two countries. If you break that down, that's about one and a quarter billion dollars a day in trade. Mexico is our second largest export market. Mexico is our third largest source of imports. Mexico is our third supplier of energy anywhere in the world. The bilateral trade, the 460 billion, not 462, 460 billion of trade in 2012 between our two countries is four times the trade that existed at the time of NAFTA.

And something that is sometimes lost in the details is the fact that what we sell to Mexico and what Mexico sells to us and what's counted as exports sometimes, what we sell to Mexico has a lot of Mexican content that we take, we assemble or we put together, we add value, and we sell it back to Mexico, and the other way around. What Mexico sells to us includes a lot of U.S. components.

So this is—you have heard many, many times diplomats talk about partnerships. Everybody likes to talk about partnerships. It's an overused term. But this is a real true partnership. This is a partnership where we make things together. We are partners in an integrated enterprise whose fortunes depend on the successful collaboration with one another. And you see it in the numbers, not just the $460 billion but the fact that Mexico—that U.S. companies have over $90 billion worth of investments in Mexico, the fact that Mexican investment in the West continues to grow and it's now at about $13 billion.

And when you get away from the numbers, what this all means is jobs and trade and a closer relationship between our two countries. And it also has, in the case of our NAFTA partners, has an added benefit, and that benefit is that by working together we strengthen our common competitiveness of the North American business.

We recently welcomed Mexico into the Trans-Pacific Partnership, the TPP. And with all three NAFTA partners now participating in the TPP, what we have now is the ability to use each other's supply chains to export goods into the other eight TPP countries.

So look, we have already a broad and deep economic relationship. We have an incredibly vibrant human relationship, a relationship that goes back hundreds of years. And all we're trying to do with this trip is to highlight the potential for deepening our relations even more. And so we will explore how we can support the Government of Mexico's reform efforts to improve economic competitiveness, how we can enhance business-to-business ties, how we can promote innovation, and how we can enhance cooperation in areas like transportation, infrastructure, and trade.

Following that, my trip, sort of personally in Mexico, I will be going to the other side of the border. I'll be going to southern Texas to—and I am sure that in Texas I will see the other side of the economic relationship. But again, it's a fluid relationship. It's a relationship that can only grow. And what we're trying to do on this trip is to highlight and to stress how interested we are and how committed we are in continuing and strengthening our economic relations. So with that, I will turn it over to your very easy questions, I'm sure.

QUESTION: Thank you for this briefing.

ASSISTANT SECRETARY FERNANDEZ: Okay.

QUESTION: When you go to Mexico, are you bringing any concrete agreements, something concrete that you can tell us, or it's more like getting to know the (inaudible)?

ASSISTANT SECRETARY FERNANDEZ: It's to—the main purpose of our trip is to stress how interested we are, to talk about how we go forward, how we deepen the relationship. So it is not necessarily to bring anything or we—it's not that we expect a concrete project to come out of it. But what we do expect is to discuss a path forward. How do we take our relationship—how are we going to do that? And that—what are the issues that are of interest to Mexico to put on the table? What are the issues that are of interest to us to put on the table?

And I suspect, which is why I'm so excited about this, that we are going to have very much of a common agenda. And so it's really about looking for a path forward.

QUESTION: Assistant Secretary, when you just mentioned both the U.S. and Mexico are going to put some issues on the table, can you please tell us—can you expand on that, what are those issues and—

ASSISTANT SECRETARY FERNANDEZ: I mean, it's something that will have to be discussed. But an issue that's of interest to all of us is: How do we streamline commerce along the border? How do we make—how do we eliminate burdensome and unnecessary regulatory disparities between the two countries? I'm sure that the issue of—just that issue, there'll be other issues of infrastructure. We'll be meeting with the Secretary of Infrastructure and Transportation. So there will be issues on that front. There will be economic issues because we will be meeting as well with the Secretary of the Economy, as well as the Finance Ministry.

So there will be issues, many issues. But again, what we're trying to do is to say okay, we have this common agenda, we have this common interest. How do we make it a reality? What else can we add to the relationship which is already quite good?

QUESTION: I understand that you—at this point I suppose that you can't be more specific, because this is the first trip with the new Government of Mexico. But I wonder if you can tell us, for example, if you would like the Mexican Government could be more open mind, for example, in the energy sector, because you're talking that you would like that Mexico could be more competitive. So—

ASSISTANT SECRETARY FERNANDEZ: Both of us need to be more competitive, not just Mexico.

QUESTION: I would like to know, what you think, what do you expect, for example, in the energy sector? You know that this is a very sensitive subject, and what do you expect? What would you like—

ASSISTANT SECRETARY FERNANDEZ: Well, look, we signed—we actually have a Transboundary Hydrocarbons Agreement, as you know, with Mexico, that was signed in February of this year. It's an agreement that's intended—that will promote joint economic exploration and development of hydrocarbon reservoirs in the Gulf of Mexico. And this is a perfect example of the kind of cooperation, kind of the common agenda that exists already between our countries. It will—from our point of view, it will enhance energy security. It will do so with a high degree of safety and environmental standards. This is something that already in Mexico the Mexican Senate has ratified. And obviously, in our Congress will implement the agreement as well, will be working to implement the agreement.

So this is a perfect example of what we will be working—of the kinds of issues that can—the kind of common agenda that we can pursue when we work together. . .

QUESTION: There are some reports of some agencies—private agencies like Stratfor [Global Intelligence] that says that there are going to be a lot of violence in 2013.

ASSISTANT SECRETARY FERNANDEZ: (Inaudible.)

QUESTION: It's Stratfor. It's this agency of security in Mexico that—

ASSISTANT SECRETARY FERNANDEZ: Okay. Okay.

QUESTION:—thinks that it's going to be (inaudible), more of the same than the last year. And do you think that the security is really a problem? Is it still a big problem?

ASSISTANT SECRETARY FERNANDEZ: Nope. I have been working in Mexico for a long time. I—so I—and I can tell you one thing, and that is—let's just start with a—something very important, which is we the United States, I on a personal basis, very much admire the work and the sacrifice of the Mexican security forces. I think the number now is 40,000 people have lost their lives in your—

QUESTION: 70,000.

ASSISTANT SECRETARY FERNANDEZ: 70,000. That's even sadder. So we very much have supported it. We have the Merida Initiative, where we have $1.1 billion worth of assistance, but also a lot of cooperation between our two agencies. Our President has several times recognized that and said that the drug problem is a shared problem, and that the illicit weapons problem is also a problem on both sides.

But that's a given. That's part of what we start with, with Mexico—that admiration for what they—for what is a very courageous fight. It's not what we do. What we're trying to do, as in the four of us who are going, are the economic agencies. And we have—we cannot lose sight of the fact that in addition to a security cooperation, we have very strong economic relations, and not just economic, but also add political and human.

And so what we are trying to highlight is the economic dimension of our relationship, because just highlighting the security relationship between our two countries is—does not do the overall relationship justice. It's a much, much more rich and historic and longstanding relationship beyond simply security.

QUESTION: Assistant Secretary, you have described a very successful relationship, but there have been, in the past, problems in trade. For example, there's—last year was this tomato affair. I don't know exactly on which faces these—I think the Commerce Department has yet—

ASSISTANT SECRETARY FERNANDEZ: Yeah.

QUESTION:—to find something. I wanted to know, in which status is this? And if you think these problems have to be addressed in order for the relationship to really go a step further?

ASSISTANT SECRETARY FERNANDEZ: Sure. Well, look, the—we have had good examples of cooperation to try to deal with issues—the trucking issue, probably you remember that. The tomato case, in accordance with our law, in accordance with the U.S. law, is something that the—that it falls within the realm of the Commerce Department. It's something that they are reviewing. It's something that we, as a Department, at the State Department, don't get involved. It's a very—it's intended to be an objective review.

All parties have been invited to submit comments. The Mexican Government and Mexican growers, in addition to a number of other stakeholders, have been in touch with the Commerce Department. And this is something that's being analyzed and that my colleague, Michael Camunez, will probably be able to speak about better than I can. But it's a process. It's a procedure objective which has a process, and that's all I can say about it. But of course, our governments have been in contact with that, as have the growers and have the other stakeholders. . .

QUESTION: So how these meetings and how this relationship can actually help with jobs here in the U.S., I mean, that's another—that's one of the biggest priorities right now for the Obama Administration, especially a couple days before the Inauguration. Are you guys looking to create an advantage here in the U.S. with these kind of relationships as well?

ASSISTANT SECRETARY FERNANDEZ: What we—jobs is our number-one priority. We, since the time that we came into office, we are—we have been told that jobs is our number-one priority at all—even at the Department of State, which is why you will have heard about the economic statecraft efforts of the Department of State.

Trade creates jobs, and if we can make it easier for countries to trade, if we can make it easier for countries to invest, if we can make it easier for countries to produce goods that have competitive advantages with other parts, other regions of the world, we will help both countries. This is not intended to be a unilateral advantage, and it's—that's not a lasting basis for a relationship. It's not a basis for a lasting relationship.

You've got to create ways for both sides to be able to trade, for both sides to be able to create jobs. The new Mexican administration also wants to create jobs. Mexico has gone through some difficult times as well. And so we intend to look for ways for us to be able to create mutual advantages for our people and to create jobs, which is why I'm so—I'm delighted that I'll be able to go to the other side of the border afterwards, because that's also—that's what we see a lot of the benefit to, right alongside the border where you have this very fluid situation, which is, I think, unique in this hemisphere, of that fluid border that we're—we create things together, we trade things together. Our families are straddled between both sides. But it's got to be a mutual advantage. Otherwise, it just does not work.

QUESTION: And if you can talk about what your activities will be at the other side of the border, or if you'll have—

ASSISTANT SECRETARY FERNANDEZ: Well, I've been asked by Congressman Hinojosa in Texas to go, and I'm delighted. I'm delighted to be able to do that, to be—because again, the benefits of what we do are visible on that side.

MODERATOR: Any more additional questions? All right.

ASSISTANT SECRETARY FERNANDEZ: Thank you, *gracias*.

MODERATOR: Thank you very much.

6

Poverty and Inequality
in the Americas

A teenage boy living on a garbage tip sitting in his makeshift shelter made from household and industrial waste outside the mexican pacific coast city of Mazatlán in Sinaloa State.

The Economics of Women and Children

In the effort to ensure long-term growth and stability in the Latin American countries of Cuba, Venezuela, and Mexico, one of the primary issues to address is the widespread poverty that disproportionately affects women and children in these countries. Development experts broadly agree that in countries where women have the same access to educational and employment opportunities as men, the gross domestic product increases significantly, which ensures long-term economic growth and political stability. Targeted programs focused on addressing the inequalities that impede women and children's access to employment and education in Cuba, Venezuela, and Mexico will greatly improve the quality of life for all citizens.

One of the key indicators of the success of an antipoverty program is the condition of the target country's most vulnerable social groups. In the case of these three Latin American countries, the two demographics demonstrating the highest rates of poverty are women and children. Many observers argue that introducing programs to address the inequalities faced by women and children—for example, improving educational resources for children and providing vocational training and opportunities for the stable employment for women—can strengthen society as a whole. Women and children continue to experience high rates of poverty in these countries despite the introduction of domestic and international cooperative programs; however, some of these programs have shown signs of success.

The United States government is presently exploring greater investment in cooperative economic programs with each of these countries. At the same time, it is seeking to expand its influence in the region, advocating democratic and free market ideals in order to promote security and stability across the region. Antipoverty programs targeting women and children in each of these countries may play an important role in these pursuits.

Cuba

The triumph of communism in Cuba, in a revolution led by Fidel Castro in the late 1950s, came about in response to a major gulf between the nation's rich and poor. When Castro took control of the Cuban government after ousting the dictator Fulgencio Batista, he moved to nationalize many of Cuba's major corporations and industries in an effort to level the economic landscape and redistribute the country's wealth. However, since the 1950s, Cuba has existed under an economic embargo imposed by the United States, and the country's economy has suffered significantly as a result. Some experts believe that the embargo is not the only factor limiting economic growth in Cuba, but that the policies introduced by the Cuban leadership in an effort to manage the economy have left behind certain segments of the population.

Cuba's women have been particularly affected by the shortcomings of these various policies. Many of the reforms introduced by the Castro regime have fostered modest growth in certain segments, but wages remain low and inequitable. Single mothers are the most vulnerable to this disparity, and the number of households with single mothers as primary earners is increasing. As is the case in many Latin American countries, women have limited access to the type of vocational training that brings in higher incomes. Cuban women consistently bear the responsibility for caring for the children and elderly living in their households. In 1975, Cuba implemented a "Family Code" that declared men and women are equal, but in practice, women are still seen as the domestic caregivers while the men are the wage-earners.

Nevertheless, many studies strongly indicate that the US embargo is having a major impact on the people of Cuba. Men and the elderly have borne the brunt of this impact, due in large part to the preferential treatment given women and children when Cuba needs to ration medical supplies and food. However, with the Cuban economy still faltering under the embargo, poverty and health issues among women and children in that nation could become more widespread.

Lifting the embargo and thereby improving the availability of a wide range of goods and supplies would greatly enhance the health and well-being of Cuba's women and children. It would also offer a potentially strong economic return for the United States, through trade in everything from educational supplies to pharmaceuticals. With Fidel Castro no longer in power and reform-minded leaders assuming more control over Cuban government institutions, many experts believe that this early "post-Fidel" era may be the right time to end a nearly sixty-year embargo against Castro's regime. This would not only thaw relations between the United States and Cuba, but would facilitate the economic empowerment of Cuban women and children and the stability of the Cuban economy.

Venezuela

As in many Latin American countries, the people of Venezuela most vulnerable to poverty are children and women. Most of those living below the poverty line in that country reside in the country's rural areas—women in these regions typically earn low wages harvesting agricultural products or working in manufacturing facilities. In the cities (where the majority of Venezuelans reside), women also earn less in most jobs than their male counterparts.

However, the Venezuelan government has made significant progress toward recognizing women's rights. Former president Hugo Chávez, in office from 1999 to 2013, took much of the credit for these efforts, as he introduced a constitution in 1999 that was gender-neutral, banned sexual discrimination, and guaranteed a wide range of services and equitable treatments under Venezuelan law. More women are now holding high-level government positions, and Venezuela's statutes include a number of provisions concerning violence against women. Venezuelan women are more likely to be literate than Venezuelan men, and more women than men are enrolled in the country's many universities. Although women comprise only about 36 percent of the country's workforce, Venezuelan law is steadily improving women's way of life.

Children, however, remain at risk of poverty and poor health. According to a recent United Nations Children's Fund (UNICEF) report, 21 percent of Venezuela's children under the age of five suffer from malnutrition. A large percentage of children in that country have little to no access to education and health care. Furthermore, according to the same report, the number of Venezuelan young people (aged fourteen and younger) with HIV and AIDS rose by 57 percent between 2005 and 2007.

Nevertheless, there are positive trends with regard to child poverty in Venezuela. UN-imposed goals for the reduction of child poverty rates have seen considerable success in Venezuela. That country's emphasis on investing money in programs promoting children's health and educational opportunities has seen successful. According to the Venezuelan newspaper *Correo del Orinoco*, the country's socialist "missions" to combat poverty and improve health are working. These missions, located in some of the country's most economically vulnerable regions, are improving the health, education, and nutrition of the nation's poorest citizens. These successes have been confirmed by the United Nations and other international organizations.

During the early 2000s, Chávez and US president George W. Bush engaged in a war of words, resulting in several diplomatic dismissals (as of 2013, neither government had an active ambassador serving in the other country). According to a number of experts, Bush's departure in 2008 and Chávez's death in early 2013 have opened the possibility of improved relations between the United States and Venezuela and increased US investments in the Venezuelan economy. Such investments would likely work to the benefit of women and children in Venezuela as well, since Chávez's successor, Nicolás Maduro, has promised to continue what he calls Chávez's "great legacy" in addressing the needs of the nation's most vulnerable populations.

Mexico

Of Venezuela, Mexico, and Cuba, Mexico is the nation with which the United States has enjoyed the warmest relations. In 1994, for example, the United States, Mexico, and Canada entered into the North American Free Trade Agreement (NAFTA), an accord that lifted most of the barriers to trade and investment among the three nations. NAFTA, by creating the world's largest free-trade zone, has since helped increase business opportunities, lower the costs of doing business, and foster economic development in each of the three participating countries.

Although the US-Mexican relationship has been bolstered by NAFTA, and the Mexican economy has benefited greatly from the arrangement, Mexico's poverty and health issues remain prevalent outside NAFTA's impact zones. According to scholars, NAFTA has greatly benefited middle- and upper-class Mexicans in Mexico City and in the northern Mexican states along the US border. However, in rural areas and the southern states, such as Oaxaca and Chiapas, there is little economic development occurring as a result of NAFTA. In these areas, the poor continue to struggle to find jobs, while the children receive substandard educations.

The plight of Mexico's poor children remains an important issue. According to UNICEF, 16 percent of Mexico's children (approximately 3.6 million) are working instead of going to school. Frequently, these jobs are low-paying and have work environments that lack the appropriate health and safety safeguards. These jobs are typically not those produced by multinational corporations as a result of NAFTA; they are local businesses in rural and underserved areas, operating in direct violation of Mexican child labor laws. Then again, Mexico's labor department, which is charged with enforcing these laws, has been strained by a lack of resources and funds in recent years. As a result, Mexico's poorest children remain vulnerable to such illegal employment standards as they seek income in the country's underserved areas.

Poor Mexican women also frequently find themselves on NAFTA's periphery. Many programs designed to improve conditions for women living below the poverty line, while modestly successful, are not effective enough in empowering women to pursue greater financial opportunities. For example, one program, taking into account the fact that Mexico's poor women are the primary providers in the household, enables women to continue their roles as domestic caregivers while working in agricultural jobs. However, it does not offer women access to job training, which would increase their administrative and technical skills. It also does not address the hours these women work at home in addition to their vocational workday. As a result, this program promotes production among poor Mexican women, but does not enhance these women's vocational capacity (which could improve their financial situations by opening more job options).

NAFTA has enhanced one preexisting program, one that has simultaneously presented opportunities for and raised questions about the welfare of women and children. Since 1965, Mexico has fostered "maquiladoras," which are manufacturing facilities along the US-Mexican border to which American businesses deliver supplies (without restrictions) for assembly and export to the United States. NAFTA has increased the number of these facilities as well as their production. As a result, more jobs are available along the border. Mexican women have been among those who have taken advantage of these jobs. Some studies of women working in maquiladoras have suggested that, while these jobs have provided much-needed income (although at low wages), they have also done little to enhance the status of women in Mexico. According to one paper, for example, maquiladora recruiters target married women and mothers because such workers focus on their jobs with their families in mind. Feminist scholars argue that this practice limits the autonomy and independence of Mexican women, widening the gender gap between men and women.

Other issues concerning Mexican maquiladoras are health and safety factors. These facilities are seen by many observers as dirty and dangerous, with typical safety measures and waste-management protocols unenforced or disregarded altogether. Not only do men and women work at maquiladoras: children do as well. In the interest of production, children under the legal age of sixteen are frequently hired, using forged and unchecked applications. Such work conditions leave Mexican children susceptible to injury, illness, and exploitation as they work for low wages in these maquiladoras.

According to a number of international studies, maquiladoras under the influence of NAFTA may have increased production, but they have not improved literacy rates, health conditions, educational opportunities, or other elements of true economic development. With Mexican women and children most susceptible to these issues (as they are across Latin America), more critical focus is being paid to the benefits and problems associated with maquiladoras and NAFTA as a whole.

Poverty in Latin America Lowest in Three Decades, U.N. Says

Associated Press, November 28, 2012

The number of people living in poverty in Latin America and the Caribbean has dropped to its lowest level in three decades due to higher wages, the UN's regional economic body said on Tuesday.

Despite lower poverty levels overall, 167 million people in the region are still considered poor. That's one million fewer than in 2011, and it represents about 29 percent of the region's population. Of those, 66 million people remain stuck in extreme poverty, the same as last year.

"Current poverty and indigence rates are the lowest for three decades, and this is good news, but we are still facing unacceptable levels in many countries," Alicia Barcena, head of the United Nations Economic Commission for Latin America and the Caribbean (ECLAC), told reporters in Santiago.

"The challenge is to generate quality jobs as part of a development model based on equality and environmental sustainability," she said.

Latin American countries that experienced some of the biggest reductions in poverty levels include Argentina, Colombia, Ecuador, Paraguay, Peru, Uruguay and Panama. The main reasons for the overall drop in poverty in the region are an increase in wages and more jobs, according to the Social Panorama of Latin America 2012 report.

"Among the different sources of household income, labor income contributed the most to changing income levels in poor households," the report said.

Women and children are especially vulnerable to poverty in Latin America. Underage minors make up 51 percent of those living under extreme poverty.

"Poverty has the face of a child in Latin America," Barcena said.

The report also found that the last decade has seen reduced inequality in income distribution, although the issue remains one of the region's main challenges.

The most recent available statistics for 18 countries indicate that, on average, the richest 10 percent of Latin America's population receives 32 percent of total income, while the poorest 40 percent receives 15 percent of total income, making it one of the world's most unequal regions.

Poverty and Inequality

Equity for Children.org, November 27, 2012

Although some data in recent years shows reducing rates of poverty, there are two major unresolved issues surrounding inequality and equity in the Latin American region. Firstly, it is necessary to focus on achieving greater equity for all, taking into account societal inclusions faced by new generations. With current development models, certain populations are experiencing exclusion, such some fifteen ethnic groups in Argentina where poverty is deep among indigenous peoples and the recent economic [situation] has led to an increase in poverty, especially in provinces in the north where estimates of income poverty ranged from around 20%[1] officially to over 40% [2] in private estimates.

At different moments of childhood, the experience of poverty and inequality varies. Groups of children and adolescents face differing consequences on their life paths during these moments, such as those who live in large urban areas of Argentina where 3 out of 10 children under the age of 18 live in homes with major health and habitat condition issues (no access to running water or lack of sewage infrastructure, overcrowding conditions, in the vicinity of landfills or polluting factories).[3] These conditions result from the misappropriation of material resources by a limited few through socio-cultural strategies that label and treat groups of poor as "different" from the rest of society. Such problems of social inequality and environmental quality of life prove to be very significant and regressive especially for adolescent girls[3].

Equidad para la Infancia advocates a reframing of human rights discussions to include the needs of children and adolescents who are most vulnerable and affected by poverty. Equidad aims to achieve equity for children. Its approach to resolving inequity in Latin America reflects ensuring all-inclusive rights in childhood and adolescence. For example, we observe patterns in children of indigenous and African descent, and who, due to their ethnicity, are highly disadvantaged and denied basic human rights.[4] This is expressed in high rates of morbidity and mortality, high education dropout and failure rates, and an exponentially higher prevalence of poverty and destitution. We also observe that adolescent girls in rural areas and both female and male adolescents from poor urban areas are more vulnerable to acts of sexual violence and criminality.

Following Lopez[5], the notion of fairness can be defined as a strategy to search for equality based on recognition of social differences. As noted though by Fitoussi and Rosanvallon (1996), equity and equality should not be competing concepts but rather work together, as equity can be utilized as a strategy for

> *The dire living conditions in slums is exacerbated by a very weak to limited state infrastructure (housing, health, education, recreation, etc.).*

achieving equality. Equity seeks equality; and equality in itself requires policies of equity.

Poverty and inequality are reproduced in different ways. According to Saraví, this is illustrated in the biographies of young people living in material poverty who experience an accumulated cycle of disadvantages. The dire living conditions in slums is exacerbated by a very weak to limited state infrastructure (housing, health, education, recreation, etc.).[6] In addition, other material difficulties that are due to a lack of work opportunity lead to an increasingly difficult and inescapable situation of poverty. Academic studies about children[7] and those civil society organizations (CSOs) that are working toward fulfilling equitable child rights are increasingly concerned with inequality and material deprivation among children and adolescents. The current social policy debate about children addresses the scope and viability of equality as a principle, given the Convention of the Rights of the Child (CRC) and its direct impact on children in the context of severe conditions of inequality in Latin America[8].

Some social policies are too focused, including those that are target interventions, which automatically exclude vulnerable groups due to a limited and partial measure that misses some issues underlying inequity. Moreover, recent income transfer programs consider the livelihood of children more broadly and contemplate the overall situation of families by seeking to achieve integrated health care and education. Beyond these activities, however, some programs still fail to acknowledge expressions of inequality such as gender discrimination[9]. For example, the high incidence of mothers and birthrates in conjunction with a lack of resources by the state providing skilled childcare space further exacerbates conditions of poverty and inequality for children.

Redefining the human rights approach from a perspective of achieving equity involves rethinking the definitions of poverty and its resulting problems, overcoming a traditional focus on quantifiable issues of income and being poor and instead considering relations maintained in poverty and the related structure of perpetuated inequality. The debate is well underway about the best ways to address society's issues of childhood poverty and inequality. It emphasizes coordinated efforts among various state sectors, academia and CSOs[10]. Unfortunately, the challenges of eliminating inequality and achieving equity in Latin America remain when thinking about living conditions for children and the general population.

Notes

1. http://www.indec.gov.ar/principal.asp?id_tema=534
2. http://www.iader.org.ar/?x=pobreza_pais

3. http://www.equidadparalainfancia.org/alberto-minujin-como-representante-de-equidad-para-la-infancia-participo-de-la-presentacion-del-cuarto-informe-del-barometro-de-la-deuda-social-de-la-infancia-422/index.html

4. Visibilidad estadística. Datos sobre población afrodescendiente en censos y encuestas de hogares de América Latina, UNDP 2010.

5. http://www.equidadparalainfancia.org/las-nuevas-leyes-de-educacion-en-america-latina,-una-lectura-a-la-luz-del-panorama-social-y-educativo-en-la-region-735/index.html

6. http://www.equidadparalainfancia.org/la-otra-inclusion-social-651/index.html

7. http://www.equidadparalainfancia.org/los-derechos-y-las-politicas-para-la-infancia-en-la-formacion-de-posgrado-de-america-latina-698/index.html

8. http://www.equidadparalainfancia.org/poblacion-infantil-y-juvenil-derechos-humanos-pobreza-y-desigualdades-610/index.html

9. http://www.equidadparalainfancia.org/programas-de-transferencias-condicionadas-de-ingresos-quien-penso-en-el-cuidado-la-experiencia-argentina-501/index.html

10. http://www.equidadparalainfancia.org/opportunities-and-challenges-in-promoting-policy--and-practice-relevant-knowledge-on-child-rights-643/index.html

Talking About Poverty with
Greg Kaufmann

By Theresa Riley
Bill Moyers.com, October 31, 2012

Theresa Riley: Last month's numbers from the U.S. Census showed poverty numbers holding steady from 2010 to 2011. That's not exactly good news since poverty levels are the worst they've been in 50 years. What should people be paying attention to in these numbers?

Greg Kaufmann: I think the biggest takeaways from the recent numbers are that only the top quintile saw its income rise in 2011; the bottom four-fifths all saw a decline. Also, only the bottom and the top saw growth in the number of full-time, year-round workers—which speaks to the proliferation of low-wage jobs and difficulty reaching the middle class. In short, I think the numbers speak to the fact that we need to stop looking at poverty as a separate phenomenon from the rest of the economy—an economy with a proliferation of low-wage jobs and a weak and inequitable recovery. Finally, the number of people living below twice the poverty line—less than about $36,000 for a family of three—rose from 103 million to 106 million Americans. That's a better representation of who is struggling in this economy than the 46 million people below the poverty line. Even at two times the poverty level people are making impossible choices between food, housing and healthcare—and forget about savings for college, for example.

Riley: What are some common misconceptions about poverty in America?

Kaufmann: That poor people don't work and don't want to work. That most people on assistance are African American (most are white). That we waged a war on poverty and poverty won (poverty would be twice as high as it is today—nearly 30 percent—if it weren't for government assistance). That the solution to families headed by single mothers is marriage. And, generally, there is a lack of recognition that most people who turn to welfare are either working low-wage jobs, are temporarily unemployed, or they need safe, affordable childcare in order to work and it's not available.

Riley: Besides the financial crisis, are there other systemic problems that are factors in the high rate of poverty?

Kaufmann: The proliferation of low-wage jobs is a huge problem. I think the fact that TANF (cash assistance) is administered differently by 50 states—and we have no uniform minimum benefit or eligibility standards—increases poverty, and also deep poverty. Prior to welfare reform for every 100 families with children in poverty 68 received cash assistance. Now it's just 27, and the benefit averages about 30 percent of the poverty line. I think the lack of affordable childcare—federal assistance for childcare currently reaches about one in seven of those who are eligible—is a huge problem for workers and also in terms of improving outcomes for children in poverty.

Riley: Why aren't people outraged by these numbers? What do you think it will take to capture the public's attention?

Kaufmann: You got me. I thought the recession would make people more sensitive to how easy it is to fall into poverty. I don't think that's happened—in fact, it seems like it's probably increased the scapegoating. I've always believed it will take presidential leadership to a) educate people about poverty; and b) take aggressive action to eradicate poverty. But these days I'm thinking it's more about us educating, agitating, organizing, and pushing—not waiting on a president. To that end, I want to do a much better job finding out and reporting on what's happening at the community level.

Riley: You started a twitter campaign #TalkPoverty encouraging people to ask the candidates questions about poverty. Any luck getting them to answer the questions?

Kaufmann: We developed the #TalkPoverty idea in early August, knowing that the campaigns would not be talking about poverty. The Twitter initiative is about pressing them on very specific, substantive questions so they can't just respond with platitudes and generalizations. The Obama campaign has said it will respond to at least some of the questions. The Romney campaign expressed openness initially, then informed me last week it will not participate—which, I know, is shocking.

Riley: Who are the visionaries—the people who are thinking creatively and realistically about how to overcome poverty?

Kaufmann: These days, I'm very much drawn to both of the Edelmans, Peter and Marian Wright. I think Angela Glover Backwell is a powerful speaker with a clear vision. I love what Witnesses to Hunger is doing—women in poverty using photographs and their own testimonials to advocate for change at the local, state and federal levels. I've been following the Coalition of Immokalee Workers for about five years now, and I'm constantly astounded by what they are achieving with farmworkers—and the collective way in which they go about their work. I'm inspired every day by advocacy groups like Half in Ten, the Coalition on Human Needs, the Western Center on Law and Poverty, who are constantly pointing out the priorities and choices we are making and what a difference they make in people's lives, for better or worse. And then there are the thinkers—at places like the Center on Budget and Policy Priorities, EPI, CEPR, CLASP, Urban Institute—I could really go on and on. But again, I'm determined at

> *Prior to welfare reform for every 100 families with children in poverty 68 received cash assistance. Now it's just 27, and the benefit averages about 30 percent of the poverty line.*

this point to really speak as much as possible with people living in poverty. The three students I talked to last month who have dealt with poverty inspired me as much as anyone in the past year.

Riley: What are a few specific measures that could be taken to reduce poverty in America?

Kaufmann: Raising the minimum wage and tipped minimum wage. For most of the '60s and '70s a full-time minimum wage job could lift a family of three above the poverty line, about $17,900 today. Not even close now. If the minimum wage had kept pace with inflation it would now be $10.55 and pay a full-time worker $21,000 annually. Why did politicians index individual campaign contribution limits to inflation but not cash assistance or the minimum wage? Something is very wrong with that picture.

Speaking of cash assistance, TANF needs serious reform if we really want to help people obtain good jobs that pay a living wage, or get the help they need if they are unable to work.

We should substantially increase spending on childcare and early education—we know that will produce better outcomes for children and increase work opportunities for parents.

The Recovery Act improved both the Earned Income Tax Credit and the Child Tax Credit. As a result, the federal EITC kept 6 million people out of poverty in 2009, half of them children. It also kept more than 3 million children out of poverty in 2010. In 2009, the Child Tax Credit protected approximately 2.3 million people from poverty, including about 1.3 million children, according to the Center on Budget and Policy Priorities. These tax credits are under fire and need to be protected.

Finally, we should reform the unemployment insurance system so it reaches more low-wage workers.

Riley: You mentioned earlier that without government assistance, poverty would be twice as high, at nearly 30 percent. A lot of the rhetoric during the campaigns has dealt with eliminating public assistance. What would this mean for our country? What does an America with 30 percent of its people living in poverty look like?

Kaufmann: Our poverty rates are already higher than other high-income countries. I would think a country with that kind of poverty is going to see a lot more crime and social unrest. I know I would do anything to feed my own kids, and if there aren't opportunities out there and there's a sense that political leadership doesn't give a damn about you—I think people will do what they have to do. But I would rather flip that and think about the positive impact we would see if we truly looked out for our brothers and sisters: when you do right by people, you feel stronger as a person and stronger as a nation. You build a sense of community, momentum and the confidence that we are all in this together. No person is viewed as "less than," and no one is dismissed as not worth fighting for.

Remarks by President Obama on Latin America in Santiago, Chile

By President Barack H. Obama
Whitehouse.gov, March 21, 2011

President Obama: Muchas gracias. Thank you so much. (Applause.) Thank you. Thank you so much. Thank you. Thank you. Please, please, everyone be seated.

Thank you. Buenas tardes. It is a wonderful honor to be here in Santiago, Chile. And I want to, first of all, thank your President, President Pinera, for his outstanding leadership and the hospitality that he's extended not only to me but also to my wife, my daughters, and, most importantly, my mother-in-law. (Laughter.)

To the people of Santiago, to the people of Chile, thank you so much for your wonderful welcome. And on behalf of the people of the United States, let me thank you for your friendship and the strong bonds between our people.

There are several people that I just want to acknowledge very briefly. We have the President of the Inter-American Development Bank, Luis Alberto Moreno, who is here. (Applause.) We also have Alicia Bárcena, who is the Executive Secretary of the Economic Commission for Latin America and the Caribbean. (Applause.)

Throughout our history, this land has been called "el fin de la tierra"—the end of the world. But I've come here today because in the 21st century this nation is a vital part of our interconnected world. In an age when peoples are intertwined like never before, Chile shows that we need not be divided by race or religion or ethnic conflict. You've welcomed immigrants from every corner of the globe, even as you celebrate a proud indigenous heritage.

At a time when people around the world are reaching for their freedoms, Chile shows that, yes, it is possible to transition from dictatorship to democracy—and to do so peacefully. Indeed, our marvelous surroundings today, just steps from where Chile lost its democracy decades ago, is a testament to Chile's progress and its undying democratic spirit.

Despite barriers of distance and geography, you've integrated Chile into the global economy, trading with countries all over the world and, in this Internet age, becoming the most digitally connected country in Latin America.

And in a world of sometimes wrenching pain—as we're seeing today in Japan—it is the character of this country that inspires. "Our original guiding stars," said Pablo Neruda, "are struggle and hope." But, he added, "there is no such thing as a lone struggle, no such thing as a lone hope." The Chilean people have shown this time and again, including your recovery from the terrible earthquake here one year ago.

Credit for Chile's success belongs to the Chilean people, whose courage, sacrifices and perseverance built this nation into the leader that it is. And we are very honored to be joined today by four leaders who have guided this nation through years of great progress—Presidents Aylwin, Frei, Lagos, and of course your current President Pinera. Thank you all, to the former Presidents, for being here, as well as President Pinera. (Applause.)

So I could not imagine a more fitting place to discuss the new era of partnership that the United States is pursuing not only with Chile, but across the Americas. And I'm grateful that we're joined by leaders and members of the diplomatic corps from across the region.

Within my first 100 days in office, one of my first foreign trips as President, I traveled to Trinidad and Tobago to meet with leaders from across the hemisphere at the Summit of the Americas. And there, I pledged to seek partnerships of equality and shared responsibility, based on mutual interest and mutual respect, but also on shared values.

Now, I know I'm not the first president from the United States to pledge a new spirit of partnership with our Latin American neighbors. Words are easy, and I know that there have been times where perhaps the United States took this region for granted.

Even now, I know our headlines are often dominated by events in other parts of the world. But let's never forget: Every day, the future is being forged by the countries and peoples of Latin America. For Latin America is not the old stereotype of a region of—in perpetual conflict or trapped in endless cycles of poverty. The world must now recognize Latin America for the dynamic and growing region that it truly is.

Latin America is at peace. Civil wars have ended. Insurgencies have been pushed back. Old border disputes have been resolved. In Colombia, great sacrifices by citizens and security forces have restored a level of security not seen in decades.

And just as old conflicts have receded, so too have the ideological battles that often fueled them—the old stale debates between state-run economies and unbridled capitalism; between the abuses of right-wing paramilitaries and left-wing insurgents; between those who believe that the United States causes all the region's problems and those who believe that the United States ignores all the problems. Those are false choices, and they don't reflect today's realities.

Today, Latin America is democratic. Virtually all the people of Latin America have gone from living under dictatorships to living in democracies. Across the region, we see vibrant democracies, from Mexico to Chile to Costa Rica. We've seen historic peaceful transfers of power, from El Salvador to Uruguay to Paraguay. The work of perfecting our democracies, of course, is never truly done, but this is the outstanding progress that's been made here in the Americas.

Today, Latin America is growing. Having made tough but necessary reforms, nations like Peru and Brazil are seeing impressive growth. As a result, Latin America weathered the global economic downturn better than other regions. Across the region, tens of millions of people have been lifted from extreme poverty. From

> *But if we're honest, we'll also admit that these dreams are still beyond the reach of too many; that progress in the Americas has not come fast enough.*

Guadalajara to Santiago to Sao Paolo, a new middle class is demanding more of themselves and more of their governments.

Latin America is coming together to address shared challenges. Chile, Colombia and Mexico are sharing their expertise in security with nations in Central America. When a coup in Honduras threatened democratic progress, the nations of the hemisphere unanimously invoked the Inter-American Democratic Charter, helping to lay the foundation for the return to the rule of law. The contributions of Latin American countries have been critical in Haiti, as has Latin American diplomacy in the lead up to yesterday's election in Haiti.

And increasingly, Latin America is contributing to global prosperity and security. As longtime contributors to United Nations peacekeeping missions, Latin American nations have helped to prevent conflicts from Africa to Asia. At the G20, nations like Mexico, Brazil, Argentina now have a greater voice in global economic decision-making. Under Mexican leadership, the world made progress at Cancun in our efforts to combat climate change. Nations like Chile have played a leading role in strengthening civil society groups around the world.

So this is the Latin America that I see today—a region on the move, proud of its progress, and ready to assume a greater role in world affairs. And for all these reasons, I believe that Latin America is more important to the prosperity and security of the United States than ever before. With no other region does the United States have so many connections. And nowhere do we see that more than in the tens of millions of Hispanic Americans across the United States, who enrich our society, grow our economy and strengthen our nation every single day.

And I believe Latin America is only going to become more important to the United States, especially to our economy. Trade between the United States and Latin America has surged. We buy more of your products, more of your goods than any other country, and we invest more in this region than any other country.

For instance, we export more than three times as much to Latin America as we do to China. Our exports to this region—which are growing faster than our exports to the rest of the world—will soon support more than 2 million U.S. jobs. In other words, when Latin America is more prosperous, the United States is more prosperous.

But even more than interests, we're bound by shared values. In each other's journey we see reflections of our own. Colonists who broke free from empires. Pioneers who opened new frontiers. Citizens who have struggled to expand our nations' promise to all people—men and women, white, black and brown. We're people of faith who must remember that all of us—especially the most fortunate among us—must do our part, especially for the least among us. We're citizens who know that ensuring that democracies deliver for our people must be the work of all.

This is our common history. This is our common heritage. We are all Americans. Todos somos Americanos.

Across the Americas, parents want their children to be able to run and play and know that they'll come home safely. Young people all desperately want an education. Fathers want the dignity that comes from work, and women want the same opportunities as their husbands. Entrepreneurs want the chance to start that new business. And people everywhere want to be treated with the respect to which every human being is entitled. These are the hopes—simple yet profound—that beat in the hearts of millions across the Americas.

But if we're honest, we'll also admit that that these dreams are still beyond the reach of too many; that progress in the Americas has not come fast enough. Not for the millions who endure the injustice of extreme poverty. Not for the children in shantytowns and the favelas who just want the same chance as everybody else. Not for the communities that are caught in the brutal grips of cartels and gangs, where the police are outgunned and too many people live in fear.

And despite this region's democratic progress, stark inequalities endure. In political and economic power that is too often concentrated in the hands of the few, instead of serving the many. In the corruption that too often still stifles economic growth and development, innovation and entrepreneurship. And in some leaders who cling to bankrupt ideologies to justify their own power and who seek to silence their opponents because those opponents have the audacity to demand their universal rights. These, too, are realities that we must face.

Of course, we are not the first generation to face these challenges. Fifty years ago this month, President John F. Kennedy proposed an ambitious Alliance for Progress. It was, even by today's standards, a massive investment—billions of U.S. dollars to meet the basic needs of people across the region. Such a program was right—it was appropriate for that era. But the realities of our time—and the new capabilities and confidence of Latin America—demand something different.

President Kennedy's challenge endures—"to build a hemisphere where all people can hope for a sustainable, suitable standard of living, and all can live out their lives in dignity and in freedom." But half a century later, we must give meaning to this work in our own way, in a new way.

I believe that in the Americas today, there are no senior partners and there are no junior partners, there are only equal partners. Of course, equal partnerships, in turn, demands a sense of shared responsibility. We have obligations to each other. And today, the United States is working with the nations of this hemisphere to meet our responsibilities in several key areas.

First, we're partnering to address the concerns that people across the Americas say they worry about the most—and that's the security of their families and communities. Criminal gangs and narco-traffickers are not only a threat to the security of our citizens. They're a threat to development, because they scare away investment that economies need to prosper. And they are a direct threat to democracy, because they fuel the corruption that rots institutions from within.

So with our partners from Colombia to Mexico and new regional initiatives in Central America and the Caribbean, we're confronting this challenge, together, from every direction. We've increased our support—the equipment, training and technologies—that security forces, border security and police need to keep communities safe. We're improving coordination and sharing more information so that those who traffic in drugs and in human beings have fewer places to hide. And we're putting unprecedented pressure on cartel finances, including in the United States.

But we'll never break the grip of the cartels and the gangs unless we also address the social and economic forces that fuel criminality. We need to reach at-risk youth before they turn to drugs and crime. So we're joining with partners across the Americas to expand community-based policing, strengthen juvenile justice systems, and invest in crime and drug prevention programs.

As the nations of Central America develop a new regional security strategy, the United States stands ready to do our part through a new partnership that puts the focus where it should be—on the security of citizens. And with regional and international partners, we'll make sure our support is not just well-intentioned, but is well-coordinated and well-spent.

I've said before and I will repeat, as President I've made it clear that the United States shares and accepts our share of responsibility for drug violence. After all, the demand for drugs, including in the United States, drives this crisis. And that's why we've developed a new drug control strategy that focused on reducing the demand for drugs through education and prevention and treatment. And I would point out that even during difficult fiscal times in the United States, we've proposed increasing our commitment to these efforts by some $10 billion this year alone.

We're also doing more to stem the southbound flow of guns into the region. We're screening all southbound rail cargo. We're seizing many more guns bound for Mexico and we're putting more gunrunners behind bars. And every gun or gunrunner that we take off the streets is one less threat to the families and communities of the Americas.

As we work to ensure the security of our citizens, we're partnering in a second area—and that's promoting prosperity and opportunity. I've been so impressed with President Pinera's pledge to lift everyone out of extreme poverty by 2020. That's an ambitious goal and an appropriate goal. And with this trip, I'm working to expand some of the trade and investment that might help achieve this goal.

Across the region, we're moving ahead with "open skies" agreements to bring our people and businesses closer together. We're moving forward with our Trans-Pacific Partnership—which includes Chile and Peru—to create new trade opportunities in the fast-growing markets of the Asia-Pacific. And as I've directed, my administration has intensified our efforts to move forward on trade agreements with Panama and Colombia, consistent with our values and with our interests.

We're also encouraging the next generation of businesses and entrepreneurs. So we'll work with the Inter-American Development Bank to increase lending. We've expanded credit under a new Microfinance Growth Fund for the Americas. We're supporting reforms to tax systems, which are critical for economic growth and public investment. We're creating new "Pathways to Prosperity"—microcredit, entrepreneurship training—for those who must share in economic growth, including women and members of Afro-Caribbean and indigenous communities.

And we're coming together, as a hemisphere, to create clean energy jobs and pursue more secure and sustainable energy futures. And if anybody doubts the urgency of climate change, they look—they should look no further than the Americas—from the stronger storms in the Caribbean, to glacier melt in the Andes, to the loss of forests and farmland across the region.

Under the Energy and Climate Partnership of the Americas that I proposed, countries have stepped forward, each providing leadership and expertise. Brazil has expertise in biofuels. Chile in geothermal. Mexico on energy efficiency. El Salvador is connecting grids in Central America to make electricity more reliable. These are exactly the kind of partnerships that we need—neighbors joining with neighbors to unleash the progress that none of us can achieve alone.

It's the same philosophy behind two additional initiatives that I'm announcing today, which will help our countries educate and innovate for the future. First, we're launching a new initiative to harness the power of social media and online networks to help students, scientists, academics and entrepreneurs collaborate and develop the new ideas and products that will keep America—the Americas competitive in a global economy.

And I'm proud to announce that the United States will work with partners in this region, including the private sector, to increase the number of U.S. students studying in Latin America to 100,000, and the number of Latin American students studying in the United States to 100,000.

Staying competitive also, of course, demands that we address immigration—an issue that evokes great passions in the United States as well as in the Americas. As President, I've made it clear that immigration strengthens the United States. We are a nation of immigrants, which is why I have consistently spoken out against anti-immigrant sentiment. We're also a nation of laws, which is why I will not waver in my determination to fix our broken immigration system. I'm committed to comprehensive reform that secures our borders, enforces our laws and addresses the millions of undocumented workers who are living in the shadows of the United States.

I believe, though, that this challenge will be with us for a very long time so long as people believe that the only way to provide for their families is to leave their families and head north.

And that's why the United States has to continue to partner with countries that pursue the broad-based economic growth that gives people and nations a path out of poverty. And that's what we're seeing here in Chile. As part of our new approach to development, we're working with partners, like Guatemala and El Salvador, who are committed to building their own capacity—from helping farmers improve crop yields to helping health care systems to deliver better care.

Which leads me to the final area where we must continue to partner, and that's strengthening democracy and human rights. More than 60 years ago, our nations came together in an Organization of American States and declared—and I quote—that "representative democracy is an indispensable condition for the stability, peace and development of the region." A decade ago, we reaffirmed this principle, with an Inter-American Democratic Charter that stated—and I quote—"the people of the Americas have a right to democracy and their governments have an obligation to promote and defend it."

Across the Americas, generations, including generations of Chileans, have struggled and sacrificed to give meaning to these words—ordinary men and women who dared to speak their mind; activists who organized new movements; faith leaders who preached social justice; the mothers of the disappeared who demanded the truth; political prisoners who rose to become presidents; and, even now, Las Damas de Blanco, who march in quiet dignity.

The people of the Americas have shown that there is no substitute for democracy. As governments, we have then an obligation to defend what has been won. So as we mark the 10th anniversary of the Inter-American Democratic Charter this year, let's reaffirm the principles that we know to be true.

Let's recommit to defending democracy and human rights in our own countries by strengthening the institutions that democracy needs to flourish—free and fair elections in which people choose their own leaders; vibrant legislatures that provide oversight; independent judiciaries that uphold the rule of law; a free press that promotes open debate; professional militaries under civilian control; strong civil societies that hold governments accountable; and governments that are transparent and responsive to their citizens. This is what makes a democracy.

And just as we defend democracy and human rights within our borders, let's recommit to defending them across our hemisphere. I understand, every nation will follow its own path. No nation should impose its will on another. But surely we can agree that democracy is about more than majority rule, that simply holding power does not give a leader the right to suppress the rights of others, and that leaders must maintain power through consent, and not coercion. We have to speak out when we see those principles violated.

Let's never waver in our support for the rights of people to determine their own future—and, yes, that includes the people of Cuba. Since taking office, I've announced the most significant changes to my nation's policy towards Cuba in decades. I've made it possible for Cuban Americans to visit and support their families in Cuba. We're allowing Americans to send remittances that bring some economic hope for people across Cuba, as well as more independence from Cuban authorities.

Going forward, we'll continue to seek ways to increase the independence of the Cuban people, who I believe are entitled to the same freedom and liberty as everyone else in this hemisphere. I will make this effort to try to break out of this history that's now lasted for longer than I've been alive.

But Cuban authorities must take some meaningful actions to respect the basic rights of their own people—not because the United States insists upon it, but because the people of Cuba deserve it, no less than the people of the United States or Chile or Brazil or any other country deserve it.

The lessons of Latin America, I believe, can be a guide—a guide for people around the world who are beginning their own journeys toward democracy. There is no one model for democratic transitions. But as this region knows, successful transitions do have certain ingredients. The moral force of nonviolence. Dialogue that's open and inclusive. The protection of basic rights, such as peaceful expression and assembly. Accountability for past wrongs. And matching political reform with economic reform, because democracy must meet the basic needs and aspirations of people.

With decades of experience, there's so much Latin America can now share—how to build political parties and organize free elections; how to ensure peaceful transfers of power; how to navigate the winding paths of reform and reconciliation. And when the inevitable setbacks occur, you can remind people to never lose sight of those guiding stars of which Pablo Neruda spoke—struggle, but also hope.

Security for our citizens. Trade and development that creates jobs, prosperity and a clean energy future. Standing up for democracy and human rights. These are the partnerships that we can forge together—here in the Americas but also around the world. And if anyone doubts whether this region has the capacity to meet these challenges, they need to only remember what happened here in Chile only a few months ago.

Their resolve and faith inspired the world—"Los Treinta y Tres." I don't need to tell you the story. You know it well. But it's worth remembering how this entire nation came together, across government, civilian and military, national and local; across the private sector, with large companies and small shopkeepers donating supplies; and across every segment of Chilean society, people came together to sustain those men down below and their families up at Camp Esperanza. It was a miraculous rescue. It was a tribute to Chilean leadership. And when, finally, Luis Urzua emerged, he spoke for an entire nation when he said, "I am proud to be Chilean."

Yet something else happened in those two months. The people and governments of Latin America came together to stand with a neighbor in need. And with a Latin American country in the lead, the world was proud to play a supporting role—sending workers from the United States and Canada, rescue equipment from Europe, communications gear from Asia. And as the miners were lifted to safety, for those joyous reunions, it was a truly global movement, watched and celebrated by more than a billion people.

If ever we needed a reminder of the humanity and the hopes that we share, that moment in the desert was such. When a country like Chile puts its mind to it, there's nothing you can't do. When countries across Latin America come together and focus on a common goal, when the United States and others in the world do our part, there's nothing we can't accomplish together.

And that is our vision of the Americas. This is the progress we can achieve together. This is the spirit of partnership and equality to which the United States is committed. I am confident that, working together, there is nothing we cannot achieve. Thank you very much. Muchas gracias.

Bibliography

Angeles-Castro, Gerardo, Ignacio Perrotini-Hernández, and Humberto Ríos Bolivar, eds. *Market Liberalism, Growth, and Economic Development in Latin America.* New York: Routledge, 2011. Print.

Becker, Thomas H. *Doing Business in the New Latin America: Keys to Profit in America's Next-Door Markets.* Santa Barbara: Praeger, 2011. Print.

Bértola, Luis, and José Antonio Ocampo. *The Economic Development of Latin America Since Independence.* Oxford: Oxford UP, 2012. Print.

Cuervo-Cazurra, Alvaro. "Economic Relationships between Latin America and Asia: A New Research Frontier." *GCG: Revista de Globalización, Competitividad y Gobernabilidad* 6.1 (2012): 16–22. Print.

Domínguez, Jorge I., Rafael Hernández, and Lorena G. Barberia, eds. *Debating US-Cuban Relations: Shall We Play Ball?* New York: Routledge, 2012. Print.

Farnsworth, Eric. "US–Latin American Relations: From Here to Where?" *Latin American Policy* 2.1 (2011): 85–89. Print.

Ferreira, Francisco H. G., et al. *Economic Mobility and the Rise of the Latin American Middle Class.* Washington: World Bank, 2013. Print.

Grandin, Greg. "Empire's Senescence: US Policy in Latin America." *New Labor Forum* 19.1 (2010): 15–23. Print.

Hinojosa-Ojeda, Raúl. "The Economic Benefits of Comprehensive Immigration Reform." *Cato Journal* 32.1 (2012): 175–99. Print.

Hornbeck, J. F. *US–Latin America Trade: Recent Trends and Policy Issues.* Cong. Research Service. *US Department of State: Foreign Press Centers.* Bureau of Public Affairs, 8 Feb. 2011. Web. 22 Apr. 2013.

Kaplan, Stephen B. *Globalization and Austerity Politics in Latin America.* New York: Cambridge UP, 2013. Print.

Kohli, Harinder S., Claudio M. Loser, and Anil Sood, eds. *Latin America 2040: Breaking Away from Complacency; An Agenda for Resurgence.* Thousand Oaks: Sage, 2010. Print.

Lowenthal, Abraham F. "Obama and the Americas." *Foreign Affairs* 89.4 (2010): 110–24. Print.

Moncarz, Raul. "The Obama Administration and Latin America: A 'New Partnership for the Americas.'" *Global Economy Journal* 10.1 (2010): 1–11. Print.

Ñopo, Hugo, Alberto Chong, and Andrea Moro, eds. *Discrimination in Latin America: An Economic Perspective.* Washington: World Bank, 2010. Print.

Rodriguez-Parrilla, Bruno. "Necessity of Ending the Economic, Commercial and Financial Embargo by the US against Cuba." *Vital Speeches of the Day* 76.1 (2010): 23–25. Print.

Sabatini, Christopher. "Rethinking Latin America." *Foreign Affairs* 91.2 (2012): 8–13. Print.

Stephen, Lynn. "Towards a Transborder Perspective: US-Mexico Relations." *Iberoamericana* 48 (2012): 85–99. Print.

Torre, Augusto de la, Alain Ize, and Sergio L. Schmukler. *Financial Development in Latin America and the Caribbean: The Road Ahead.* Washington: World Bank, 2012. Print.

Urbonas, Tomas A. *Politics and Economics of Latin America.* Vol. 7. New York: Nova Science, 2010. Print.

Villarreal, M. Angeles. *US-Mexico Economic Relations: Trends, Issues, and Implications.* Cong. Research Service. *Federation of American Scientists.* Federation of Amer. Scientists, 9 Aug. 2012. Web. 22 Apr. 2013.

Websites

Embassy of the United States: Mexico

http://mexico.usembassy.gov/

The Ambassador to Mexico, E. Anthony Wayne, leads a wide range of activities and programs in support of diplomatic relations with the Mexican government and its citizens. The website provides news and information on business, policy, education, and culture. Information for travel and tourism as well as visa applications is provided as well.

Organization of American States (OAS)

http://www.oas.org/

The OAS is the world's oldest regional organization, bringing together all thirty-five independent states of the Americas. The organization focuses on the promotion of four areas: democracy, human rights, security, and development. The OAS website provides information on major issues and concerns in the region, identifies strategic partners, and presents mission statements from member states.

United States–Mexico Chamber of Commerce (USMCOC)

http://www.usmcoc.org/

A nonprofit business association, the USMCOC is a bilateral organization to promote trade, investment, and joint ventures in the two countries. In 1996, the chamber established the Cultural and Education Foundation to promote educational and cultural exchanges that would foster future business leaders. The organization's website provides information on events, business opportunities, and programs to support their mission.

Wilson Center: Latin American Program

http://www.wilsoncenter.org/program/latin-american-program

The Woodrow Wilson International Center for Scholars brings together experts and scholars to join in conversation and debate on issues of international importance. The Latin American Program promotes research and dialogue in the areas of democratic governance, citizen security, and trade and economics. In addition, the Mexico and Brazil institutes promote United States relations in these regions.

Index

❖